Connecting Young Adults to Catholic Parishes

Connecting Young Adults to Catholic Parishes

Best Practices in Catholic Young Adult Ministry

Committee for Laity, Marriage, Family Life, and Youth
United States Conference of Catholic Bishops

United States Conference of Catholic Bishops
Washington, D.C.

The document *Connecting Young Adults to Catholic Parishes: Best Practices in Catholic Young Adult Ministry* was developed as a resource by the Committee for Laity, Marriage, Family Life, and Youth of the United States Conference of Catholic Bishops (USCCB). It was reviewed by the committee chairman, Archbishop Roger Schwietz, OMI, and has been authorized for publication by the undersigned.

Msgr. David J. Malloy, STD
General Secretary, USCCB

Cover image: Rob Porazinski/Photodisc/Getty Images.

First printing, March 2010

ISBN 978-1-57455-546-2

Contents

Preface

In *Sons and Daughters of the Light: A Pastoral Plan for Ministry with Young Adults*,[1] published in 1996, the Catholic bishops of the United States outlined three invitations and four goals for young adult ministry. The pastoral plan invited young adults to holiness, community, and service. The four goals were framed in terms of connecting: with Jesus, with the Church, with the mission of the Church in the world, and with peers.

This book, *Connecting Young Adults to Catholic Parishes: Best Practices in Catholic Young Adult Ministry*, builds upon the theme of connecting by sharing the lived reality and experiences of many people who were involved in young adult ministry throughout the years preceding and following the publication of *Sons and Daughters of the Light*. *Connecting Young Adults to Catholic Parishes* is designed to be a resource to enable all parishes across the United States to become "young adult user-friendly."

Much research, reflecting, writing, rewriting, editing, and re-editing have gone into the production of this book. These pages attempt to capture the reality of so many people who have shared their experiences in young adult ministry. This book also draws upon the expertise of the staff from the Center for Ministry Development (CMD), as well as the board of directors and members of the National Catholic Young Adult Ministry Association (NCYAMA), who continue to serve as a vital resource in the field of young adult ministry.

Without wishing to slight the countless numbers of people who have implemented the invitations and goals of *Sons and Daughters of the Light* with much heart and dedication, we would be remiss in not mentioning Fr. Charles Pfeffer and Sr. Diane Guy, SND, in particular. Both were leaders in the field of young adult ministry who contributed much. Both have been called home to our God, and we remember them with fondness for their invaluable insight and love for young adult ministry.

It is our hope that *Connecting Young Adults to Catholic Parishes* becomes a valuable tool for all parishes to use in strengthening their ministry to young adults. Without the giftedness of our young adults, our parishes would lack the energy and vitality and insight that make them the strong communities they are called to be.

---

1   See United States Conference of Catholic Bishops, *Sons and Daughters of the Light: A Pastoral Plan for Ministry with Young Adults* (Washington, DC: USCCB, 1996).

In meeting you, the young adult members of the Church, we are more aware of your capability to love and serve. We invite you to continue to give of yourself, your time, your energies, and your talents for the good of others. We will be praying that the Holy Spirit guide you and the Church as together we grow in the love of Jesus Christ.[2]

Archbishop Roger Schwietz, OMI
Chair, Committee for Laity, Marriage, Family Life, and Youth

2   *Sons and Daughters of the Light*, vii.

Introduction

What would our Catholic parishes be like if no young adults were present? Parishes certainly would not be as life-giving or dynamic. Young adults give to the Church their own unique way of looking at faith and life, their idealism that is tempered by real-life experiences, and their passions and dreams for themselves and for the world. Young adults are a vital part of the intergenerational faith community. They provide energy and hope to older adults, asking their elders the "why" of the Catholic faith in holy and healthy ways. They serve as role models and mentors for adolescents and children who look up to them.

Young adults are new parents searching for ways to share faith with their little ones. They are newly married couples learning what it means to live a sacramental married life. They are single adults seeking a vocation or embracing single life. And they are young priests and sisters and brothers who are living out their call to ordained or consecrated life.

The variety of young adults in the Church is incredible. Young adults are factory workers and executives, college students and soldiers, employed workers and the unemployed. Some are career-driven; others are still searching for their careers; some are in the military; some are migrant workers; a small number are in prisons or rehab centers. Today's young adults represent the most culturally diverse generation ever seen in the United States. They include the wealthy, the middle-class, and the poor. And they may or may not be engaged in faith communities.

The Church needs these young adults, just as they need the Church. The mutuality of this need provides Catholic parishes with tremendous opportunities. A pastor in Omaha, Nebraska, greeted a young woman after Mass and personally welcomed her to the parish, not suspecting that in a few years she would be a member of the parish pastoral council. A young man with a high-powered job in the business world gave it up to fill the hunger in his heart, not anticipating that his choice would change the lives of hundreds of young adults and hundreds of pastors whom he would train in Catholic leadership.

Young adults contribute to the richness of parish life, but they may not automatically connect with, or stay connected with, the Church in the way generations before them did. It takes a conscious effort on the part of each community of faith to welcome the gifts and meet the needs of the young adults who live within their boundaries.

PURPOSE OF THIS BOOK

This book, *Connecting Young Adults to Catholic Parishes: Best Practices in Catholic Young Adult Ministry*, was developed to help faith communities implement *Sons and Daughters of the Light*, the pastoral plan issued by the Catholic bishops of the United States to promote ministry with young adults.[1] *Connecting Young Adults to Catholic Parishes* seeks to help parishes make a better connection with young adults. It is the result of years of vision development and of action by young adults and by those who walk with them on the journey of faith. This book is meant for all those whose ministries touch the lives of young adults, particularly in parishes. It provides strategies for being more responsive to the needs and the gifts of young adults in specific aspects of parish life—and then in the entire Catholic community.

This book complements *Young Adult Works*, the five-binder comprehensive resource developed by the Center for Ministry Development through its Ministry with Young Adults: A National Catholic Initiative ("the Initiative"), which provided specific programs and resources focused on ministry to and with young adults.[2] *Connecting Young Adults to Catholic Parishes* goes further by focusing on making parishes more responsive to young adults and by encouraging the integration of all young adults into Catholic communities of faith. This book helps parishes that strive to be more young adult–responsive to (1) identify what they are already doing to provide services to young adults, (2) assess how responsive they are to young adults, (3) make changes to become more responsive, and (4) offer particular programs and resources to meet the unique needs of young adults. Only then can parishes credibly invite young adults into their communities, welcome them unconditionally, and challenge them to take the initiative for making ministry with their peers the best it can be.

The first chapter of the book, "Creating a Young Adult–Responsive Church," is meant for all ministries. Each succeeding chapter focuses on a particular aspect of church life as it relates to young adults and includes real-life examples of successful ministry with them. Experts in ministry with young adults from across the country, many of them young adults themselves, share their insights into how the various elements of ministry with young adults can be developed more strongly in positive, creative, and faithful ways. Most chapters include

---

1   See United States Conference of Catholic Bishops (USCCB), *Sons and Daughters of the Light: A Pastoral Plan for Ministry with Young Adults* (Washington, DC: USCCB, 1996).
2   See Ronald Bagley, CJM, John Roberto, Susan Stark, and Joan Weber, eds., *Young Adult Works* (Naugatuck, CT: Center for Ministry Development [CMD], 1997).

a special section at the end, "The Campus Connection," which explores the chapter's topic in the context of campus ministry. Finally, the concluding chapter, "Taking the Next Steps," summarizes the Initiative team's projections for the future and is helpful to all ministries. You may wish to read the first and the last chapter, and then other chapters as needed for your particular ministry.

In many chapters, the general issues raised are also addressed through the specific lenses of culture and cultural diversity. In addition to observations about ministry with young adults from African American and Asian/Pacific Islander communities, many segments throughout the book (including Chapter 12, "Young Adult Ministry: Hispanic/Latino Perspectives") give special attention to ministry with Hispanic/Latino young adults. In the year 2000, Hispanics/Latinos accounted for more than 45 percent of Catholics under the age of thirty in the United States[3]—and for more than 35 percent of Catholics of all ages in the United States.[4] Those numbers are expected only to grow over the next decades.

While many parishes may never be able to offer comprehensive ministry to their young adults—due to demographics, lack of resources, or other factors—all parishes can be more responsive to young adults. This book is for everyone working in church ministry who recognizes the gift that young adults are to the Church, as well as the urgency of meeting them in the context of their lives, welcoming their gifts, and supporting them on the journey of faith.

Ultimately, ministry with young adults must and will continue to grow and be refined by young adults themselves—not merely by those who minister to and with them. May this resource provide inspiration and encouragement for the journey.

---

3   See Instituto Fe y Vida Research and Resource Center, *Changing the Face of Ministry with Catholic Hispanic Youth and Young Adults* (Stockton, CA: Instituto Fe y Vida).

4   See *www.usccb.org/hispanicaffairs* and the U.S. Census Bureau.

CHAPTER ONE

Creating a Young Adult– Responsive Church

How do parishes welcome the gifts and meet the needs of the young adults in their midst? This chapter provides parish leaders with insights and strategies for outreach to young singles and couples, and it invites parishes to become more responsive to young adults. Using Sons and Daughters of the Light *as a framework, the chapter challenges readers to be more aware of the opportunities that already exist for connecting with young adults.*

The Catholic bishops of the United States, in their pastoral plan *Communities of Salt and Light*, define the parish in the following way:

> The parish is where the Church lives. Parishes are communities of faith, of action, and of hope. They are where the Gospel is proclaimed and celebrated, where believers are formed and sent to renew the earth. Parishes are the home of the Christian community; they are the heart of our Church. Parishes are the place where God's people meet Jesus in word and sacrament and come in touch with the source of the Church's life.[1]

Parishes that live up to this challenging description are already responsive to young adults because they offer what young adults look to the Church to provide: a deeper relationship with Jesus, inspiration, a sense of hope, opportunities to do justice, rituals that touch their hearts as well as their minds, and connections between their lives and their faith.

A young adult–responsive parish has Jesus at its core. Everything the community does, from Sunday liturgy to parish potlucks, serves as a way to connect parishioners with Jesus. This connection in itself is appealing to young adults, who seek a personal relationship with Jesus that is supported by the Word of God and the church community. In the discussions during

---

1   United States Conference of Catholic Bishops (USCCB), *Communities of Salt and Light: Reflections on the Social Mission of the Parish* (Washington, DC: USCCB, 1994), 1.

Ministry with Young Adults: A National Catholic Initiative ("the Initiative"), young adults described how much they value a community of faith that talks more about Jesus than about church structures and systems. *Sons and Daughters of the Light*, the bishops' pastoral plan for young adult ministry, witnesses to this reality in its first two goals: connecting young adults with Jesus, and connecting young adults with the Church—the connection with Jesus being primary.

Throughout the years of the Initiative, participants worked hard to identify what it means to be responsive to young adults in a parish. *Sons and Daughters of the Light* describes the relationship between parishes and young adults:

> Often, the first community that Catholics connect with is the parish. This may be where they were baptized, where they stop by when they are in town, or where they hope to marry. Pastoral care for young adults requires that parishes be a *home* for young adults where they are personally touched in their faith journey. Here is where most young adults experience life cycle events—birth, marriage, and death—and struggle with the challenges of their lives—leaving home and coming back.[2]

As the Introduction to this book acknowledges, not every parish has the population, resources, or personnel needed to do comprehensive ministry with young adults. But *every* parish can be more responsive to the needs and gifts that young adults bring. Vast resources, more staff, and a large budget are not necessary; what is required is being a joyful community of faith: living the Gospel with integrity, caring for each other, and reaching beyond the community to care for those most in need. Young adults are drawn to a community that radiates the joy first described in the Acts of the Apostles, where Resurrection is real and the Good News is taken to heart:

> The community of believers was of one heart and mind, and no one claimed that any of his possessions was his own, but they had everything in common. With great power the apostles bore witness to the resurrection of the Lord Jesus, and great favor was accorded them all. There was no needy person among them, for those who owned property or houses would sell them, bring the proceeds of the sale, and put them at the feet of the apostles, and they were distributed to each according to need. (Acts 4:32-35)

---

2   USCCB, *Sons and Daughters of the Light: A Pastoral Plan for Ministry with Young Adults* (Washington, DC: USCCB, 1996), 27.

This description of the first Christian community challenges Catholics today to show the same fidelity and to embrace the call to be Easter people in all aspects of their lives. In a world in which young adults have witnessed the effects of hatred and despair, a Church that offers them hope for the future and joy in the present is a Church to which they can say "yes."

AWARENESS IS A FIRST STEP

Young-adult–responsive parishes are, first and foremost, aware that young adults are present, regardless of their degrees of participation or attendance at Sunday liturgy.

That assertion may seem obvious. Yet many church leaders who participated in the Initiative initially reported having few young adults in their parishes—only to be proved wrong after actually conducting a young adult census. For example, the Archdiocese of Omaha decided to do a diocese-wide census to determine the number of young adults in the twenty-three counties of northeast Nebraska. One pastor reluctantly agreed to do the census, although he reported that he had few young adults. Once the census was completed, however, he came back to share that young adults were the largest age group in his parish.

Young adults are not on the radar screen of many parish leaders. Both the Initiative and *Sons and Daughters of the Light* attempted to heighten awareness. An initial step in becoming a young adult–responsive parish is educating the parish—staff, volunteers, and parishioners at large—about the young adults in its midst. Each parish can help to validate this reality and increase its awareness by conducting its own census.

RESPECTING THE *ADULT* IN YOUNG ADULTS

Healthy parishes recognize that people in their late teens, twenties, and thirties are *adults*, whose gifts parishes need and whose unique developmental issues deserve parishes' attention. In these parishes, young adults are not patronized or otherwise treated like second-class citizens. They are listened to. Their faith journeys are not just tolerated—they are celebrated and affirmed.

Regardless of whether young adults are searching for answers to their faith questions or are embracing a faith for which they have already found answers, the Church welcomes them. It is a home for their faith. Parishes in tune with young adults follow Jesus' model of unconditional acceptance and love, inviting young adults into a community where they are welcomed, known, and cared for by name.

As the Catholic bishops of the United States expressed in their adult faith formation statement *Our Hearts Were Burning Within Us,*

> a living faith is a *searching* faith—it *"seeks understanding."* Adults need to question, probe, and critically reflect on the meaning of God's revelation in their unique lives in order to grow closer to God. A searching faith leads to deepening conversion. Along the way, it may even experience doubt. Yet the essence of this quality of adult faith is not doubt, but search—a trusting, hopeful, persistent "seeking" or "hunger" for a deeper appropriation of the Gospel and its power to guide, transform, and fulfill our lives.[3]

Parishes that are responsive to young adults appreciate this searching faith. They know that, amid the doubts articulated by young adults, a holy search for truth and meaning is progressing.

Welcoming parishes see young adults as a treasure that the Church cannot afford to lose. They invite young adults into active involvement and significant leadership positions—on the pastoral council or the finance committee, in liturgical planning, in religious education and youth ministry, as RCIA sponsors or catechists. And responsive parishes offer young adults the training and support they need to be successful in their leadership. Parishes that have invited young adults into active participation and have supported them along the way have reported a renewed sense of life and vibrancy in their communities. Many who participated in the Initiative commented on the keen sense of stewardship in their young adults. When young adults' spiritual hungers are fed, they in turn feed others—by volunteering their time, giving of their treasure very generously, and offering their unique talents to the community of faith.

---

3   USCCB, *Our Hearts Were Burning Within Us: A Pastoral Plan for Adult Faith Formation in the United States* (Washington, DC: USCCB, 1999), no. 52, quoting *Catechism of the Catholic Church*, no. 158.

DIVERSITY AS A GIFT

To be responsive to young adults is to recognize that young adults are diverse in every way. They represent every vocational call to ministry—lay ministry, consecrated life, or ordained ministry. They also represent every life decision: marriage (with or without children), single life (including newly single life, through divorce, separation, or the death of a spouse), religious life, or ordained ministry. They are rich in cultural diversity, represent every socioeconomic and educational level, and are present in all professions. Each one of them deserves unconditional welcome by the Catholic community.

Diverse Age Groups

Responsive parishes pay attention to the three distinct age groups that constitute young adulthood:[4] eighteen to twenty-five, middle to late twenties, and thirties. These age groups are general classifications that may vary between different cultures.

The first group, ages eighteen to twenty-five, includes those who are in college, the military, or their first full-time job. They are the least likely to be present in parish life—possibly because they are figuring out their own faith, independent of their parents' influence. The responsive parish looks for ways to stay connected with these young adults as they graduate from high school so that they know they always have a home for their faith. Ritualizing their passage into young adulthood, offering an open house in the rectory at Christmastime, sending birthday cards, or e-mailing the bulletin or online daily meditations are several ways in which parishes can maintain their connection with the youngest adult population. Using podcasts to share the daily Word or various prayer experiences is another way to address the spiritual needs of this age group. Strategies for evangelizing the youngest adults that do not center on meeting as a group are often more likely to engage them than are group programs located at the church.

The second young adult age group consists of those in their middle to late twenties. Since many in this group are still single, they are the most likely to attend programs and events and are eager to discuss faith issues with their peers. Responsive parishes look for ways to involve these young adults in leadership and to offer them opportunities to share faith with each other. In today's society, most people discern their vocational call in the period from the

---

4   See Robert Gribbon, *Developing Faith in Young Adults* (Washington, DC: The Alban Institute, 1990), 3, 4.

middle twenties to early thirties. Consequently, parishes have a tremendous opportunity to provide workshops and retreats on discernment that will give young adults a prayerful setting in which to discern God's call to "holiness, community, and service."[5]

The third group includes young adults in their thirties, who are likely to be the busiest and most settled of all young adults. Because so many of them are starting families or establishing themselves in their careers, they are more likely to attend events and programs targeted to their unique needs (e.g., young mothers or fathers) than to come to generic programs. They are ready to make a long-term commitment to a faith community that addresses their needs and invites them to share their gifts.

Diverse Faith Lives

Young adults are also diverse in their faith lives. Some are actively involved in their parishes; others come occasionally. Still others are angry with, alienated from, or indifferent to their Catholic faith. Some are drawn to traditional faith practices; others are looking for new ways to express their spirituality. Labels like "conservative" or "liberal" are irrelevant to today's young adults, who seek a faith that is meaningful to them as individuals.

Taking this diversity seriously means that parish leaders spend time listening to their own young adults to hear their life stories and understand their faith issues. Too often parishes try to connect with young adults by creating programs for them to attend. Yet, as the bishops note in *Sons and Daughters of the Light*, "there are many opportunities to touch the lives of young adults, and these should be seen as moments for evangelizing outreach. Some of these may require a change in the way we approach evangelization so our outreach is more dynamic, taking the Church into the community where young adults gather rather than waiting for these men and women to come to us."[6] Faith communities that understand young adults form relationships with them before extending an invitation to attend programs. Staff members and parishioners invite young adults to share their stories, their struggles, and their questions in an atmosphere of acceptance and love. They recognize that proselytizing is not the first step in connecting with young adults—the first step is to encounter young adults in the circumstances of their lives.

---

5   *Sons and Daughters of the Light*, 17.
6   *Sons and Daughters of the Light*, 34.

This was Jesus' method two thousand years ago, and it is just as effective today, as *Sons and Daughters of the Light* describes:

> Young adult men and women experience a spiritual tension arising from the contrast between contemporary society and the desire to live according to the will of God. They speak at times of a wariness toward organized religion. Although they desire a deeper spiritual life, this attitude and other influences from contemporary society push them to question and doubt what has been part of their lives. The Church needs to respond to this doubting and questioning by encouraging a dialogue that welcomes challenges from the young adult to the Church and from the Church to the young adult, so that each may grow in discipleship.[7]

Another way in which effective parishes evangelize young adults is through "entry points"—moments or points of contact when young adults approach the parish. Not even the best catechetical session, spiritual formation program, or service project can be done with young adults until they are present in parishes, so entry points are crucial. They can mean the difference between whether a young adult joins and fully participates in a parish or instead leaves the Catholic Church forever.

CONNECTING FAITH AND LIFE

Young-adult–responsive parishes take seriously the *National Directory for Catechesis*, the bishops' directory for catechetical formation and ministry in the United States, and its call to "bring about in the believer an ever more mature faith in Jesus Christ, a deeper knowledge and love of his person and message, and a firm commitment to follow him."[8] One way the parish can support young adults' discipleship is by being bridge builders: that is, by connecting the life experiences of young adults with the Gospel and the two-thousand-year Tradition of the Catholic Church. Effective parishes already make an intentional faith-life connection for all parishioners through the priests' homilies, the parish Web site, the bulletin, and the programs offered to the adult community. For example, when a presidential election is on the horizon, many parishes

---

7   *Sons and Daughters of the Light*, 13.
8   USCCB, *National Directory for Catechesis* (Washington, DC: USCCB, 2005), § 19.A.

share with adult members the bishops' most recent statement on faithful citizenship.[9] Parishes that are responsive to young adults make sure to include young adults in these efforts. These parishes are not afraid of the tough questions that young adults ask, because they know the questions deserve mature and honest answers. Effective parishes trust and understand the Church's good reasons for doing what it does, and they share these reasons honestly and openly with young adults. Church leaders carry out what Kenda Creasy Dean and Ron Foster call "double exegesis" in *The Godbearing Life*: they "use contemporary language with faithfulness and clarity to bring the power of the [Gospel] into the present" and balance it by "drawing out the Gospel's meaning for the theological struggles at work" in the lives of the faithful.[10]

ADULT EDUCATION THAT INCLUDES *YOUNG* ADULTS

Parishes that look at adult religious education from the perspective of young adults recognize that all catechesis offered to the adult community needs to be responsive to young adults. In their pastoral plan *Our Hearts Were Burning Within Us*, the bishops challenge the Church to focus on adult faith formation.

When the religious-education director is planning an event for adult education, he or she needs to be aware of the catechetical hungers of young adults and act accordingly. Publicity should be directed to younger as well as older adults and might invite participants to "try before they buy" when a series of workshops is offered. In the workshops themselves, a straight lecture approach will not be effective with young adults. Rather, young adults, who tend to be experiential learners, deepen their faith when they engage in the process of sharing faith. Catechetical efforts that employ contemporary technology (e.g., an online video or a podcast) will also appeal more directly to young adults' learning style.

Responsive parishes stay current with new ways of connecting young adults with the Church and its mission in the world. For example, in November 2003, the bishops published a short statement to young adults about stewardship, in which they issued the following challenge: "this is a call to

---

9   The USCCB issues a faithful citizenship statement every four years, just before each U.S. presidential election season. See *FaithfulCitizenship.org* for more information.

10   Kenda Creasy Dean and Ron Foster, *The Godbearing Life* (Nashville, TN: Upper Room Books, 1998), 178.

young adults everywhere to renew the face of the Earth. This is a call to listen to the voice of the Spirit speaking of gratitude and responsibility. This is an invitation to Catholic stewardship."[11] Several midwestern parishes used this brochure as an opportunity to engage young adults in dialogue through an evening of reflection. The statement includes four sets of questions for young adults, focusing on the gifts that young adults bring to their world and on the challenge to bring out the gifts they see in others.

CARPE DIEM

Young-adult–responsive parishes practice a *carpe diem* philosophy, forming young adults in faith whenever they can. They invite young adults to the Church in order to work through the issues confronting them in the world—from same-sex marriage to cohabitation, from just war to economic injustice. Young adults are given a supportive community where they can discuss their struggles with the challenges of church doctrine and with political systems that disappoint them. Through the lenses of the Gospel and Catholic social teaching, young adults are encouraged to listen to God's Word as it is spoken in today's world. For example, when war breaks out, responsive parishes invite young adults to come together to discuss war from a Catholic perspective—bringing in the Church's rich teachings on when war can be morally justified. A parish in the San Francisco area offered young adults a chance to gather and discuss war when U.S. troops were sent overseas, and almost two hundred young adults showed up.

YOUNG ADULTS AND SERVICE: ADDING THE THEOLOGICAL REFLECTION

The Center for Applied Research in the Apostolate (CARA), in a survey[12] taken for the Initiative, identified service as a feature of parish life that attracts young adults. Most parishes already offer opportunities for young adults to live out their gospel call. These opportunities include service within the parish (e.g., visiting parishioners who are unable to leave home, or working as members

---

11   USCCB, *Stewardship and Young Adults: An Invitation to Help Change the World* (Washington, DC: USCCB, 2004).

12   See Mary E. Bendyna, RSM, Mary L. Gautier, and Paul Perl, *Meeting the Challenges of Ministry with Young Adults in a New Millennium: An Evaluation Project for the Ministry with Young Adults—A National Catholic Initiative* (Washington, DC: CARA, 2000), 121.

of St. Vincent de Paul) as well as service beyond the parish (e.g., working as a parish team at a Habitat for Humanity site).

Whatever the service, responsive parishes offer young adults the chance for theological reflection after their service project so that they see the connection between what they have done and who they are as disciples of Jesus. Providing a journal, leading a discussion of the experience in the van on the way back to the parish or campus, and concluding the experience with prayer are ways to connect the service to faith. Questions like "What happened to your heart today?", "How were you the Body of Christ for the people you served?", and "How were they the Body of Christ for you?" remind young adults that such service reflects their baptismal call to serve others—it is not merely a résumé-booster (the reason that one Initiative participant gave to explain the service she did in college). The Church has a unique opportunity here to help young adults make the connection between their service to others and the challenge issued by Jesus in Matthew 25:40: "Amen, I say to you, whatever you did for one of these least brothers of mine, you did for me."

The *Young Adult Guide to Service*, in Binder Five of *Young Adult Works*[13] (the comprehensive five-binder resource developed after the Initiative to help faith communities do young adult ministry), is a reproducible booklet that young adults can use to reflect on service from many different perspectives. It was developed as a tool to help those young adults who are likely to serve—but unlikely to come to church for service opportunities—to reflect on service through the lens of faith.

YOUNG ADULTS AND TECHNOLOGY

Responsive parishes know that using technology is an especially effective way to reach out to young adults. These parishes put energy and effort into creating, maintaining, and regularly updating a dynamic parish Web site. They offer online reflections on each day's readings or provide links to other appropriate Web sites for prayer, discussion, reflection, and retreat experiences (e.g., directing young adults to *www.usccb.org* to get a podcast of the daily readings). They use social networking Web sites to connect and update interested young adults. They may even get a group of young adults to create and promote an

---

13   See Joan Weber, *Young Adult Guide to Service,* in *Young Adult Works,* eds. Ronald Bagley, CJM, John
        Roberto, Susan Stark, and Joan Weber (Naugatuck, CT: Center for Ministry Development [CMD],
        1997), Binder 5.

online video that relates to faith and life. As stated by one creative team at the 2000 Ministry with Young Adults Symposium,

> the "Faith Internet" reaches out to people without judging and enables them to respond as they feel called by the Spirit. Like a Web site, the Church is only as effective as its links. It transmits the presence of God and receives the presence of God wherever people are. It is open and accessible to everyone. The image of the Church as a web includes celebrating, teaching, acknowledging, and personal relationships.[14]

INCORPORATION, NOT SEPARATION: THE TWENTY-FIRST–CENTURY GOAL

Certainly, parishes that are responsive to young adults offer them the context and the support they need to progress through their unique developmental issues. Yet the ultimate goal of responsive parishes is *not* to create a separate sub-parish for young adults. Rather, these parishes integrate young adults into the life of the intergenerational faith community.

Young adults engage in leadership and participation at all levels of parish life. They enrich the faith lives of all age groups. They can be particularly effective in mentoring adolescents, in part because young adults represent the independence for which youth yearn—they are at a stage of life that youth long to reach—and because they are young enough to remember the struggles of adolescence better than older adults might. (In contrast, older adults share few early experiences with today's teens, because of all the rapid changes in the world in the last few decades.) Young adults are also a gift to older adults; they share life stories with the elderly, share leadership with the middle-aged, and give both generations a sense of hope. The Church is in good hands with young adults. Their inspiration and energy and the new ways they have discovered to live the Gospel are sources of renewal for all of us within the community of faith.

One team at the 2000 symposium described the type of community that is responsive to young adults: "the Church is a body in which people's gifts are identified and lifted up. The Church should discover, recognize, develop and

---

14   John Roberto and Joan Weber, eds., *Meeting the Challenges of Ministry with Young Adults in a New Millennium* (Naugatuck, CT: CMD, 2000), 22.

share the gifts of young adults for the mission of Christ in family, community, workplace, church, and the world."[15]

In their book *The Search for Common Ground*, James Davidson and his colleagues describe what unites younger and older Catholics. In a three-year research project, they found that pan-Vatican II beliefs—long-standing doctrines such as the Trinity, Incarnation, and the Resurrection (imbedded in the Nicene Creed) as well as the beliefs in Mary as the Mother of God and in the Real Presence of Christ in the Eucharist—are the foundation of the greatest unity among Catholics. Davidson and colleagues found that another area of common ground centers on the Church's social teachings: for example, most Catholics embrace the principle of concern for the poor.[16]

Young-adult–responsive parishes build on these areas of common ground between young adults and other generations. They engage young adults in faith sharing with the "wisdom people" who honestly and openly share their own journeys and their fidelity to the Catholic Tradition.

At the same time, these parishes pay attention to the findings presented in the book *American Catholics*: the findings that young adults contribute to trends like "declining levels of attachment to the Church as an institution" and "declining levels of religious practice."[17] This research—reported by William D'Antonio, James Davidson, Dean Hoge, and Katherine Meyer—indicates a lower level of agreement with church teachings among young adults than that seen in older generations. These scholars raise a key question: What can church leaders do to increase agreement with church teachings? In response, they offer three suggestions:

1. "Leaders need to build relationships among Catholics . . . the stronger these relationships; the more likely Catholics are to embrace church teachings. . . ."

2. "Leaders need to communicate the Church's core values in ways that speak to people's needs. . . . they need to understand the life circumstances and lifestyles of today's Catholics. . . ."

3. "Leaders need to make the acceptance of church teachings as attractive and rewarding as possible. Agreement with church teachings

---

15   Roberto and Weber, *Meeting the Challenges of Ministry*, 21.

16   See James D. Davidson et al., *The Search for Common Ground: What Unites and Divides Catholic Americans* (Huntington, IN: Our Sunday Visitor, 1997), 42-43.

17   William V. D'Antonio, James D. Davidson, Dean R. Hoge, and Katherine Meyer, *American Catholics: Gender, Generation, and Commitment* (Walnut Creek, CA: AltaMira Press, 2001), 28.

should be associated with opportunities and benefits that are not available to people who disagree. . . . They should maintain relationships with people who are not ready to embrace church teachings; listen to their questions, doubts, and concerns; try to interpret church teachings in meaningful ways; and strive toward a convergence of views."[18] In striving toward mutual understanding of views, leaders must be careful to be true to Catholic Tradition, while maintaining open lines of communication.

These three suggestions offer good advice for all parishes, but particularly for those trying to be more responsive to the young adults in their midst.

CONCLUSION

The Initiative held listening sessions with young adults across the country to determine how they characterize a young adult–responsive Church. When asked, "What are you looking for in the Church today?", young adults named the following ten elements:

1. A sense of community and belonging (a faith community where "everybody knows your name")
2. Dynamic liturgies
3. Spiritual growth and enrichment
4. Religious education and Catholic identity
5. Guidance and direction in life
6. Acceptance and support
7. Opportunities for service and leadership
8. Social activities
9. A community that shares common values
10. Inspiration and rejuvenation

This book, *Connecting Young Adults to Catholic Parishes*, shares many different ways in which Catholic communities can provide these opportunities and resources to young adults in the context of parish life.

---

18   *American Catholics*, 139-140.

CHAPTER TWO

Prayer and Spirituality

How can parishes guide and support young adults on their
spiritual journeys? This chapter uses real-life stories to help
parishes fulfill the bishops' call to offer spiritual direction and formation
to young adults. It explores opportunities for sacraments, retreats, prayer,
and other faith experiences with young adults, in both group and
individual settings and in both traditional and innovative formats.

*One of the defining characteristics of today's young adults is their
hunger for a personal spirituality.*[1]

Church life at the start of the twenty-first century, as illuminated in the
listening sessions of Ministry with Young Adults: A National Catholic Initiative ("the Initiative"), includes young adult Catholics who are as spiritual as
any previous generation. While not necessarily attracted to organized religion,
they want the same spiritual growth opportunities that other adults seek. In
prayer, they acknowledge God's power and goodness, their own need for and
dependence on him, and the truth that God has created them to love and to
be loved. Their spirituality engages their views of life and their unique ways
of living out those views at home, at work or school, during recreation, and in
their economic and social lives. For Catholic young adults, spirituality centers
on their relationship to God in Jesus Christ.

Today's young adults are drawn to the exploration of spirituality. The parish can support young adults as they deepen their relationship with God. It
connects them with the Catholic faith, which can play a vital role in their
spiritual lives by guiding and directing young adults toward Christ.

The sacraments of the Church provide the strength that young adults need
in order to live faithful lives in the world. In the Eucharist, in which they share
in Christ's sacrifice and in which they are nourished by the Body and Blood of
Christ, young adults find answers to the deep yearnings of the human heart.
Parishes that are responsive to young adults know that the Eucharist awakens

---

1   "A Spiritually Challenging Vision," in *Young Adult Works*, ed. Ronald Bagley, CJM, John Roberto, Susan
     Stark, and Joan Weber (Naugatuck, CT: Center for Ministry Development [CMD], 1997), Binder 3, 7.3.

within those celebrating it a taste for prayer; this knowledge inspires responsive parishes to offer young adults the varied and rich tradition of prayer within the Church.

SCENARIOS

- Lisa, a recent college graduate who now works full-time, was very involved in youth ministry at her parish and in a diocesan retreat program. She was also active in campus ministry at her university's parish. Last year, she moved to a new area and is seeking a way to connect with a faith community again.

- Jose was involved in his parish as a child, through the prompting of his mother. However, after Confirmation he "graduated" from religious education. After high school he stopped going to Mass. Around his thirtieth birthday, he sensed something was missing from his life.

- Tim and Jim, twin brothers, went on a young adult retreat sponsored in their diocese, at the encouragement of Tim's girlfriend. Tim enjoyed the weekend but does not want to make any life changes at this time, as he is enjoying his college experience. Jim, however, cannot wait to get involved with the Church, perhaps by serving as a lector or religious education teacher in campus ministry or at a parish, or perhaps by starting a young adult group.

- One Sunday during the sign of peace, an African American young adult reached out to shake the hand of a little boy who was about five years old. As she reached for his hand, he pulled it back, turned to the man standing next to him, and said, "She's black." The young woman never did get that handshake.

- Suzanne is a divorced thirty-two-year-old mother of two children, ages three and six. She barely has enough time to buy groceries, between her job and the kids' activities. She knows she should focus some time and energy on her faith, but she just does not see when she can.

Each of these young adults is at a different point on the path to God. All have had different life experiences, yet all hunger for a deep faith that can give meaning to their lives at work and at home. The Catholic Church has a wonderful opportunity to offer them a "vision of life based on a faith that calls each of them to holiness" and to help them "develop their spiritual life rooted in a personal relationship with Jesus Christ as their redeemer and savior."[2] Does your parish take advantage of this opportunity? Do young adults feel welcomed there? What programs and services can they find in your parish to assist them in their progress toward God?

In their pastoral plan *Sons and Daughters of the Light: A Pastoral Plan for Ministry with Young Adults*, the Catholic bishops of the United States identify four goals, the first of which is *connecting young adults with Jesus Christ*.[3] Of that goal's three objectives, this chapter addresses the first: *spiritual formation and direction*.[4] The bishops, in their pastoral plan, challenge the Church to support young adults in a variety of ways as they strive to deepen their spiritual lives.

SPIRITUAL FORMATION OF YOUNG ADULTS

Most adults seek a connection between their faith and their day-to-day lives. What is unique about many young adults today is that they feel a disconnect between a Catholic identity that is based on spirituality and a Catholic identity that is based on involvement with the structures of the institutional Church. Some young adults look for God in places outside the Church, trying Eastern meditation, yoga, Native American spiritual practices, or prayers from other traditions. Some have spiritual awakenings when they engage in activities not traditionally seen as "religious." For example, young adults in the Initiative shared that reading a particularly moving book, seeing a Broadway show, or experiencing a beautiful sunset made them feel as spiritually fulfilled as sacramental practices did.

Parishes have a real opportunity to provide a forum in which young adults can gather to share how they find God in their experiences. This opportunity can, in turn, serve as a reminder to parishes that young adults are more than capable of seeking God and of taking initiative in their own spiritual practices.

Some young adults experience a spiritual tension between the values of contemporary society and their personal desire to live faithful lives. This tension can arise out of their current relationship status (single, dating, engaged,

---

2   United States Conference of Catholic Bishops (USCCB), *Sons and Daughters of the Light: A Pastoral Plan for Ministry with Young Adults* (Washington, DC: USCCB, 1996), 17, 28.

3   The other three goals are as follows: (2) connecting young adults with the Church, (3) connecting young adults with the mission of the Church in the world, and (4) connecting young adults with a peer community. See *Sons and Daughters of the Light*, 28-41.

4   See *Sons and Daughters of the Light*, 28. Objective 2, religious education and formation, is addressed in Chapter 4 of this book, and Objective 3, vocational discernment, is addressed in Chapter 5 of this book.

married, separated, divorced, or widowed), their employment status (working full-time or part-time, working multiple jobs, being unemployed or underemployed, studying in college or vocational training centers, being imprisoned, or serving in the military), or their family life (living with family of origin, married without children, married with children, or single with children). Tensions between contemporary social mores and faith may arise out of many other aspects of life as well.

While the challenge may seem overwhelming, the good news is that young adults want a strong prayer life and want spiritual development. The Church can provide a variety of opportunities for young adults to connect: through the sacraments, prayer, study, retreats, and creative outreach. Offering young adults meaningful faith experiences—and inviting them to articulate the ways in which they find God in non-traditional settings—can help them make the connection between their spiritual yearnings and their Catholic identity.

MEETING YOUNG ADULTS IN THEIR OWN LIVES: SEARCHING FAITH

Developmentally, young adults are asking questions, seeking answers, and looking for ways to fit faith into their everyday lives. John Westerhoff identifies four stages of faith through which people move as they grow spiritually:

1. *Experiential faith*—Faith usually seen in the small child
2. *Affiliative faith*—Faith that usually occurs in later childhood and early adolescence
3. *Searching faith*—Faith that develops, for most people, in late adolescence or early young adulthood
4. *Owned faith*—A fully embraced adult faith, which some people never achieve[5]

Most young adults have moved from affiliative faith to searching faith, wherein they question, experiment, and test belief statements. This is a necessary step to reaching owned faith. Westerhoff points out that stages can't be skipped. A person can only achieve owned faith—making a personal commitment to one's beliefs—by working through all three previous stages.

---

5   See John Westerhoff III, *Will Our Children Have Faith?* (New York: Seabury Press, 1976).

Young adults in the third stage, the searching stage, need a responsive parish where they can find answers to their questions. Responsive parishes offer "safe places" where young adults can ask questions, and they offer resources to help young adults seek answers. And when parishes commit to the spiritual needs of young adults in this way, the parish can expect some of the young adults to commit in turn to the parish community.

Many young adults have not had the depth of experiential faith that previous generations had. Some young adults were raised by Baby Boomer parents, who decided not to raise their children in the Catholic faith but instead to let them choose their own religion as adults. Others grew up with parents who were lapsed Catholics, not engaged in the practices of the Catholic Church. These experiences change the nature of the searching stage of spiritual growth for today's young adult Catholics. As a result, young adults have an even greater need for parishes to provide profound, holy experiences that lift up young adults, help them grow closer to God, and help them fulfill their need for experiential faith.

PRAYER THAT ENGAGES YOUNG ADULTS

Each young adult is unique, but the vast majority of those who were interviewed in the Initiative shared that prayer was an important part of their spirituality. The Catholic Church is blessed to have such a wide variety of prayer styles to offer. From Benedictine chants to guided meditations, the Church can engage the prayer lives of young adults through its rich, diverse Tradition. The prayers of the Church have stood the test of time and are meaningful for today. They are suitable for young adults of every time and every culture.

Sons and Daughters of the Light recommends that faith communities "provide opportunities for young adults to learn and experience different forms of personal and group prayer."[6] Key here is the emphasis on learning *and* experiencing. Responsive parishes not only talk to young adults about prayer, but also offer dynamic experiences that lift up young adults. Variety is critical to engaging this diverse population.

---

6   *Sons and Daughters of the Light*, 28.

The following examples show how the Church has engaged young adults with different prayer experiences:

- The Cathedral of Christ the King in Atlanta, Georgia, held a four-week evening series on various forms of prayer. Each session began with a brief talk on one type of prayer and then led into an experience of that form of prayer. The series was open to the whole parish, but it attracted a number of young adults.

- St. Dominic Parish in the Archdiocese of San Francisco has held a weekly young adult Rosary. The parish provides prayer sheets, instruction booklets, and rosaries so that everyone can participate.

- During Lent, the St. Ignatius Young Adult Group in Boston, Massachusetts, has sponsored a weekly "Soup and Stations" program for the entire parish. Community is built through the meal and in prayer.

- St. Clement Parish in Chicago, Illinois, has offered a "centering prayer" time every Saturday morning—a wonderful opportunity for young adults to learn how to get in touch with the voice of God through silence and centering.

- Regular prayer in community by young adults from Sagrada Familia Parish in Cleveland, Ohio, has led them into a weekly ministry of taking food to the homeless on Saturday nights.

- Catholic Underground, an event combining evening prayer, adoration, benediction, and faith-inspired culture, is popular in the Northeast. Hundreds of young adults have gathered together to experience sacred silence and the presence of Christ through eucharistic adoration.

- Journaling as a prayer tool—introduced through either a parish bulletin article or an adult faith formation session on the topic—has proven enriching for many young adults. Young-adult-responsive parishes have provided specific resources, such as *Discovering Your Light: Common Journey of Young Adults*, for young adults to use as starting points for their journaling.[7]

---

7   See Margaret O'Brien, *Discovering Your Light: Common Journey of Young Adults* (Mineola, NY: Resurrection Press, 1991).

Seasonal journals have also helped young adults make the connection between everyday life and the liturgical year. *Waiting with Hope*[8] is an Advent journal that was developed as part of the Initiative. Written by young adults for young adults, it includes Scripture readings, a reflection, and a key question for each day. *Journey to New Life*[9] is a Lenten journal that has the same format.

Popular Piety and Today's Young Adults

Popular piety expressions that are found among a significant number of young adults today create a wealth of possibilities for parishes to enrich young adults' prayer lives. Some are drawn to traditional prayers of the Church, like the Rosary, novenas, or the Stations of the Cross. Parishes can be responsive to young adults by offering the experience of traditional prayers. These can be attractive both to young adults who already know and love these forms of prayer and to those who may not have experienced such forms before.

For example, a parish may offer a Rosary or the Stations of the Cross during a mission trip or young adult service project. The motif of prayer in such contexts is justice. The parish might use prayer resources from the Catholic Campaign for Human Development (CCHD) at the United States Conference of Catholic Bishops (USCCB) for praying both the Rosary and the Stations from a justice and peace perspective. Young adults who directly serve the poor, as well as those who learn how to advocate with elected representatives for the rights of those whom they serve, might find resources like the *Novena for Justice and Peace, Unity in Diversity: A Scriptural Rosary*, and the *Way of the Cross Toward Justice and Peace*[10]—all available from the USCCB—to be a powerful witness to their faith.

In 2002, the Year of the Rosary, Pope John Paul II proclaimed the Mysteries of Light, or Luminous Mysteries. These events focused the Church's attention—including the attention of many young adults—on the Rosary as a prayer practice. The Church offers different ways to meditate on the decades that connect well with young adults. The Luminous Mysteries can connect

---

8   See Ron Bagley, CJM, ed., *Waiting with Hope: Reflections by Young Adults for Every Day of Advent* (Naugatuck, CT: CMD, 1997).

9   See Ron Bagley, CJM, ed., *Journey to New Life: Reflections by Young Adults for Every Day of Lent* (Naugatuck, CT: CMD, 1997).

10   USCCB–CCHD, *Novena for Justice and Peace* (Washington, DC: USCCB, 1998); USCCB Committee on Migration, *Unity in Diversity: A Scriptural Rosary* (Washington, DC: USCCB, 2008); USCCB–CCHD, *Way of the Cross Toward Justice and Peace* (Washington, DC: USCCB, 1998).

the public mission of Jesus to the challenges young adults face as they attempt to lead faithful lives in the world. Young adults also appreciate hearing the history of the Rosary as a prayer practice. Knowing why and how the Church prays the decades enhances the spirituality of the young adult.

The Liturgy of the Hours, Holy Hours, novenas, the Divine Mercy devotion, and adoration of the Blessed Sacrament are among other traditional forms of prayer that appeal to young adults who hunger for a quiet space in the midst of their noisy lives. Parish leaders can respond to young adults' hunger by emphasizing the primacy of such prayer forms. The parish can invite young adults to services that already exist or offer special gatherings just for young adults to introduce them to the Hours or other prayers. For example, one parish in the Midwest had great success in gathering young adults at a local coffee shop or park to pray the Liturgy of the Hours before work in the mornings.

The traditional prayer forms offered by many religious communities also appeal to young adults. Parishes can tap into the resources of these communities to connect their young adults with ancient religious practices, or with modern interpretations of these practices. As an example, young adults could join the local Jesuit community in a version of the spiritual exercises of St. Ignatius. Or they might pray the psalms throughout the day in the Benedictine tradition. Some could find a home for their prayer life in imitating St. Francis of Assisi, who gave priority to prayers of praise and thanksgiving.[11] St. Francis also found deep spiritual fulfillment in meditating on the crucified Jesus, something many young adults find powerful in their own lives.

Some young adults find that particular traditions of prayer (e.g., Franciscan, Benedictine) are helpful in deepening their prayer lives because the traditions emphasize themes or aspects of Catholic teaching that are especially relevant to them as individuals. Books like *Prayer and Temperament*[12] and *Who We Are Is How We Pray*[13] offer suggested ways of praying, based on different types of personality.

---

11   See Gloria Hutchinson, *Six Ways to Pray from Six Great Saints* (Cincinnati: St. Anthony Messenger Press, 1982), 10.

12   See Chester P. Michael and Marie C. Norrisey, *Prayer and Temperament: Different Prayer Forms for Different Personalities* (Charlottesville, VA: The Open Door, 1984).

13   See Charles J. Keating, *Who We Are Is How We Pray: Matching Personality and Spirituality* (Mystic, CT: Twenty-Third Publications, 1987).

Praying with Various Cultures

Because today's young adults have grown up with more diversity than any previous generation, they respond well to and are enriched by prayers from different cultural traditions, including the traditional Catholic prayers. Serenading Our Lady of Guadalupe on the morning of December 12 can be moving and holy for many young adults. They may appreciate the renewal and faith demonstrated in a sage purification or blessing from the Native American tradition. They may wish to integrate Asian or Pacific Islander rituals such as burning incense, participating in centering prayer, and meditating; or they might incorporate the oral tradition of storytelling and the cultural gifts of song, music, and movement from the African American community into an evening of reflection, a prayer service, a parish concert, or a scriptural discussion. Finally, many young adults from a variety of cultures find devotions to the Blessed Virgin Mary appealing.

Parishes can help young adults prepare for a liturgical season or religious holiday (e.g., Lent, Advent, or All Souls' Day) by inviting young adults and older adults to a discussion on the spiritual traditions that various cultures practice for these seasons or holidays. Parishes might encourage parishioners to set up home altars and might teach favorite traditional prayers, novenas, and songs from those cultures. They may share pictures and memories of particular regional practices, like the Hispanic/Latino practice of *Los Penitentes* in New Mexico, or incorporate a traditional practice such as living Stations of the Cross (*Via Crucis*) into existing parish prayers.

Parish leaders can connect with young adults by seeking opportunities to learn about and appreciate rich spiritual traditions from the young adults' own cultures. For example, if there is a cultural museum nearby, or if traveling exhibits of arts or culture come to the area, a parish might arrange an intergenerational visit and include young adults as facilitators or organizers. The group can look for forms of prayer and piety in the exhibits and then meet to reflect and discuss impressions over a meal afterward. Leaders can encourage young adults to discuss their own spiritual practices in relation to their families' practices: what traditions they miss, what traditions they continue to observe, those they would like to reinstate, and those they would like to incorporate from another culture.

To support all these efforts, parish leaders might consider a partnership with other parishes of differing cultural populations, sharing ways of celebrating faith across boundaries and across generations.

Other Prayer Experiences

Taizé prayer,[14] used by parishes and campuses across the country, attracts large numbers of young adults. The ecumenism of Taizé, the opportunity for quiet meditation, the simplicity of the prayers, and the inclusion of simple chants and Scripture all appeal to young adults. Parishes can offer Taizé prayer without undue effort, simply by providing an environment with icons and candles, acquiring some of the simple chants, and having someone coordinate the music. Young adults themselves can conduct the services.

Charismatic prayer also appeals to some young adults. This prayer experience takes its name from the word "charism," which means "gift." Persons engaged in charismatic prayer speak of "being baptized in the Spirit," which means that through this prayer they are conscious of the activity of the Spirit within their lives. While many parishes do not themselves have groups that focus on this particular style of prayer, they can steer interested young adults toward neighboring parishes that do.

Nature has always been a holy place for prayer. Young adults can certainly connect with the holiness in nature without the parish's help, but the parish might consider creating a setting for outdoor prayer, such as a grotto, a rosary garden, or a labyrinth walk like those used in medieval Christianity to symbolize the journey toward heaven. The whole parish benefits from such an undertaking.

RETREATS WORK

Jesus took time away to pray, and in today's busy world, young adults need these opportunities as well. Retreats have always been attractive to young adults, but the hectic pace of life can make committing to an entire weekend retreat next to impossible. Parishes and campuses have successfully met the needs of young adults with nontraditional or creative retreat formats that accommodate busy schedules.

- Parishes can offer twilight retreats (held one evening, with dinner included), mornings of reflection, or days of recollection, in addition to overnight and weekend retreats.[15]

---

14   To learn more about Taizé, see *www.taize.fr.*
15   Section 8B in Binder 4 of *Young Adult Works* provides six fully developed retreats for college students and young adults that a parish could easily adapt to its own setting.

- St. Joseph Parish in Austintown, Ohio, has held an annual men's renewal weekend and women's renewal weekend for all interested adults. The weekend retreats attract both single and married participants.
- Many dioceses have a Charismatic Renewal program or offer the Life in the Spirit seminar, which introduces adults to the role of the Holy Spirit in their faith lives.
- Creighton University has developed an "Online Retreat in Everyday Life," available at *www.creighton.edu/CollaborativeMinistry/cmo-retreat.html*. This Ignatian retreat has reached thousands who don't have the time to "go away" physically, yet who hunger for spiritual renewal. People can do the daily reflections whenever their schedules permit.
- A nearby campus ministry program might offer a Busy Person's Retreat that young parishioners can join or that can be adapted for use in any faith community. This unique design offers a personal, individual retreat experience. During a chosen week, the retreatant continues with everyday life, yet he or she meets for an hour each day with a spiritual director and commits to reading Scripture throughout the week. (See *Young Adult Works* for one complete format for offering a Busy Person's Retreat.[16])
- Retreat opportunities offered by nearby religious communities and/or the diocese can specifically address young adults' needs. For example, in Chicago and Cincinnati, Charis retreats[17] (weekend retreats that explore Catholic identity and faith questions for young adults in their twenties and thirties) are based on the Spiritual Exercises of St. Ignatius. The three-day Teens Encounter Christ (TEC) retreat format,[18] based on the Paschal Mystery of Jesus and focusing on themes of dying, rising, and going forth, was adapted for young adults in the Archdiocese of Atlanta. The Humility of Mary Sisters in Villa Maria, Pennsylvania, publicize a number of different retreats in the Dioceses of Erie, Pittsburgh, and Youngstown.
- Many young adults are ready for a more reflective monastic retreat. If a monastery is located within driving distance of the

---

16 See "Busy Student Retreat," in *Young Adult Works*, Binder 4, 8B.3–8B.21.

17 For more information about Charis retreats, see *www.charisretreats.org*.

18 For more information about Teens Encounter Christ retreats, visit the TEC Conference at *www.tecconference.com*.

parish, gathering a small group of young adults to attend can provide a life-changing opportunity that might encourage someone to go who would not go alone.

PILGRIMAGES

Pilgrimage is an ancient practice in the Church that has been enjoying great renewal. Ever since Pope John Paul II began the tradition of World Youth Day, young adults have been increasingly drawn to join large gatherings of faithful Catholics. Many parishes have taken groups of young adults to World Youth Day events in locations like Denver, Rome, Toronto, Cologne, and Manila. Often the groups make side trips as part of the overall pilgrimage experience (such as a trip to Assisi when World Youth Day was held in Rome, or to Lourdes when Paris hosted the event).

The Archdiocese of San Francisco organizes annual pilgrimages of young adults to different churches within the archdiocese. Any parish could easily do the same, perhaps initiated and organized by the parish young adult group itself. The young adults might choose five or six churches around the diocese, call to make sure the doors will be open when they come, and select prayers to say at the churches. Holy Thursday is a special opportunity for making this kind of pilgrimage.

Pilgrimages to any shrine can be wonderful opportunities for the spiritual growth of young adults, as pilgrims dedicate themselves to solidarity and simplicity during the journey.

SPIRITUAL READING

More books written today on spirituality are targeting people in their twenties and thirties. With the abundance of resources available online and in libraries, bookstores, and media centers, locating resources that are in keeping with church teaching can be difficult. Faith communities can point young adults toward good Catholic resources and holy, healthy Web sites (e.g., *www.usccb.org*, *www.americancatholic.org*, *www.sacredspace.ie*).

The parish library might include appropriate books on Catholic spirituality that resonate with young adults on their own spiritual journeys. In addition to providing contemporary works, young adult–responsive parishes include books on the lives of the saints, remembering that young adults hunger for genuine heroes and role models of faith. Of course, once the parish library has resources that appeal to young adults, the parish must spread the word to young adult parishioners. Offering a book discussion group for young adults to talk about spiritual readings is one way to draw them into spiritual study.

Consider more ways to engage young adults with good spiritual reading.

- On their own initiative, a group of young adults from St. Augustine's University Parish in St. Augustine, Florida, began reviewing the lives of the saints together, especially the younger saints, finding inspiration in the extraordinary things the saints did as young adults.
- Many Christian bookstores have prayer rooms or study spaces. Parishes can contact local Christian or Catholic bookstores to see if the stores will host a regular book club discussion.
- Some parishes provide links on their Web sites to national Catholic Web sites (e.g., the Web site of the USCCB) for daily meditations, Scripture readings, and saints of the day. A podcast of daily readings from the *New American Bible* can be found at *www.usccb.org/nab*. Other sites also have podcast meditations that users can download and listen to at their convenience.
- When new parents attend baptismal preparation sessions, young adult–responsive parishes provide them with resources on praying at home as a family.

PRAYER PARTNERS

A middle-aged woman who participated in the Initiative hearings shared a story about giving a talk at a gathering of young adults in Omaha, Nebraska. She told the young adults that her grandfather, born in 1884, had such impaired vision in his eighties that he could no longer read. But he prayed the Rosary so many times a day that the beads of his rosary were worn down to almost nothing. She related that she had found this encouraging as a young adult—knowing that her grandfather was praying for her when she got caught up in the busy pace of her life. Young adults at her talk resonated with this story to the point where they asked their parish staff if they could organize prayer partners. Parish staff matched interested young adults with seniors (many of them unable to leave their homes) in the parish. The partners didn't meet often, since that wasn't the point. But they did keep in touch by phone. And, of course, they prayed for each other. It was a beautiful cross-generational experience for both persons.

FORMING FAITH-SHARING GROUPS OF YOUNG ADULTS

Catholic communities are called by the bishops to "form bible study and reflection groups that are both peer and intergenerational."[19] Young adults are looking for ways in which the Word of God relates to their daily lives. Some want more academic learning about the Scriptures; others desire faith-sharing sessions based on the lectionary. Still others want to gather to discuss specific topics, such as the relationship between faith and work, or Catholic social teaching. Some illustrations follow. (See Chapter 10, "Forming Faith Communities of Young Adults," for still more ideas.)

- St. Gregory Parish in Plantation, Florida, has offered a discussion series on different books of the Bible.
- St. Julie Billiart Parish in San Jose, California, has facilitated a Bible study for college-aged young adults on Monday nights to suit the students' schedules and energy levels.
- Holy Faith Catholic Church in Gainesville, Florida, has offered its Little Rock Scripture Study at various times of the day to accommodate the varied schedules of the parishioners—a great way to encourage young adults to join.
- St. Catherine of Genoa Parish in Boston, Massachusetts, has encouraged young adults to discuss inspirational books through "spiritual book report nights."
- Small-group sessions to study the documents of Vatican II have proven effective in many places with young adults, who never experienced the pre-Vatican II Church.
- Small Christian communities, both peer and intergenerational groups, can provide spiritual renewal for young adults. Resources are available through RENEW International.[20] *Young Adult Works*[21] offers seventeen small-group catechetical sessions on core themes of Catholic faith, as well as twelve spiritual formation sessions.

---

19   *Sons and Daughters of the Light*, 29.
20   See *www.renewintl.org* for information.
21   See *Young Adult Works*, Binder 3, 7.1-7B.196.

SPIRITUAL DIRECTION FOR YOUNG ADULTS

Sons and Daughters of the Light challenges parishes to "make available opportunities for personal spiritual direction/formation, and provide the necessary training of spiritual directors/facilitators."[22] Some parishes print the names of spiritual directors in the bulletin or on the parish Web site so that interested adults can find a spiritual director. Others draw on the resources already offered by their diocese. For example, the Diocese of Salt Lake City's Spirituality Office helps people to find a spiritual director and provides training for potential spiritual directors. Parishes that are responsive to young adults maintain a relationship with the office in their diocese that offers similar services.

Of course, many young adults have never been educated in what spiritual direction is or what a spiritual director does. Offering a mini-workshop on the benefits of spiritual direction would be a gift—not just to young adults, but to the entire adult faith community. Use the illustrations below to generate other possibilities for offering spiritual direction to young adults.

- Connect young adults with the religious communities in your area. Some offer retreats and spiritual direction. Many have religious men and women eager to assist with retreat facilitation or to speak about their communities' particular charisms.
- Encourage parishioners to be "spiritual companions" to one another. A senior adult might pair up with a young adult to share faith stories, struggles, and hopes.
- Provide information for parishioners to connect to national or international organizations with spiritual dimensions, such as Pax Christi,[23] the National Catholic Young Adult Ministry Association,[24] or Catholic Relief Services[25] (among others).
- Parish Web sites with good links to spiritual Web sites and resources provide a great service to parishioners, especially to young adults, who tend to be most active on the Internet.

---

22   *Sons and Daughters of the Light*, 29.
23   See *www.paxchristi.net*.
24   See *www.ncyama.org*.
25   See *www.crs.org*.

CONCLUSION

Fr. Brett Hoover, CSP, founding director of Paulist Young Adult Ministries, compares the faith journey of the young adult to a "spiritual road trip."[26] Parishes and campus ministry programs that are responsive to young adults provide road maps, directional signs, rest areas, and filling stations along the journey. Responsive faith communities support young adults who are developing their spiritual life and their personal relationship with Jesus. These communities welcome searching, exploring, questioning, and experimenting, even as they provide opportunities for young adults to do each of these within the community. They invite young adults into the sacraments, particularly the Eucharist. They provide opportunities for prayer, study, and retreats. And they remember that young adults want the same thing other age groups want: to grow spiritually. In faith communities that connect young adults with opportunities for prayer and Catholic spirituality, young adults become holy, and their holiness touches and improves all Catholics' lives.

26   Brett C. Hoover, *Losing Your Religion, Finding Your Faith: Spirituality for Young Adults* (New York: Paulist Press, 1998), 13.

THE CAMPUS CONNECTION

There are certainly as many ways to pray as there are believers. Nothing is truer for today's college students, who find themselves in increasingly diverse settings. They are simultaneously drawn to both familiar and unfamiliar prayer forms. Whether at a large or small institution, college students away from home for the first time initially seek out that which is familiar. Often, the Church on campus is that place. There, students can breathe easily, because once they set foot in the chapel or church—or whatever space the campus ministry uses for liturgy—they know they are home. They know the look and feel, the gestures and the postures—and, of course, the prayers. For some students, the Church is just enough connection to home that they feel all right with being away from home. Having this experience of shared prayer gives students the strength and confidence to explore all that is new about college life.

College is often the time in life when young adults express the desire for new and more meaningful prayer experiences. For Catholic college students, this need can be met in a number of ways. Providing opportunities for students to gather outside of Sunday worship can be as simple as arranging a weekly prayer hour. The style and form of the prayer can rotate with each gathering or perhaps each semester. Asking what kind of prayer the students themselves would like to lead is essential to the program's success. When communal prayer does not necessitate a sacramental minister, a student should be invited to lead.

Many college campus ministries across the country are successfully using a variety of styles of prayer. One popular prayer form is Taizé (also discussed elsewhere in this chapter). Within communities made up of students from all over the world, campus ministries must offer forms of prayer that can enable people with little common language to actively pray together. Taizé is directed toward the goal of communal prayer for a diverse community. The use of the Taizé songs in prayer implies an overall style of celebration in which there is a spirit of recollection and an atmosphere of silence, the manner of the presider is welcoming, and the elements of the prayer space are arranged simply. Small groups can perform the music of Taizé with a simple guitar or keyboard accompaniment or with voice alone. It is a way of saying what words cannot say and of expressing a spiritual animation that swells from the depths of the human heart. Many

Newman centers and campus ministries are using this prayer form. Go to *www.taize.fr* for more information.

Other campuses use contemporary music to draw students together for communal prayer. Many tap the talent from among their own students who have knowledge of what Christian music best resonates with their peers. The time used for this gathering can be structured in a praise-and-worship format that some campuses offer on a regular basis. A concert format can be used once or twice at the beginning of the semester to generate interest. This may inspire students to come forward to host their own gatherings. Texas Tech University's campus ministry has held a weekly program called "The Rock," which features the music of a contemporary Catholic band, then a selected speaker who leads a time of teaching and prayer. The Web site for Texas Tech's Catholic student center, *www.raidercatholic.org*, offers other ideas for a parish church serving a large university community.

In addition to communal prayer experiences, students are also drawn to individual prayer. On campuses where a chapel is available, times can be set aside for traditional devotions such as adoration of the Blessed Sacrament, Stations of the Cross, or the Rosary. These can be scheduled regularly (e.g., once a week), seasonally (e.g., during Advent and Lent), or periodically (e.g., every first Friday). In response to the increasingly strong desire of students to deepen their personal relationship with God, many campuses offer individual spiritual direction. Sometimes a brief experience—a week or just a few days—can both accommodate students' busy schedules and give them enough of a taste that they will initiate a longer commitment themselves. The Newman Center at West Chester University in Pennsylvania offers a unique program called Thirty Days with the Saints. This program, developed by a campus minister, offers otherwise very busy students the opportunity for focused prayer and communal reflection online. Participants commit to reading and reflecting on a daily meditation, prayer, and thought for the day. They can then connect with others "on the journey" through e-mail. This enables participants to experience personal prayer while remaining connected with others, but without gathering in a formal setting.

Campus ministers who take seriously the command to pray always need to help those in their care to do the same. Remaining flexible and creative is important when working with college students in their prayer lives. There is a wealth of Catholic prayer forms, all of which are valuable. Campus ministers can respond to students' needs by exposing them to as many of these expressions as possible.

CHAPTER THREE

Catechesis and
Young Adult Ministry

How can parishes catechize today's young adults and foster love and receptivity for lifelong learning in the faith? This chapter describes experiences from parishes throughout the United States that are embracing this challenge with faithfulness, energy, and creativity. By employing real-life examples and referring to foundational resources, this chapter explores the aims, topics, and context for catechesis with young adults. It offers practical examples and strategies for developing leadership and provides models for catechesis that address the current challenges.

One million Catholics, most of them young adults, gather from around the globe to celebrate **World Youth Day**. Inspired by the leadership of the Holy Father and surrounded by thousands of people their own age who share their faith, the young adults open their hearts to Christ. Bishops and cardinals meet with smaller groups of these young adults in catechetical sessions. Consequently, the young adults' faith deepens as they learn more about God and their Catholic religion. Liturgical experiences, culminating in a Mass celebrated by the Holy Father, send the young people back to their own countries on fire for their faith.

Meanwhile, **small groups of Catholic young adults** gather in various spots across the United States to deepen their knowledge of the Catholic faith. One group gathers at a coffee shop in a large city to explore the *United States Catholic Catechism for Adults*[1] with peers, while another group focuses on a booklet from RENEW International, a group that fosters spiritual renewal by supporting individuals and small communities. A Hispanic/Latino group gathers at a local parish to explore the role of the saints in the group members' lives. College students gather in the residence hall of a local university to study Scripture.

St. Michael the Archangel Catholic Community in Cary, North Carolina, has engaged in **catechesis with young adults** between the ages of eighteen

---

1   See United States Conference of Catholic Bishops (USCCB), *United States Catholic Catechism for Adults* (Washington, DC: USCCB, 2006).

and twenty-five. Much of the community of Cary consists of young families. The parish has had a full-time director of adult faith formation who believes, as does the parish, that this job includes being the parish contact for young adult ministry. Together they have made sure that parish-wide catechetical structures—such as small Christian communities for Lenten faith-sharing, organizations like the Knights of Columbus, and adult faith formation groups—include young adults.

Theology on Tap[2] celebrated its twenty-fifth anniversary in October 2005. The success of the program, which began in the Archdiocese of Chicago and has spread to numerous dioceses across the country, relies on contribution from a speaker, interaction with the young adult audience, and socializing in a casual environment like a bar or pub. Theology on Tap addresses topics of concern to young adults: everything from war to morality to stewardship. Speakers range from bishops and cardinals to theologians and teachers to prominent sports figures and media personalities.

Spirits and Wisdom was founded by a young adult parishioner in Raleigh, North Carolina. The Office of Young Adult Ministry in the diocese has partnered with this young adult leader to host events at various locations in the Raleigh-Durham area on the second Tuesday of each month. Young adults have gathered for dinner, drinks, fellowship, and a presentation on a catechetical topic they have chosen. Spirits and Wisdom targets those who want to grow in their experience of faith and in their knowledge of the teachings of the Catholic Church.

Each of these examples illustrates an opportunity for young adults to deepen their relationship with Jesus and broaden their knowledge of the Catholic faith. Throughout the listening sessions of Ministry with Young Adults: A National Catholic Initiative ("the Initiative"), young adults named Catholic identity and religious education as vitally important to them. The Initiative's list of what young adults seek from the Church, recounted in Chapter 1, "Creating a Young Adult–Responsive Church," places religious education and a sense of Catholic identity fourth.[3] Young adults hunger for meaning in their

---

2   For information on bringing Theology on Tap to your area, see *renewtot.org*. For additional information, including how to order the *Theology-on-Tap Manual*, see *www.yamchicago.org* or write to the Young Adult Ministry Office, Archdiocese of Chicago, 711 W. Monroe Street, Chicago, IL 60661.

3   See Ronald Bagley, CSJ, John Roberto, and Joan Weber, *Becoming a Young Adult Responsive Church* (Naugatuck, CT: Center for Ministry Development [CMD], 1997), 12.

faith lives, and the Church owes them the "what" of the Catholic faith as well as the "why" behind Catholic beliefs. This chapter explores the nature of catechesis, the challenges of catechizing young adults, and some effective strategies for deepening young adults' relationship with Jesus Christ as members of the Catholic Church in the twenty-first century.

THE AIM OF CATECHESIS WITH YOUNG ADULTS

The *General Directory for Catechesis* (GDC) describes the aim of catechesis as putting people "not only in touch, but also in communion and intimacy, with Jesus Christ."[4] The *National Directory for Catechesis* (NDC), the bishops' foundational resource for catechetical leaders in the United States, echoes this goal, stating that the object of catechesis is "communion with Jesus Christ. Catechesis leads people to enter the mystery of Christ, to encounter him, and to discover themselves and the meaning of their lives in him."[5] The Catholic bishops of the United States reinforce this goal for young adults in their pastoral plan *Sons and Daughters of the Light*, identifying the first goal of ministry with young adults as "connecting young adults with Jesus Christ." Parishes are called "to foster the personal and communal growth and education of young adults toward a relationship with Jesus Christ leading to Christian maturity."[6]

Nothing is more important in catechesis with young adults than their relationship with Jesus. All catechetical efforts with young adults must build from this foundation and work toward this goal. Parishes and communities can develop conversations, programs, and other religious-education endeavors that will help young adults to seek and to find relationship with Jesus in the parish setting.

One young adult woman who had left the Catholic Church after growing up Catholic and attending Catholic schools told the Initiative staff that she had left the Church because the Church talked too much about the Church and not enough about Jesus. She didn't feel supported in developing a personal relationship with Jesus. Even though the purpose of the Church's catechesis is always to help the faithful to be transformed by Christ, this story reinforces what the Church already says about good faith formation—it is

---

4   Congregation for the Clergy, *General Directory for Catechesis* (GDC) (Washington, DC: USCCB, 1997), no. 80, quoting Pope John Paul II, *Catechesi Tradendae*, no. 5.

5   USCCB, *National Directory for Catechesis* (NDC) (Washington, DC: USCCB, 2005), § 19.B.

6   USCCB, *Sons and Daughters of the Light: A Pastoral Plan for Ministry with Young Adults* (Washington, DC: USCCB, 1996), 28.

about the young adult and Jesus Christ. The NDC states that "the inspiration for catechesis for young adults is Christ's proposal to the young man: 'Come, follow me' (Mt 19:21)."[7]

Effective young adult catechesis follows the way of Jesus when it engages the head (the cognitive or believing part of the person), the heart (the trusting or affective part), and the hands and feet (the doing or active part). Effective catechesis engages young adults in learning Jesus, not just in learning about him. As one of the seven elements of ministry with young adults identified in the Initiative,[8] catechesis draws young adults into a deeper experience of the presence of the living God. Simultaneously, it draws them into the life of the Church and into an understanding of their own giftedness, of the Church's needs and mission, and of the world's hungers. Finally, it helps them to see the convergence among all these things.

When the Church offers quality catechetical efforts to young adults, the Church itself benefits. Catholics are called to experience a deeper conversion, to realize that "we can all learn from [young adults]," and to invite young adults "to expand [their] leadership role in witnessing."[9]

Catechesis with young adults is inseparable from evangelization. In fact, in Hispanic/Latino ministry the term "evangelizing catechesis" is used frequently.[10] As one Hispanic/Latino leader expressed to the authors of this chapter, young adult catechesis "has to do with falling in love! If we are captured by the love of Jesus, we will want to know more and grow in the Christian way." Parishes that are responsive to the catechetical needs of all young adults offer well-prepared "evangelizing experiences" (e.g., retreats, processions, service and justice trips, small group experiences, times for music and worship). Such experiences help young adults to meet Jesus in community, in nature, in cultural celebrations, in the poor, and in confronting situations of injustice. Any or all of these encounters may appeal to different young adults at different times.

Young adults deserve *systematic* and *intentional* catechesis that covers the core content of the Catholic faith: the gospel message and the call to be disciples of Jesus; Catholic identity, rooted in the Creed; the sacraments, focusing on their meaning as well as how to participate fully in them; the church

---

7   NDC, § 48.C.
8   The other six elements are community life, evangelization, justice and service, liturgy and sacraments, leadership, and prayer and spirituality.
9   USCCB, *A Letter to College Students from the Catholic Bishops of the United States* (Washington, DC: USCCB, 1995), 5.
10   See USCCB, *Encuentro and Mission: A Renewed Pastoral Framework for Hispanic Ministry* (Washington, DC: USCCB, 2002), no. 30.

year, including the feasts and seasons within the liturgical calendar; prayer that engages them in both traditional and contemporary, individual and communal ways of praying; moral formation and moral decision making; and the call to be people of justice and service in the world. This intentional catechesis will look very different from catechesis with children and youth. It respects the "adultness" of young adults, who may have a deeper sense of what they need from the Church to grow in faith. Some of them never received the foundations for a living faith; others received the foundations, but have left them behind. All young adults need to engage with the teachings of the Church through the lens of their life experience as adults.

In addition to intentional programs of religious formation, the GDC acknowledges the power of "occasional catechesis" that "seeks to interpret determined circumstances of personal, family, ecclesial, or social life and to help them live in the prospect of faith."[11] One of the most effective occasional strategies for catechesis with young adults involves bringing them together to reflect on, discuss, and learn the Church's teachings on issues they are encountering now in their own lives or in the world. They want to hear, for example, the reasons for the form of the Mass or Divine Liturgy—the meaning behind the gestures and the prayers, the truth of the Real Presence. They want to know the origins of Catholic doctrine. They want, in other words, to know *why* the Church believes, says, and does what it believes, says, and does. And they want to address current topics—from cloning to abortion, from war and peace to corporate greed—through the lens of faith.

Effective catechesis helps young adults to make the connection between their faith and their everyday lives. As the NDC states, "Effective catechesis will assist young adults in examining their lives and engaging in dialogue about the great questions they face. Catechesis with young adults helps them to make these crucial decisions in accord with God's will and their Catholic Faith."[12]

---

11   GDC, no. 71.
12   NDC, § 48.C.

TOPICS FOR YOUNG ADULT CATECHESIS

Our Hearts Were Burning Within Us, the bishops' pastoral plan for adult faith formation, recommends basing catechetical efforts with adults on the lived realities of adults' lives: "Start by listening to adults and let the stories of their lives and the hungers of their hearts inspire pastoral care and inform catechetical programming."[13] The Initiative staff listened to young adults across the United States in order to learn their stories and identify their hungers. The young adults expressed deep desires: for relationships, for meaning and purpose in life, for a sense of accomplishment that is compatible with faith and hope, for heroes, for guidance and direction, for Sabbath and time away from the hectic pace of life, for a sense of belonging to a supportive community, and for the opportunity to serve others.[14] Parishes can respond to young adults by addressing each of these hungers in the course of faith formation.

Sons and Daughters of the Light identifies particular topics that young adults want and need to explore in catechesis:

> Choose themes for catechesis and faith formation that include church teaching or church life, such as church tradition, theology, theology of the sacraments, Scripture studies, the role of women in the Church, and Catholic identity. Also, consider issues that include relationships, intimacy, sexuality, family life, culture, workplace ethics, morality, personal faith, and dealing with life's pain.[15]

The *National Directory for Catechesis* identifies important themes in young adult catechesis:

> the formation of conscience, education for love, vocational discernment, Christian involvement in society, missionary responsibility in the world, the relationship between faith and reason, the existence and meaning of God, the problem of evil, the Church, the objective moral order in relation to personal subjectivity, the relationship between man and woman, and the social doctrine of the Church.[16]

---

13   USCCB, *Our Hearts Were Burning Within Us: A Pastoral Plan for Adult Faith Formation in the United States* (Washington, DC: USCCB, 1999), no. 80.

14   See Dennis Mahaney, "Connecting Young Adults with Jesus," in *Young Adult Works* (Naugatuck, CT: CMD, 1997), Binder 2, 6.211-6.213.

15   *Sons and Daughters of the Light*, 29.

16   NDC, § 48.C.

THE SIX TASKS OF CATECHESIS

As the *General Directory for Catechesis* states,

> The object of catechesis is realized by diverse, interrelated tasks. To carry them out, catechesis is certainly inspired by the manner in which Jesus formed his disciples. He made known to them the different dimensions of the Kingdom of God: "to you it has been given to know the secrets of the Kingdom of heaven" (Mt 13:11). . . .
>
> The faith demands to be known, celebrated, lived and translated into prayer. Catechesis must cultivate each of these dimensions. The faith, however, is lived out by the Christian community and proclaimed in mission: it is a shared and proclaimed faith.[17]

Using the six tasks of catechesis from the GDC as a framework, consider the following suggestions for effective practices in faith formation with young adults:

1. *Knowledge of the Faith.* Offer social evenings with a speaker. Popular informal formats include the Theology on Tap series, "pizza with a purpose," or welcome nights. Develop thematic small faith-sharing groups that focus on Scripture, the lectionary readings, or issues of life and faith. Some parishes have found *Catholic Updates* to be great resources for discussions with young adults, since they provide church teaching about current issues in a concise and accurate way.[18] Appropriate teaching videos or Web sites can also help to supplement faith formation outside group settings.

2. *Liturgical Life.* Educate young couples preparing to receive the Sacrament of Matrimony and new parents preparing for the Baptism of a child about the meanings of, reasons for, and effects of the sacraments. Conduct whole-parish preparation for the celebration of a sacrament as well. For example, your parish might integrate children's First Reconciliation with the parish-wide Advent Reconciliation service, prepare everyone for the event through homilies, and offer guidance about making an

---

17   GDC, no. 84.
18   To obtain more information about *Catholic Updates*, contact St. Anthony Messenger Press, *www.americancatholic.org.*

examination of conscience in the bulletin the week before the event. RCIA, teaching Masses, and retreats (online or in person) foster liturgical catechesis, as do guides for sacramental celebrations that provide clear explanations of the ritual moments and symbols. As the NDC says, "Catechesis with young adults draws them into the liturgical life and mission of the Church."[19]

3. *Moral Formation.* Discuss ethical issues, and provide resources young adults can use to learn the scriptural and doctrinal foundations for the Church's positions on these issues. Hold forums on morality using Scripture, especially the Ten Commandments and the Sermon on the Mount, as a guide; also, use the lectionary readings for each Sunday to shed light on contemporary moral issues. The NDC points out that "catechesis with young adults should form them in Christ, helping them to make moral decisions in light of the teachings of Christ and the Church."[20]

4. *Prayer.* Awe-inspiring experiences of prayer with catechetical connections include the Liturgy of the Hours, novenas, the Rosary, and prayers from different spiritual traditions (e.g., Franciscan, Benedictine, Ignatian, Taizé) or cultures. These prayer experiences are usually offered for the entire parish, but parishes could make a special effort to invite young adults to participate. Or parishes could offer these traditional prayers just for young adults at times that accommodate their schedules (e.g., Taizé prayer at 10 p.m.). A meditation from a young adult about his or her prayer experiences could be disseminated online or in a newsletter for young adults. Unpacking the richness of the Our Father in a printed or spoken reflection—for example, using the *Catechism of the Catholic Church* (nos. 2759-2865) or Part IV of the *United States Catholic Catechism for Adults* as a resource—can deepen the prayer lives of young adults.[21]

5. *Communal Life.* Provide opportunities to reflect on the practices of community life (e.g., simplicity, hospitality, humility) through exploring models of these practices in the Communion of Saints. Offer experiences of communal living on service trips or in

---

19   NDC, § 48.C.
20   NDC, § 48.C.
21   See *Catechism of the Catholic Church*, 2nd ed. (Washington, DC: USCCB, 2000); USCCB, *United States Catholic Catechism for Adults* (Washington, DC: USCCB, 2006).

religious communities of men and women. Conduct a small-group reflection on the parish community itself: e.g., before a major event, such as a parish anniversary, review church teachings on community and the call to participation. Challenge young adults to become part of the intergenerational faith community in the parish by sharing both the privileges and the responsibilities of belonging (e.g., they benefit from the wisdom of older adults; they inspire the faith of teens; they participate in stewardship by sharing their time, treasure, and talent with the whole faith community).

6. *Missionary Spirit.* Catholic social teaching can be woven into the service projects that young adults already do. Other opportunities include peer ministry training, short-term mission trips, workshops on the skills of advocacy from a faithful perspective, discussions to help young adults connect with local missionaries and contemporary martyrs (such as the four American women murdered in El Salvador in 1980), and forums on living one's faith in the workplace. The Church can communicate a thirst for justice to young adults by offering programs that fulfill the dual mission of evangelization and justice. Pope John Paul II in *The Church in America* observes that "growth in the understanding of the faith and its practical expression in social life are intimately connected. Efforts made to favor an encounter with Christ cannot fail to have a positive repercussion in the promotion of the common good in a just society."[22]

CONTEXT FOR YOUNG ADULT CATECHESIS

Our Hearts Were Burning Within Us reminds catechetical leaders that effective catechesis must be "cognitive, experiential, and behavioral" and that "it requires development in 'the threefold dimension of word, memory, and witness (doctrine, celebration, and commitment in life).'"[23] Catechesis with young adults sometimes takes place in a retreat setting; at other times it resembles a debate. Sometimes a guest speaker presents the teaching; at other times young adults use a print or Web resource to launch the discussion. Sometimes

---

22 Pope John Paul II, *The Church in America* (*Ecclesia in America*) (Washington, DC: USCCB, 1999), no. 69.
23 *Our Hearts Were Burning Within Us*, no. 21, quoting GDC, no. 262a.

catechesis with young adults is prayerful and reflective; in other cases, young adults engage in active discussion about issues of faith.

The environment must be welcoming, not intimidating or judgmental. As the *National Directory for Catechesis* describes, young adults "need a non-threatening place where they can freely express their questions, doubts, and even disagreements with the Church and where the teachings of the Church can be clearly articulated and related to their experience."[24] Picture a room with couches or comfortable chairs and a prayer center that includes the Scriptures, a candle, and a symbol of the topic being discussed (e.g., a scale model of a plow, when the topic is just war doctrine and the Scripture includes the call to "beat swords into plowshares"). The facilitator might illustrate key points in the talk through a PowerPoint presentation. Or young adults themselves could direct the discussion. With or without a facilitator, they might dig into a church document or Scripture and explore the meaning of the text with each other in an animated, lively conversation. Imagine the vibrant young adult catechesis that could take place in such an atmosphere.

In creating the parish environment for young adult catechesis, invite young adults to express their faith in their own cultural traditions. Incorporate opportunities for young adults to enjoy and create visual, musical, written, and dramatic expressions of themes like vocation, faith-life questions, and response to God's call. Lively, culturally inclusive films, photography and other visual art, and dramatizations can proclaim faith and invite reflection in a way that engages young adults holistically. Such works can reach many different types of learners as well as the non-literate or less literate.[25] The Hispanic/Latino community offers engaging examples in the dramatization of the Passion and the Stations of the Cross during Lent and Holy Week. With careful preparation that incorporates analysis of contemporary suffering, as well as reflection, social analysis, Bible study, and faith sharing after the dramatization, these practices can form an engaging catechesis for young adults on many levels and at the same time allow them to minister to the greater community.

Sons and Daughters of the Light describes the context in which effective faith formation with young adults occurs:

> During the listening process, many young adults spoke of their desire
> for effective adult religious education to help them make good moral

---

24   NDC, § 48.C.

25   For books, music, and videos in Spanish, contact La Red, the National Catholic Network de Pastoral Juvenil Hispana, at *www.laredpjh.org.*

decisions. They said that they need a forum not only where misgivings and doubts can be expressed freely but also where the teachings of the Church can be clearly articulated in response. . . . Many young adults told us that what is most convincing is an open but well-reasoned discussion, informed and fortified by the minister's confidence in the wisdom of the Church.[26]

The NDC suggests several settings in which young adult catechesis can be done: "a series of evening or weekend sessions, special one-time presentations, days of recollection, retreats, discussion groups, Scripture study groups, mentoring relationships, hands-on social justice programs, and mission education projects can all be attractive means for involving busy young adults."[27] Parishes would benefit from assessing their current efforts at reaching out to young adults and providing faith formation in different settings. They should also address settings for catechesis with young adults from different cultural backgrounds. For example, in a parish with Hispanic/Latino parishioners, parish leaders can assess where and how their parish ministries are forming Hispanic/Latino young adults through Sunday liturgies, retreats, Bible studies, sacramental preparation for children, marriage preparation, RCIA, justice work, community service, dramatic presentations during the Church's liturgical seasons, and so forth. Once the assessment is complete, parish leaders would then reflect on ways to be more responsive to Hispanic/Latino young adults' faith formation needs and develop simple plans and commitments to improve current ministries. The same assessment would be applicable for any cultural group found in a particular parish.

For all young adults, relevant catechesis provides a forum in which they can search for truth with openness and acceptance. As an example, in 1997, the Diocese of Raleigh brought in Fr. John Cusick, young adult ministry director in the Archdiocese of Chicago, to lead the annual Winter Fest conference and luncheon with priests and pastoral administrators. Fr. Cusick, in his remarks, explained how he deals with the "why should I?" question that young adults raise in relation to church rules. For example, he said, "The question about the Sacrament of Reconciliation is not so much whether you have to go, but rather for you to ask yourself, 'If not this way, then how do I get free?'"

---

26   *Sons and Daughters of the Light*, 29.
27   NDC, § 48.C.

How can catechists invite young adults to figure out the "why" behind traditional Catholic practices? Effective catechesis with young adults challenges them to personally evaluate the teachings for their lives and to move from cognitive knowledge (head) to valued and lived faith (heart and hands). Catechists must also be prepared to share their personal "whys" with young adults: why do they themselves participate in the sacraments, for example, and why do they treasure this aspect of church teaching?

MODELS OF CATECHESIS

Young adults deepen their relationship with Jesus Christ in many kinds of peer settings, including retreats, classes, online environments, social sessions, and presentations by speakers. But they are also part of the larger faith community, and they enjoy learning with other generations.

Event-Centered Learning

Many parishes in the United States have moved to event-centered, lifelong faith formation as a supplement to their core catechetical efforts.[28] When parishes *prepare* their members to celebrate the events of the liturgical seasons, *engage* them in each event, and then *reflect* on the meaning of the event in their lives, all generations, including young adults, understand their Catholic identity more deeply.

Preparation for an event in the life of the Church requires gathering the generations together to help them understand the meaning and purpose of the event. In intergenerational, event-centered learning, various age groups come together in prayer to experience the meaning of the event for which they are preparing. They learn in greater depth through group activities, in either intergenerational groups or age-specific groups. When age groupings are used, parishes need to provide young adults with catechesis that employs engaging and experiential adult-learning methods. Planners can ensure that the catechetical methods used are responsive to the learning styles and needs of young adults by including a significant number of young adults on the planning team.

Take preparation for the Feast of the Annunciation (March 25) as an example. The whole parish could gather to learn about discernment. Young

---

28   See *www.generationsoffaith.org* for a description of this particular way to conduct intergenerational catechesis.

adults who are working to discern God's call could study Mary's "yes" to God's invitation and then apply it to their own lives. If they have already discerned their vocations, they can focus on discernment in other areas of life—choosing where to live, where to work, where to worship, or how to practice stewardship of time, treasure, and talent. When young adults engage in discernment rather than mere decision making, they celebrate the meaning of the Annunciation on a deeper level and carry their learning into everyday life. (See Chapter 4, "Discernment and Vocation," for more on vocation and other major life decisions.)

Adult Faith Formation

Our Hearts Were Burning Within Us challenges the Church in the United States to *"engage adults actively in the actual life and ministry of the Christian community."*[29] The bishops go on to say that adults "do not grow in faith primarily by learning concepts, but by sharing the life of the Christian community."[30] Catechesis that engages young adults with older adults will enable them to better understand Catholic teaching by providing them with opportunities for dialogue about living the faith over the course of a lifetime. Young adults sometimes think differently, in ways that the older members of the Church cannot conceive of, thereby offering a tremendous gift to the Church. By asking penetrating questions, young adults challenge the Church to remember—and to share in a way that makes sense to younger generations—why Catholics follow certain traditions and ways of life. Older members of the faith community, in turn, bring their own gifts to young adults. They know the Tradition and the practices of the Catholic faith very well and can share why and how to keep them, because they have faithfully done so for many years.

Young Adults as Catechists

An old saying asserts that the best way to learn something is to teach it. When young adults serve as catechists, they can fulfill this saying. Young adults can draw younger learners—adolescents and children—into a deeper relationship with Jesus. From the example of young adults, the youngest Catholics learn that faith is a lifelong journey, something pursued by even young adults—the people who are in a time of life that younger Catholics can't wait to reach.

---

29   *Our Hearts Were Burning Within Us*, no. 83.
30   *Our Hearts Were Burning Within Us*, no. 83, quoting International Council for Catechesis, *Adult Catechesis in the Christian Community*.

More mature learners discover new ways to live their faith as they learn from younger teachers, who approach faith in fresh ways. And young adults can also grow in faith when they connect with and learn from each other. In all these situations, young adult catechists confirm and strengthen their faith when they share it with other people. Preparing lesson plans and seeking answers to tough questions forces catechists to embrace and deepen their own knowledge of the faith.

CHALLENGES IN CATECHESIS WITH YOUNG ADULTS

Working with Diverse Learning Styles

Putting young adults in touch and in intimacy with Jesus is not always easy in today's world. More mature church leaders recognize that the world is changing at such a rapid pace that life experience now is very different from what it was even ten years ago. This evolution challenges catechists to change methods to meet the learning needs of today's young adults. Dynamic faith communities provide experiential opportunities to a generation that values "trying before buying." Learning in these communities is relevant and energetic, often making use of visuals.

One experiential, engaging method of catechesis is shared Christian praxis. Shared praxis begins by capturing the interest of the learner through a focusing activity or reflection. The five movements of praxis are as follows:

- Identify the life experiences of the learner that connect to the element of faith.
- Invite learners to share that experience with each other.
- Present the faith story through lecture, drama, scriptural proclamation, or some other method.
- Encourage learners to embrace the faith story and to integrate it into their everyday lives.
- Invite learners to decide how they will live differently as a result of their faith.

Praxis, done well, builds the bridge between faith and life.

Rite-based learning is another way to engage young adults in catechesis. The Catholic Church has the Tradition to share faith through the richness of symbols, practices, and rituals. As an illustration, young adults can attain a deeper understanding of their baptismal call by exploring the words of the Rite of Baptism; studying the meanings of the symbols of water, oil, the white garment, and the baptismal candle; and then discussing how to live out their baptismal call at work and at leisure, with family and with friends.

Catechesis with young adults is enriched by paying attention to the numerous studies of learning styles that have been published over the last two decades. Particularly helpful is the concept of the seven intelligences and corresponding learning styles analyzed by Howard Gardner. These intelligences can be described as follows:

- *Verbal-linguistic intelligence* calls for word-based methods, both spoken and written. Lectionary-based catechesis is ideal for young adults who learn through language.
- *Logical-mathematical intelligence* calls for sequential, cause-and-effect, rational learning methods. Church history is one content area to which logic-minded young adults readily respond.
- *Visual-spatial intelligence* calls for involving learners in images and three-dimensional learning. The Catholic Church's abundance of rituals, symbols, and artistic depictions should be used in teaching young adults who learn visually.
- *Musical intelligence* calls for learning that includes melody and rhythm. Contemporary and traditional religious songs that take their lyrics directly from Scripture make an ideal teaching opportunity for musical young adults.
- *Bodily-kinesthetic intelligence* calls for hands-on learning and physical activity. A desert retreat or experience of ritual would be effective with young adults who learn by doing.
- *Interpersonal intelligence* calls for learning that engages learners with other people. Teaching or supporting other learners helps interpersonally gifted young adults to deepen their own faith.
- *Intrapersonal intelligence* calls for learning that includes opportunities for reflection, journaling, meditation, and goal setting. Young adults who show intrapersonal intelligence are ready for deeper forms of soul searching.[31]

---

31   See Howard Gardner, *Frames of Mind: The Theory of Multiple Intelligences* (New York: Basic Books, 1993).

Those who design young adult catechetical programs are encouraged to spend time studying the seven intelligences and offering a variety of methods to share faith with young adults.

Respecting Cultural Diversity

In this culturally diverse Church and world, those who catechize young adults are most effective when they respect and value each cultural group. Catechesis that does not resonate with people's cultural identity diminishes their full understanding of their own humanity.

Catechists in the African American community, for example, must approach their ministry with the realization that African American young adult Catholics are simultaneously rooted in both the larger African American community and the larger Catholic community. Catechesis must reflect and resonate with both sets of sensibilities.

For another example, the Hispanic/Latino community in the United States is growing, and many of its members are Catholics. In their pastoral document *Encuentro and Mission*, the bishops of the United States call on catechists to "make the formation of young Hispanics, especially young adult Hispanics, an urgent priority."[32]

In all cases, catechists should be mindful of cultural customs and habits that may not be the same as their own. For example, many young adults who are foreign-born, or who are the children of foreign-born parents, may not be in the habit of registering in a parish. This presents an opportunity for evangelizing and catechizing. Parishes might introduce the idea of registering and then encourage young adults to commit to ministries and share in the financial support of the community. This formation could help young adults explore the meaning of stewardship, including the benefits and challenges of giving and participating.

Successful catechesis with young adults from all cultural backgrounds relates the historical and existential realities of their lives to the Revelation of God and the mission of the Church. In this way, catechesis enables young adult Catholics to rise to their full stature in the image and likeness of God.

---

32   *Encuentro and Mission*, no. 55.

Fitting into Busy Schedules

Catechesis with young adults must compete with their hectic schedules—all the commitments that drain their limited time: work, study, family, social life, and recreation. To meet this challenge, catechists can do what Kenda Creasy Dean and Ron Foster call "backdoor theology"[33]—that is, provide faith formation in the midst of life. For example:

- Hold faith-formation breakfasts or lunches at coffee houses, so that young adults can stop in on their way to work in the morning or during their lunch hour.

- Use sacramental preparation, particularly marriage and baptismal preparation, as opportunities to share faith with young couples or young adult parents.

- Practice *carpe diem*, that is, seize the moment. When young adults experience the death of a parent or grandparent, talk with them about Catholic beliefs about life after death when planning the funeral. When an armed conflict breaks out, invite young adults to come together within a few days to discuss war from the perspective of faith.

- After watching or playing a sports game, talk about and reflect on competition and gospel values.

- Use media to teach. Bestsellers provide opportunities for discussion of values that are complementary with or contrary to gospel values.

- Include short moments for formation, faith sharing, and/or reflection within other meetings or parish gatherings that might have a mainly social or practical purpose. For example, at the beginning of a meeting of the young adult team, get in the habit of reading one of the readings of the day and the short reflection found on Creighton University's Daily Reflection page.[34] Alternatively, read a short passage from a church document, or play a recording of a song. After the reading, take a moment of silence. Provide copies of the text or lyrics for those who might wish to revisit the

---

33   Kenda Creasy Dean and Ron Foster, *The Godbearing Life: The Art of Soul Tending for Youth Ministry* (Nashville, TN: Upper Room Books, 1998), 180-181.

34   See *www.creighton.edu/CollaborativeMinistry*.

reflection on their own, and ask for brief feedback to evaluate the effectiveness of the moment.

The more the Church connects faith formation to the everyday lives and busy schedules of young adults, the more young adults will want to participate in the Church. If young adults feel that the experience and insights they gain in learning the faith story help them at work or at home or in their social lives, they are much more likely to participate—and may become catechetical leaders themselves.

Another strategy for providing catechesis within the busy lives of young adults is establishing a presence in their regular schedules. Spirits and Wisdom, the young adult faith-formation model described at the beginning of this chapter, usually meets once each month at the same time and place. Consistency in time and place helps young adults to plan accordingly. And because Spirits and Wisdom is usually advertised throughout the region, a larger number of young adults can gather from many parishes within the radius targeted by the marketing.

The timing of catechetical offerings makes a difference in whether young adults attend. Try offering a simple meal with an evening program; this can eliminate the pressure to rush from work to home to parish. Ask young adults what time works for them, which day of the week is best, and whether Sunday mornings are good for them (before or after Sunday liturgy).

Parishes can find creative ways to bring the faith story to young adults who cannot or will not take the time to come to group programs. Consider the following strategies:

- Offer online learning—e.g., send a small nugget of Catholic doctrine via e-mail, or post one on the parish Web site, each day.
- Direct young adults to Web sites that have catechetical material, such as www.americancatholic.org or www.bustedhalo.com.
- Create podcasts of Catholic teachings, and offer them to young adults on the journey.
- Encourage young adults who are already involved to reach out and catechize their peers.
- Weave catechesis into other activities in which young adults already participate (e.g., service projects).

While none of these activities takes the place of in-depth, intentional catechesis, each one provides support for it.

Marketing Events

Marketing catechetical events to young adults requires creativity and a multi-pronged approach. Catechetical leaders must always ask themselves, "Who is our target population, and how can we reach the people in it?"—keeping in mind that catechists are not called to tend only to faithful churchgoers. Many faith-formation programs overlook prisoners, military men and women, the unchurched and non-practicing, and those young adults who attend Mass only at Christmas and Easter. Young-adult–responsive parishes reach out to these young adults. They advertise in bars and gyms, apartment complexes and coin-operated laundries, coffee shops and malls.

Marketing for parish programs must also respond to the perceptions of young adults. Include young adults on the design team to share ideas with older adult leaders, some of whom may not know what styles of advertising text and visuals attract the attention of young adults. For example, consider getting the word out about catechetical opportunities through an e-mail distribution list. Through personal testimony, blogging, social networking Web sites, videos posted online, and word of mouth, young adults themselves can help to draw their peers to catechesis.

Ultimately, young adults will come to those programs that sound relevant to their daily lives. By emphasizing what participants will gain from attending a session, catechists can attract busy people who have a limited amount of free time and are practical in their choices.

Countering the Message of the Dominant Culture

Helping young adults to understand that there is a defined and specific *Catholic* identity is a challenge for those who facilitate young adult faith formation. How do catechists help young adults to be open to the grace of God in a world filled with individualism and moral relativism? The belief that Jesus (or Catholicism) is simply one of many paths to God is widely held among today's young adults. As the *National Directory for Catechesis* describes, "Many young adults have been captivated by the consumerism and materialism of the society in which they grew up and have become apathetic and cynical. Young adulthood is sometimes a world of boredom, disillusionment, and indifference to the Church. Young adults are often 'the first victims of the spiritual and cultural crisis gripping the world.'"[35]

One way the Church can support young adults in hearing the Catholic message among all the other voices in their lives is by providing good reflection tools for critiquing the secular culture in which they live. Young adults could gather in the parish to view a contemporary film, identify the actions in the film that support Catholic values as well as the actions that contradict them, and discuss ways the characters in the movie could have acted to be authentic disciples. Or they could explore the in-depth meaning of a Catholic value, such as respect for the life and dignity of every human person, and then name the ways in which the culture supports or contradicts this value.

LEADERSHIP IN CATECHESIS WITH YOUNG ADULTS

Catechesis with young adults—like all other ministries with young adults—needs to be done by faithful disciples. Ideally, many of the catechists for young adults should themselves be young adults, since peer ministry is a hallmark of this generation. Therefore, parishes that are responsive to young adults intentionally recruit and train young adults for the ministry of catechesis. In these parishes, young adults are part of the parish or campus adult faith-formation team. As the bishops explained in *Our Hearts Were Burning Within Us,*

> teams include qualified representatives of all the major parish demographic and cultural groups. This representative team will recognize the gifts and talents of each group and address the varied learning needs and interests of the multi-cultural and generational community more effectively. The adult faith formation team is encouraged to coordinate its efforts with those of other parish ministries engaged in formation (e.g., children and youth catechesis, young adult ministry, family life, pro-life, liturgy, social action, and ecumenism) in order to weave diverse parish efforts into a more cohesive approach.[36]

Parishes have sometimes been blind to the young adults in their midst. Leaders in parishes that seek to be responsive to young adults are aware of young

---

35   NDC, § 48.C, quoting GDC, no. 181.
36   *Our Hearts Were Burning Within Us,* no. 143.

adults and work constantly to discover their gifts and talents and to invite them into catechetical leadership.

Older adults are also needed to share faith with young adults. If the goal of catechesis is intimacy with Jesus that leads to discipleship, who better to share faith than those who have been faithful disciples for a long time? Seniors and middle-aged adults can help young adults understand that conversion is truly a lifelong journey.

Questions that parishes might ask themselves in looking for leaders in the catechesis of their young adults include the following:

- How do we identify and invite faithful young adults who are knowledgeable in their faith and comfortable sharing it to be catechists?
- How do we invite faithful older adults who can inspire young adults to be catechists for young adults?
- How do we offer them the training they need to succeed in this ministry?
- How do we make the training of catechists friendly to young adults?

The Diocese of Raleigh has focused on the catechetical formation of young adult leaders by offering yearly leadership retreats for these leaders to support one another, pray together, inspire one another, network, receive catechetical formation and evangelization, revisit *Sons and Daughters of the Light*, and plan their calendars. These retreats have helped all participating parishes: both those that want to start ministry with young adults and those that desire to continue the faith formation of their young adults.

Many young adults in the diocese are trained professionals who have large circles of influence and high levels of responsibility in their careers, but who can nonetheless be plagued with a sense of inadequacy about applying their gifts to the service of the community. For example, one leader for a diocesan service-learning trip to Jamaica was a physician who directed a large clinic. However, she was reticent about taking on the responsibility of the trip because she felt ill-equipped and unempowered to lead a faith-formation experience. Only after being reminded repeatedly of her baptismal call to be priest, prophet, and servant leader—and of her high level of competence in secular circumstances—did she make the connection that she could indeed serve the Church as a catechist and as the trip leader.

Young-adult–responsive parishes invite faithful, gifted young adults to take leadership in the faith formation of their peers. These parishes set up young adults for success by giving them training both in the content of the Catholic faith and in effective, engaging methods of imparting Catholic doctrine. This training needs to be both accessible and flexible. For example, parishes might offer online training sessions about doctrine or church history, which young adult catechists can complete independently according to their own time constraints. Parish leaders might also demonstrate methodologies, rather than merely talk about them. When young adult catechists engage in actual experiences of a method, they can not only grasp how to practice it, but also learn firsthand its strengths and weaknesses for sharing faith with their peers. If young adult catechists and other parish catechists attend diocesan workshops and certification programs together, it is important that the program trainers be conscious of the group's demographics and adjust their methods accordingly.

A parish must make intentional efforts to recruit young adult catechists from all the cultures represented in the parish community. Consider the following strategies to help ensure that Hispanic/Latino young adults, as one example, are invited to and trained in catechetical leadership. Imagine how you could tailor these ideas to meet the needs of other cultural groups in your parish.

- Observe the talents of Hispanic/Latino young adult parishioners who are especially comfortable and creative with groups and who have an uplifting spirit and natural gifts for facilitating communication and encouraging participation. Make a special effort to have one-on-one meetings with these individuals, and get to know their perspectives on faith and on the Church. Suggest more focused formation to involve them more deeply in parish life.
- Organize a ministry career fair in your diocese or region for Hispanic/Latino young adults. Identify funding for those who are interested to volunteer, to pursue professional ministry, and/or to study theology. Invite and challenge these young adults to take the next step.
- Raise funds to be able to offer quality formation resources and opportunities to young adult Hispanic/Latino parishioners, vol-

unteers, and staff. Send them to regional and national conferences and trainings, and support them in pursuing ministry degrees.[37]

CONCLUSION

"Catechesis" comes from the Greek word "*katekhein*," loosely meaning "to echo." Catholic Christians are called to be Easter people, whose song is "Alleluia." Catechists in young adult–responsive parishes want the song of every young adult's heart to echo "Alleluia," to echo—despite and amidst the challenges of life—the joy of knowing and experiencing God's unconditional love for each of us, a love evidenced by the Crucifixion and Resurrection of Jesus.

The late Mary Dowling, former director of the Office of Faith Development in the Diocese of Raleigh, in North Carolina, stated many times that "the most important thing that *we* can do is make sure the faith development directors in the parishes realize that the most important thing that *they* do is the formation of their catechists and leaders." Focusing on the formation of leaders for the evangelization and catechesis of young adults cultivates healthy, mature, balanced, and effective young adult ministry. This focus also offers a wonderful way to attract young adults, to equip them for ministry and mature Christian living, and to cultivate and support the parish-based, peer-led young adult ministry called for in *Sons and Daughters of the Light*.

---

37   Contact Foundations and Donors Interested in Catholic Activities (FADICA), *www.fadica.org*.

THE CAMPUS CONNECTION

Catechesis—coming to know and understand the Catholic faith—is vital for every type of Catholic ministry, but especially for ministry with young adults, many of whom are just beginning to develop a personal and adult faith. At Catholic colleges, catechesis may be provided through the theology department. On secular campuses, catechesis normally happens through the efforts of the Catholic student center or the local parish. Whatever the setting, campus ministries have an unparalleled opportunity to help students mature intellectually in the Catholic faith—or to discover it for the first time.

To meet the needs of an ever more diverse population of students, campus ministers can choose from a wide array of group formats that have proven successful at other schools. A group that meets for catechesis may resemble an adult catechetical program, similar to those found in many parish settings. It may be very academic, with instructors who require readings and assign papers. It may be very simple, making little demand on participants. It may range from a general overview of the Catholic faith to profession-specific issues.

For example, some campus ministries offer a program that focuses on Catholic doctrine. Some pair this program with the Rite of Christian Initiation of Adults (RCIA) process, so that Catholic students interested in learning more about their faith participate in the same sessions as students interested in becoming members of the Catholic Church. Others offer a separate program, sometimes called "Catholicism 101"; these programs frequently use the *Catechism of the Catholic Church* as a resource and meet weekly during a semester. In either type of program, topics may be covered systematically, or they may be chosen by the students or campus minister. As a supplement or an alternative to such programs focused on Tradition, campus ministries may offer Scripture study groups. Still other types of groups may meet to share faith or to cover and discuss topics of interest to the participants.

Such informal groups can work well on either Catholic or secular campuses. At secular institutions, Catholic campus ministries have found that more formal and in-depth alternatives for religious education can help the Church to reach more students. At the University of Kansas, for example, the St. Lawrence Catholic Campus Center (*www.st-lawrence.org*) established the Catechetical Institute for any student who would like to learn more about the Catholic faith, have a better understanding of the Bible, and develop a daily relationship with Christ through prayer. Several hundred students have participated in the weekly classes, which are organized into a comprehensive four-year curriculum. The first year gives an overview of the Catholic faith as expressed in the Creed and the *Catechism of the Catholic Church*. In the second year, students consider a virtue-centered approach to moral theology, and they study Pope John Paul II's theology of the body. The third year begins with a deeper exploration of the Deposit of Faith and continues with an investigation of Catholic spirituality; participants study the Doctors and mystics of the Church as well as the liturgical prayer of the Church. The fourth year is devoted to the study of the four Gospels. The practice of *lectio divina* is introduced, and students learn to read the Scriptures in light of Tradition and the Magisterium.

The Corpus Christi University Parish at the University of Toledo (*www. ccup.org*) has found another creative way to establish a catechetical presence on campus. The parish has funded the Chair in Catholic Studies at the University of Toledo. The Catholic studies program that the chair oversees has allowed students at this secular institution to receive academic credit for studying topics in Catholicism. This program has created a direct relationship between the university and the Catholic campus ministry, and it has given Catholic studies a place among the other educational programs at the university.

An important part of any campus ministry's mission is to connect Catholic faith with high intellectual pursuit and achievement. Campus ministers must address how a Catholic intellectual's faith informs, and is informed by, his or her scholarship. To help incorporate scholarship and faith, the St. Thomas More Chapel and Center at Yale University (*www.yale.edu/stm*) has established Catholic Faith Fellowships. The St. Thomas More Chapel has offered three annual endowed fellowships, one in each of the following areas: faith and science, faith and culture, and religion and law. The fellowships have served to elevate credible and vibrant Catholic intellectual discourse by inviting nationally recognized thinkers of notable accomplishment to spend a full day at the Chapel, meeting with students. Each visit culminates with a lecture open to the whole university community. Numerous other Catholic scholars and theologians have also given lectures through the program.

At the University of Illinois in Chicago, the John Paul II Newman Center has established the Integritas Institute (*www.integritasinstitute.org*). The Institute has provided a forum for study and discussion in the areas of healthcare ethics, business and professional ethics, and public service leadership. The Institute has also sought to assist students with incorporating the Christian virtues of mercy, justice, charity, and truth into their professional lives. Finally, the Institute has established the Cardinal Newman Dialogue as a forum for discussion on some of the most pressing moral issues of our time. In these ways, the Institute has helped both Catholics and non-Catholics to better understand the Catholic tradition.

Clearly, catechetical ministry in a campus setting can take different forms. In light of the diverse settings, situations, and groups of students it serves, each campus ministry needs to discern which model or models will work best to help it form mature, faith-filled Catholics who can transform the world for Jesus Christ.

CHAPTER FOUR

Discernment and Vocation

How can parishes support young adults in making faithful decisions, particularly with regard to their life vocation? This chapter explores different ways of teaching young adults discernment and theological reflection. One of the authors, Sr. Christine Wilcox, uses her own vocational story to highlight ways in which parishes can invite young adults into openness to the Spirit as they discern God's call to them as single, married, religious, or ordained members of the parish community.

Because young adults today have grown up in a secular society, one that is often inattentive to the voice of God, the art of discernment is one of the most crucial skills that the Church can share to help young adults connect faith and life. Discernment is a practice of decision making that incorporates into the process deep listening for the movement of God's Spirit. "The word discernment comes from the Latin word *discernere* which means to distinguish, to sift out, to separate what may be from God and what may come from egocentric interests or cultural pressures."[1] When young adults *discern*—not just *decide*—how to spend their money, how to use their leisure time, what career to enter, and ultimately to what vocation God is calling them, the Holy Spirit becomes an intimate part of their everyday lives. Parishes can help young adults to master the discernment process, particularly vocational discernment.

DISCERNMENT AND YOUNG ADULTS

Discernment is a primary life task for young adults. It is particularly important in today's world, where, as Pope Benedict XVI has repeatedly noted, relativism and secularism are rampant. For the teenager, discernment primarily focuses on discovering one's personal worth and values and on using one's gifts. The task for the young adult is to discern with whom and in what context he or she is called to use these gifts in every aspect of adult life: career, companions,

---

1   Kathleen Bryant, RSC, *Vocations Anonymous: A Handbook for Adults Discerning Priesthood and Religious Life* (Chicago: National Coalition for Church Vocations, 1996), 23.

mates, vocation, local involvement, and all that goes with becoming a fruitful, healthy, happy, and holy adult.

Discernment vs. Decision Making

The parish community that is responsive to young adults recognizes its opportunity to play a significant role in the discernment process. In a world that celebrates having a multitude of choices, young adults can benefit from programs that directly offer skills and strategies for holy decision making. Identifying the difference between *decision making* and *discernment* helps young adults to hear God's will for their lives more clearly. Decision making involves making a choice, arriving at a solution, coming to a conclusion. It may include seeking advice, weighing options, or reviewing pros and cons, but the person makes the final choice. Discernment, on the other hand, always involves listening to the Holy Spirit through prayerful reflection. It includes consulting with faithful mentors or with Sacred Scripture; it means reflecting on the God-given talents and the limitations that are part of the person's identity. Discernment involves patiently waiting for God's response, not rushing into a decision just to get it done. It sometimes includes trying out a decision for a day or a week, living as if the discernment were accomplished, and seeking the inner peace that indicates the choice was a holy and good one.

As one way to help young adults explore the difference between deciding and discerning, parishes might offer young adults evening workshops or twilight/weekend retreats on discernment. Invite speakers—preferably young adults—who can witness to the power of discernment in their own lives.

The findings from Ministry with Young Adults: A National Catholic Initiative ("the Initiative") demonstrated that young adults respond particularly well to such concrete invitations to discern. As a direct result of the Initiative, for example, the dioceses of northern California jointly hosted a four-part young adult ministry training program entitled Principles and Practices in Ministry with Young Adults. Almost all of the participants were explicitly invited by their pastor, the peer lay leader or minister of their young adult community, or the diocesan director of young adult ministry. All of the participants responded positively to the invitation and the opportunity. Most have since furthered their ministry in the Church by putting their learning into practice in their parish.

In the Principles and Practices program, one session of the first course was devoted to discernment. Reflective music (e.g., Jesse Manibusan's "Open

My Eyes, Lord") set the tone. Next, participants were asked to recall a recent important decision and to spend quiet time reflecting on how they made the decision. After reflection, they gathered in groups to share their decision-making processes and to determine whether they had truly discerned their choices or had just decided what to do. Instructors presented key elements of discernment—the need for prayer, listening to the wisdom of Scripture and Tradition, taking time to live with the decision before acting—and the young adults were invited to add their own elements to the list. Then the last weekend in the Principles and Practices program included a session on discerning gifts, in which young adult participants explored their gifts for ministry and learned how to discover gifts in their peers.

This exploration proved to be an effective part of the Principles and Practices training; young adults responded to it with enthusiasm. One young woman discerned the need to move on from a destructive personal relationship. A young man switched from deciding to discerning where to live. He was struggling with whether to live at home with his parents, buy a condo, or rent an apartment. He found that discernment helped him to look at issues he hadn't considered before, such as the needs of his parents and the practice of stewardship in how he spent his money. Two other young women who participated in Principles and Practices have changed their careers since completing the course. Through the training, they became aware that God was calling them to dedicate their lives to serving the mission of the Church. The first young woman is currently discerning and walking with a local religious community. The second has discerned a call to work exclusively with young adults in the Church. She is currently practicing this call as a volunteer minister and is actively seeking a lay-ministry position in which she can more deeply fulfill this call.

Another great resource for discernment for all ages comes from the St. Catherine of Siena Institute:[2] the two-and-a-half-day Called and Gifted Workshop, in which Institute teachers have led members of parishes and dioceses through a "gifts inventory" and discernment. As the opening lines of the Institute's *Discerning Charisms* workbook assert, "you can't discern in a vacuum."[3] Fulfilling part of the Institute's mission to "foster the proclamation of the gospel to all the world by ensuring that lay Catholics are equipped to effectively

---

2   The Institute was founded in July 1997 as a program of the Western Dominican Province.
3   Eryn Huntington and Sherry Anne Weddell, *Discerning Charisms: A Workbook for Navigating the Discernment Process* (Seattle: The Siena Institute Press, 2000), 5.

carry out their unique and essential part in this mission,"[4] the workshop has helped participants to discern and identify the charisms[5] and gifts given to them by God. The Institute's instructors have been trained to continue the discernment in one-on-one and small-group settings, so that the lay members of the community are prepared to discover and use their gifts for the greater mission of the Church in the world.

Participants in the Called and Gifted Workshop have reported a greater understanding of and excitement about their role in God's plan. Some of the qualities that have made the Institute's program successful in parishes include (a) its design, which is geared specifically for working adults and others leading busy lives, (b) its rootedness in Catholic Tradition and magisterial teaching, and (c) the humor and personal stories used by the instructors to fully engage participants throughout the whole process.

At the beginning of the 2000 Jubilee Year, the Archdiocese of San Francisco invited the Institute to offer the Called and Gifted Workshop specifically for young adults from the Bay Area. More than two hundred young adults participated in the workshop. Not only was this the largest group of participants the Institute had ever addressed, it was also the first exclusively young adult group. At the end of the weekend, when invited to give a free-will offering to offset the costs of the training, the attendees offered the highest average per-person donation that the Institute had received up to that point. By their enthusiasm and generosity, these young adults made clear their desire and need for skills, work, and opportunities related to discernment.

Theological Reflection

A vital way to foster discernment is to encourage young adults to experience deeper theological reflection on vocational issues. For example, many parishes offer service opportunities to their young adults. But if these projects are not followed with reflection on how the service connects to the Catholic faith, they are no different from projects young adults might do through their workplaces—or, as one young adult stated in the Initiative, mere service activities that look good on a résumé. Instead, if young adult participants are invited to answer questions like "How were you the Body of Christ for the people

---

4   *Discerning Charisms*, 97.
5   A charism is "a specific gift or grace of the Holy Spirit which directly or indirectly benefits the Church, given in order to help a person live out the Christian life, or to serve the common good in building up the Church" (*Catechism of the Catholic Church*, 2nd ed. [Washington, DC: Libreria Editrice Vaticana–United States Conference of Catholic Bishops (USCCB), 2000], Glossary).

you served today?" and "How were they the Body of Christ for you?", they can more clearly see the connection between the gospel call to serve and their actual service.

The "Spiritual Development" section of *Young Adult Works*,[6] a binder series from the Center for Ministry Development, provides parishes with a template for designing short sessions (running an hour and a half to two hours) for doing theological reflection in groups. Young-adult leaders identify an issue in their lives—and the lives of their peers—that currently demands attention. Then the young adult community is invited to gather for one session (with no further commitment asked) to reflect on the issue from a perspective of faith. The facilitator, preferably a young adult, shares his or her story as it pertains to the issue and then invites the other young adults to consider all the sources of input they experience on the issue, asking, "What are the voices you hear regarding this issue? What does your family say you should do? Your friends? Your colleagues at work? Your heritage?" Then they are invited to listen for the voice of God amidst the other voices and to reflect on what God is saying to them.

This process works because it meshes with the busy lives of young adults. Issues bubble up spontaneously. No ongoing commitment is required. Young adults come because the particular issue being discussed relates to them. Very rarely does someone feel like an outsider, because different people show up each time an issue is addressed.

Young-adult–responsive parishes that want to try this process might begin by sharing the template in *Young Adult Works*[7] with young adult leaders. The young adults could decide, with their peers, which issue to address, and then use the template to plan the discussion. They might publicize the gathering by putting an announcement in the bulletin, e-mailing young adults in the community, or posting notices in places where young adults gather. Word of mouth is, as always, the most effective way to get people to come.

Parishes that have never tried this type of gathering might first want to experiment with one of the ten pre-planned sessions in *Young Adult Works*, using issues that young adults have already identified as being key in their lives—such as dealing with rejection or moving away from home.

---

6   See "Spiritual Development," in *Young Adult Works*, ed. Ronald Bagley, CJM, John Roberto, Susan Stark, and Joan Weber (Naugatuck, CT: Center for Ministry Development, 1997), Binder 3, Section 7A.

7   See "A Process for Spiritual Reflection," in *Young Adult Works*, Binder 3.

Here are some examples of strategies for supporting young adults on the journey of vocation and discernment:

- Teach the practice of the Examen of Conscience (an Ignatian spiritual exercise, originally taught in Spanish) to teach listening, attentiveness, and the rhythm of discernment throughout life. Practice it often at young adult gatherings, and offer to lead it during other parish gatherings.[8] The practice can be as simple as taking time to check in with each other before a young adult team meeting, to share highs and lows of the week or month since the group last met, and to observe, in silence or aloud, how God is speaking to each young adult through these joys and sorrows.

- Incorporate spiritual direction into evaluation after activities. Ask questions about the Holy Spirit, life, and vocation. After a team leadership experience, evaluate both the practical and spiritual aspects of the event. Ask everyone: Did the team meet its goals? How effective were the techniques and methods? How well did the team model *"pastoral de conjunto"* ("communion in mission")?[9] What can be improved? What did team members learn about those present? Who shows leadership potential? And take time to ask each team member: What were your personal highs and lows (consolations and desolations)? What does this tell you about yourself or your team? About what God desires for you or the group? What did this experience of leadership tell you about your interests, talents, needs? What does it lead you to want to do, to practice, or to learn more about?[10]

- Work with nearby religious communities to host service trips for a weekend or week if possible. The trip's structure should include challenging and simple living, hard work meeting real community needs, nightly reflection, social analysis, prayer, and discernment. The trip could involve a mixed or a single-sex group.

- Arrange time for young adults to shadow the work or ministry of religious or of their lay colleagues. Build in time for religious or

---

8   See Dennis Linn, *Sleeping with Bread: Holding What Gives You Life* (New York: Paulist Press, 1995).

9   *"Pastoral de conjunto,"* translated "communion in mission," is a collaborative ministry model valued in Hispanic/Latino ministry. See USCCB, *Encuentro and Mission: A Renewed Pastoral Framework for Hispanic Ministry* (Washington, DC: USCCB, 2002), no. 33.

10   For more on incorporating spiritual direction into activity evaluations, refer to the recommendations in *Sleeping with Bread*, 7, 30.

lay ministers to share their stories of commitment, community, vocation, and vision of the Church. Emphasize how much young adults are needed by the Church and the world.

- Host an evening on stewardship, and use the questions presented in the bishops' statement *Stewardship and Young Adults: An Invitation to Help Change the World*:

    — "What resources, talents, and abilities has God given me? Do I use them in service to others? How might I take the next step to become a more effective steward?"
    — "What qualities in the life of Jesus provide a model for living and an example of good stewardship? How might they compare to my own life and lived experience?"
    — "If I am to work to be an effective Christian steward, with the help of God's grace, what will it cost me in terms of personal sacrifice and hardship? Am I willing to take the next step?"
    — "How am I reaching out to invite others to recognize their gifts? What opportunities do I provide for them to employ those gifts for the good of the community?"[11]

DISCERNING THE UNIVERSAL CALL TO HOLINESS

In their pastoral plan for young adult ministry, *Sons and Daughters of the Light*, the Catholic bishops of the United States invite young adults "to continue to give of yourself, your time, your energies, and your talents for the good of others."[12] They promise to pray for the guidance of the Holy Spirit as young adults continue to grow in the love of Jesus Christ.

"Every Christian has a vocation, and the call to holiness is required of all"[13]—so affirmed the 2002 Third Continental Congress on Vocations. *Sons and Daughters of the Light* provides a beautiful interpretation of "vocation" as

---

11   USCCB, *Stewardship and Young Adults: An Invitation to Help Change the World* (Washington, DC: USCCB, 2004).

12   USCCB, *Sons and Daughters of the Light: A Pastoral Plan for Ministry with Young Adults* (Washington, DC: USCCB, 1996), vii.

13   *The Executive Summary of the Pastoral Plan for the Third Continental Congress on Vocations to the Ordained Ministry and Consecrated Life in North America*, 2, www.usccb.org/vocations/summary.pdf (henceforth cited as *Executive Summary*). In 2002, more than a thousand interested parties from all walks of Catholic life attended this Congress on Vocations in Montreal, Canada. The congress resulted in documents and a pastoral plan that offer direction for the Church in the United States as it continues to create, develop, and nurture a culture of vocation throughout all branches of church life.

the call to holiness, community, service, and Christian maturity lived out in the various states of life.[14] Yet when many people, young adults included, hear the word "vocation," the first association that comes to mind is priesthood— the primary synonym for "vocation" in the Church for decades. By continuing to broaden the understanding and use of the concept of vocation to include all aspects of discerning God's will in one's life, the Church will better enable all Catholics to integrate the concept, and the invitation it conveys, into their own lives.

Young adulthood is the time when one searches for, works to discern, and responds to one's vocation: single life, marriage, religious life, diaconate, or priesthood. *Sons and Daughters of the Light* reminds the Church of its responsibility to provide young adults with opportunities for this discernment and to invite them "to share their stories and be affirmed in the importance of their lives within the Church."[15] The bishops clearly articulate a vision for vocational ministry in each aspect of the Catholic community. In this vision, the parish community is not only an important companion—it is a mentoring, affirming presence for the young adult who is discerning whether to get engaged, whether to join a religious community or enter the seminary, or whether to make a commitment to single life.

SETTINGS FOR FOSTERING YOUNG ADULT DISCERNMENT

Campus Ministry

Young adults can be moved to discern a deeper call to vocation and service through opportunities for short-term commitments, group discernment efforts, and invitations to serve using their own strengths and talents. Young adults who attend campus ministry activities find many such opportunities to grow in Catholic leadership.

A notable resource for colleges and universities seeking to formalize their discernment work with students was a 2000-2007 Lilly Endowment initiative called Programs for the Theological Exploration of Vocation (PTEV). In 2000, for example, PTEV awarded Boston College a significant grant to establish Intersections, a program designed to help students explore their vocational

---

14   For a full explanation of the bishops' message on vocation, see "A Vision of Faith for Young Adults," in *Sons and Daughters of the Light*, 17-22.

15   *Sons and Daughters of the Light*, 15.

choices at significant points in their college years. One of the most significant aspects of Intersections, the Halftime Retreat, offers sophomores the opportunity to reflect on their college experiences and their personal vocation choices. A thirty-minute video featuring a popular theology professor, Fr. Michael Himes, invites students to consider three questions:

1. What brings me joy?
2. What am I good at?
3. Does the world need me to do it?[16]

After the video, the Intersections workshop pairs college juniors and seniors with faculty and staff members for one-on-one mentoring, a process that can help students to discern life decisions as well as vocations.

See the special "Campus Connection" section at the end of this chapter for more ideas about how to foster vocational discernment on campus.

Parish Life

Parishes could organize an outreach program like the Intersections workshop discussed above. Consider posing Fr. Himes's three questions in a twilight retreat or an evening of reflection offered for young adults. By exploring these questions in the context of a retreat experience, young adults in the parish often come to a clearer understanding of the gifts they have to offer in service to the world.

In addition, parishes could provide mentors for young adults who are looking at a particular calling. A young man thinking about priesthood could be mentored by a faithful, joy-filled priest; a young couple discerning marriage could be mentored by a couple who have embraced the sacramentality of their union for many years.

Whatever method it uses to foster young adult discernment, the parish community should participate significantly in creating the culture of vocation. Whenever anyone is encouraged to discern and answer the call to holiness in his or her life, *all* are encouraged. However, "to hear and respond to God's love presupposes a living relationship with the One who calls our name unceasingly."[17] In every aspect of parish life, the invitation to deepen one's

---

16   For a fuller exposition of these three questions, see the Boston College Intersections Project, "Three Key Questions," *www.ptev.org/hints.aspx?iid=5*. For more information on the initiative Programs for the Theological Exploration of Vocation, see *www.ptev.org*.

17   *Executive Summary*, 3.

relationship with God is critical to the fulfillment of God's call to us as Christians and as a Catholic community. The executive summary of the 2002 Congress on Vocations indicates that young adulthood encompasses

> key years during which young people consolidate their faith-stance and make life decisions for education, career, and relationships. The Church needs to be innovative in finding new ways to reach out to young Catholics during this important period of their lives. Possible initiatives include: "Catholic updates" in various settings, "theology on tap" programs for students and young working Catholics, credit courses in Catholic colleges, theological reflection on various elements of contemporary pop culture, and social action groups in which outreach is combined with personal and theological reflection.[18]

To be more attentive to the development of vocations in the lives of young adults, a parish might consider the following strategies.

- Create a parish vocation committee charged with evaluating all parish programs and activities in light of the "preferential option for the young" called for by the Congress on Vocations.[19] (The organization Serra International has tools for the development of such committees and other programming.[20])
- Invite young adults into positions of leadership in the parish community, and support and mentor them in these positions.
- Develop venues in which priests, sisters, brothers, and lay leaders can share their stories of discernment and their life experiences in these roles.
- Develop and host young adult–friendly weekend and evening retreats in which young adults can discuss and learn discernment strategies. Gather young adult members of small ecclesial communities for a day, morning, afternoon, or evening of retreat or reflection on baptismal calling and the needs in the world. Present options for local ministry, e.g., volunteering in hospitals, jails, youth detention centers, shelters, or alternative high

---

18   *Executive Summary*, 5.
19   *Executive Summary*, 3.
20   See *www.serra.org* for information on Serra International, an organization that fosters vocations to the priesthood and vowed religious life through prayer, awareness, affirmation, and support.

schools; participating in gang outreach or community organization; or coordinating music, liturgy, drama, or catechesis. Have
people involved in these ministries come to explain what is
needed for each ministry. Present handouts with contact information that individuals and groups can use to follow up.

- Invite the parish community to "call by name" those young
adults who may have a religious vocation. Provide opportunities
for these young adults to discuss, and to grow in, this call.

- Develop a dinner program in which older parish leaders take
turns hosting young adults for dinner in order to mentor them
and grow in personal relationships. Parish leaders must be sure
to attend to their own vocations in order to model happy, healthy,
and holy leadership.

- Become a more hospitable, welcoming community. Invite others
to join your community, and offer opportunities for them to serve
people in your area who need the Church's social outreach.

- Initiate or develop a program, similar to Theology on Tap or Holy
Grounds, at which young adults can gather for conversation, discernment, and growth in spirituality in a familiar or comfortable
setting. Make sure that this endeavor has an educational dimension. Theology on Tap is a program initiated in Chicago that
brings young adults together either at a parish or in a local pub
or bar for discussion about theological, spiritual, or religious topics. Holy Grounds is a similar program that brings young adults
together in a coffeehouse setting.[21]

- Organize a pilgrimage (or *peregrinación*, a popular custom from
the Hispanic/Latino community). Groups can make a pilgrimage to a destination far away (e.g., to the Basilica of the National
Shrine of the Immaculate Conception in Washington, D.C.; the
Basilica of Our Lady of Guadalupe in Mexico City; Archbishop
Romero's tomb in San Salvador; or the site of the first Eucharist
celebrated in the United States in St. Augustine, Florida)—or they
can make a simple trip to a church or shrine not far away from
the parish. Incorporate service with justice/solidarity action: e.g.,

21   For more on Theology on Tap, see Archdiocese of Chicago Young Adult Ministry, "The Theology-on-Tap
Report presented to the U.S. Bishops," *www.yamchicago.org/yam-TOT04-BishopReport.htm*. For more on
Holy Grounds, see Archdiocese of Atlanta Young Adult Ministry, "Holy Grounds," *www.yam.org/events/
hg.php*.

with prisoners, victims of violence, or area farm workers or other struggling workers. The value comes from having a community religious experience to prepare for. Be intentional about asking God to illuminate participants about his call to them as individuals and as a community. Teach prayer and discernment principles before and during the trip. Include testimonies from people who integrate faith and justice into their everyday lives. Prepare readings on how to live the call to discipleship in society today.

- Host or attend a ministry/volunteer fair. Many religious colleges and universities hold such fairs for students. Creighton University in Omaha has hosted a fair for local community groups to meet with interested students each August, and it has offered a post-graduate volunteer fair each September.[22] Many religious communities offer opportunities for volunteer service around the country or overseas (the Capuchins, Christian Brothers, Vincentians, Jesuits, Dominicans, Columbans, and so on) that do not require that young adult participants be college graduates.[23] Service gives young adults lessons in self-awareness and the world's needs; it helps them develop contacts and job skills. It allows them to taste a lifestyle that incorporates faith with justice, and it provides valuable guidance in discernment.

- Research, and encourage applications to, grants that may be available for young adults based on their culture of origin. For example, while the choice to devote an extended period of time exclusively to service is not common among the growing community of Hispanic/Latino young adults, AmeriCorps has offered an education grant that can help a young Hispanic/Latino adult to make this choice.[24] Challenge Catholic foundations to channel resources into recruiting young adults from diverse cultures for religious and peace-building work.

- If your parish has a significant number of Hispanic/Latino young adults, invite Spanish-speaking career counselors (from an area community college, for example) to a parish workshop to speak and present tools for career discernment found in books like

---

22   See the Web page for the Creighton Center for Service and Justice, *www.creighton.edu/ccsj*.

23   See *Response*, the Catholic Network of Volunteer Service's excellent annual guide, available at *www.cnvs.org*.

24   See the AmeriCorps Web site, *www.americorps.org*.

What Color Is Your Parachute? and *Do What You Are*.[25] Convey the belief that God wants people of all cultures to have equitable opportunities, to develop their talents and gifts as fully as possible, and to play their part in a just society. This discernment process can also be fruitful when conducted in separate gender groups, as each has particular family expectations and pressures to navigate in the Hispanic/Latino community. Invite reflection, journaling or drawing, and debate on questions such as "Is there a difference between God's will and my will for my life? How important is it to respond to the needs in the world? Can I take steps toward my own fullness of life that will also serve the needs of my community? What steps do I want to take to better develop my interests and use my gifts and talents in the world? What help do I need in order to take my next steps (e.g., improve my English, go back to school, apply for a different job)?"

- During a novena of Our Lady of Guadalupe or another special feast day or memorial for the Hispanic/Latino community, invite someone familiar with Fr. Virgilio Elizondo's theology of the vocation of the Mestizo Pueblo to give a presentation. This will lift up the whole Hispanic/Latino community and will especially challenge young adults. Parishes can adapt this strategy to the needs of other specific cultural groups in the community. Or they might adapt it to reach a broader young adult audience through similar workshops on the feasts or memorials of saints who are known for their particular discernment experiences: e.g., St. Elizabeth of Hungary, St. Elizabeth Ann Seton, or especially St. Ignatius, who did his discerning as a young adult.

SPECIFIC VOCATIONS

Considering Ordination or Religious Life

While many in parish communities bemoan the seeming shortage of priests and religious in their churches, some parishioners say they would not encourage

---

25   See Richard Bolles, *What Color Is Your Parachute? A Practical Manual for Job-Hunters and Career-Changers* (Berkeley, CA: Ten Speed Press, 2003); and Paul D. Tieger and Barbara Barron-Tieger, *Do What You Are* (Boston: Little, Brown, 1995).

people they know to discern a call to religious or ordained life. This reluctance presents a critical challenge.

Parishes can directly invite young adults to consider whether God has called them to ordination or religious life. Given opportunities to serve and to learn more about religious or ordained vocational choices, young adults do respond—but many young adults have never been invited even to consider such a call. The Center for Applied Ministry in the Apostolate (CARA) reported that only one out of six young adults born between 1963 and 1983 even *considers* a religious vocation, compared to one out of three people born in or before 1962.[26] Since the mass media do not always portray priests, religious, and lay ministers in a positive and accurate light, parishes and church leaders must make passionate, committed priests, sisters, and brothers more visible and present in young adults' lives. When the Congress on Vocations asked young adults what they would need in order to consider a religious vocation, the young adults responded that they need to hear people living religious or ordained lives share their passion for their vocation—why they love being priests, sisters, or brothers.[27]

Each local Catholic community offers numerous resources to support the parish in developing the culture of religious vocation to which the Catholic bishops of the United States and the Holy Father call us all:

- Diocesan and religious community vocation ministers
- Diocesan lay leadership schools and programs
- Diocesan young adult ministry offices and programs
- The USA Council of Serra International, and local chapters of Serrans
- Knights of Columbus

Because reaching out to young adults in the context of their lives is critical to the effectiveness of any ministry with them, young adult–responsive parishes might explore and share with young adults the numerous Internet resources for discerning a call to religious or ordained life. The Internet presents a multitude of Web sites for individual religious communities, but significant national sites include the following:

---

26   See Center for Applied Research in the Apostolate (CARA), *CARA Working Paper Number 1: Young Adult Catholics in the Context of Other Catholic Generations* (Washington, DC: CARA, 2000), 2.

27   See *Executive Summary*, 9.

- National Religious Vocation Conference: *www.nrvc.net* (and its extraordinary annual resource guide at *www.vocation-network.org/guide*)
- United States Conference of Catholic Bishops' Committee on Clergy, Consecrated Life, and Vocations: *www.usccb.org/vocations*
- National Coalition for Church Vocations: *www.nccv-vocations.org* (including a catalog with numerous materials that parishes can use to promote and develop vocation awareness)
- Vocations Online: *www.vocationsonline.org*
- Busted Halo, a service of Paulist Young Adult Ministries: *www.bustedhalo.com*
- Catherine of Siena Institute: *www.siena.org*
- Programs for the Theological Exploration of Vocation: *www.ptev.org*
- Boston College Intersections Program: *www.bc.edu/intersections*
- Catholic Vocations Ministry of the Archdiocese of Melbourne: *www.catholicvocation.org.au* (includes particularly useful information for parishes)

For young adults who identify with particular cultural experiences, accepting the invitation to religious life or priesthood may be complicated by their respective culture's perceptions of the Church. For example, some members of the African American community may be hesitant to support a young man's or young woman's call if they perceive the Church as being somehow hostile or unfriendly to that young man or woman. Seminary directors and other vocations leaders need to be sensitive to and aware of this possibility and need to work to reassure community leaders that they have these young adults' best interests at heart. They can educate the community about the under-representation of African Americans in the Catholic clergy and religious orders, for example, and can use materials that specifically promote vocations among African Americans.[28] Similar challenges can exist in other cultural groups as well. Parishes that are responsive to young adults of all cultures understand and address these challenges. They make sure to welcome and include all of God's people, finding effective ways to invite them into vocational discernment within the Church.

---

28   See *Executive Summary*, 9.

Seeing Single Life as a Vocation

Another challenge in vocational discernment occurs when single life is not recognized as a calling from God. Yet the *National Directory for Catechesis* calls people who say "yes" to God's call to single life "dedicated" singles.

More people in the United States are remaining single. Fortunately, today's young singles are less likely to encounter the negative stereotypes about adult singles (especially women) that previous generations grew up with. (Some readers will remember the Old Maid card game, where the loser was the one left without a partner and with only a single card of the "old maid"—and she wasn't pretty!) But despite the increasingly positive understanding of single life, many Catholics still do not see single life as a true vocation or a permanent commitment, sometimes treating it instead as a default or interim status. Parishes can change this perspective. For example, priests can be sensitive in their homilies by including examples of people who live alone, rather than assuming that everyone lives in a family setting. Homilies, bulletin inserts, and catechetical sessions provide opportunities to discuss single life as a holy call from God. Parish leaders can also pair older singles with young adults who feel called to remain single. These mature mentors can share the gifts and the challenges of single life. They can also clarify the difference between "single and looking" and "single and committed to staying that way."

Some parishes celebrate "Singles Sunday" to educate the entire parish community—not just young adults—about the potential for holiness in the single life. The liturgy on this Sunday includes special petitions for the singles in the community. Singles are invited to participate as liturgical ministers. If the day includes a longer program, testimonies by faith-filled singles and workshops on saints who were single can inspire young adults who may be feeling as though being single is the default vocation or a second-class status. It can reassure them that not having found someone to marry, or not feeling called to be a nun or priest, does not mean they do not have a vocation.

Discerning the Vocation of Sacramental Marriage

The majority of young adults will marry. Once they become engaged, most will go through a marriage-preparation program. These programs help the couple to discern their relationship's strengths and shortcomings and their own readiness to marry. They also help the couple to hone their relationship skills in order to launch their marriage on the right track.

Immediate preparation for marriage has great value, but it also has limitations. Once a couple has announced their engagement, and wedding plans have been put into motion, substantive relationship patterns are difficult to change, and true discernment about whether they should marry is hampered. Most immediate marriage preparation is based on the premise that the couple will follow through with their wedding plans.

Into a serious relationship and subsequent engagement, each young adult brings a particular set of skills for communication and conflict resolution, and particular attitudes toward commitment, sexuality, faith, and spirituality. The formation of effective skills and attitudes is crucial to the success of immediate marriage preparation during engagement and to a healthy start for a couple's marriage. This formation prior to engagement is called "proximate" preparation for marriage.

Young adults have an intense interest in relationships, particularly their own. They are discovering that mature romance can be truly fulfilling, but also quite complicated. Many have already discovered that sex complicates a relationship and complicates life. Most young adults, while not saying as much aloud, are constantly looking for help and direction, ideas and strategies, about how to navigate the waters of romantic relationships. They do their proximate preparation for marriage on their own. Yet when a parish or campus ministry program offers opportunities for young adults to explore mature relationships, they come, ready and anxious to learn and share.

Young adults in today's society bring specific needs to their dialogue with the Church on love and marriage. First, they need opportunities to talk about their own views on marriage and covenantal commitment. Some have not witnessed healthy marriage. They may need opportunities to talk about effective ways to resolve conflict in relationships, since many have never learned those skills. They also need opportunities to discuss the sacramental nature of marriage and its importance in the community. Many have absorbed the secular view of marriage as merely a private agreement between two persons. For this reason, they may also need opportunities to talk about cohabitation and sexual activity outside of marriage. Some have adopted the prevailing attitude that cohabitation is a necessary precursor to marriage, just like trying on a pair of shoes is necessary before buying them. Yet most are not aware of the detrimental effects of cohabitation. As a result, many have had hurtful experiences.

The Church has much wisdom to share about relationships, sex, and marriage. Those who minister responsively to young adults take advantage of every opportunity to share this wisdom. They put a priority on providing safe and healthy forums where young adults can talk about their hopes, dreams, confusions, and questions about relationships that lead to marriage.

PERSONAL WITNESSES TO
THE VOCATIONAL JOURNEY

Call to Religious Life

One of the authors of this chapter, Sr. Christine Wilcox, shared her own experience of how she discerned her call to religious life after she spent time away from the Church and then returned to a vibrant Catholic community:

> I returned to the Catholic Church during my sophomore year of college: a return initiated by a friend's persistent, annoying invitation to Mass. After finally agreeing to go, I discovered a spiritual home in the Catholic Church that I hadn't even known I'd been missing. However, not until graduate school did I feel able to commit to my faith, when I joined an adult Confirmation class and became more integrated into the Catholic community at my campus Newman Center. There, I was invited to find some way to serve the community by discerning my gifts, then focusing on how one of them might serve others. I became a lector.
>
> Proclaiming the Word in Sunday liturgy sparked the process of discovering my own vocation, God's call and gift to me, as a Dominican sister. Over the next several years at the Newman Center, I was invited again and again to deepen my commitment to service in this Catholic community. Each invitation—to participate on the liturgy committee, to coordinate the young adult group—was issued *in person* by someone in the community who knew me. And each invitation moved me closer to being able to hear God's call to religious life. My spirituality and faith were deepened within this community because it was responsive to the needs and life development of its young adults.
>
> At age twenty-eight, I had met only two religious sisters. Vocation to religious life wasn't even on my radar. Through active participation in a Newman Center, my parish community, I developed a deep relationship of love with God and the Church. Through the

invitation, encouragement, and development of my call in this local community, I was opened to hear God's call in another way. While I didn't know many religious sisters, I did get to know two religious priests, and their lives of healthy community, happy ministry, and challenging growth in the church community helped me see options for my own life other than the wifehood and motherhood that I had always assumed would be my path.

After a communal prayer experience in which I heard the voice of God ask me to consider being a sister, I approached a priest friend who had known me for several years. He was able to respond sincerely, "Sounds like vocation to me," and proceeded to tell me that he had been waiting for this conversation for a while.

Call to Marriage

Sean Lansing, a young adult who has worked for the Center for Ministry Development as the coordinator of Young Neighbors in Action, a national service-learning program for adolescents, described his vocational discernment in this way:

> I was a junior in college with no plan or desire to get married. I had much bigger ideas about what I was going to do with my life to change the world, and none of them included settling down and getting married—that I knew for sure. My vocation to marriage found me; I certainly was not looking for it.
>
> I started dating my wife, and it did not take long before we both realized the potential for our love. I struggled early in our relationship with the thought of how getting married might tie me down and close doors of possibility. As our relationship grew and our love matured, I came to realize that the opposite was true. Our marriage, our love, our vocation to each other allowed us to become better people and to experience life more fully than I could have imagined.

A Single's Call: Freedom in Commitment

A young adult who was interviewed during the Initiative shared her story of eagerly wanting to get married in college and her mid-twenties. She yearned to be a wife and a mother. But as her late twenties approached, she began to hear God's call to something else—single life. At first she was dismayed, thinking of how much she wanted those babies. She was afraid she would be unhappy if she followed God's call to single life. But she said her ultimate surrender came when she asked herself, "Would God ask me to do something that would make me miserable?" The answer was a resounding "no!" So she began to pray about what being single means from the perspective of faith. What she discovered was the opportunity to do God's will in a unique way— balancing the challenge of not being selfish with her time (since she was not accountable to a husband, children, or a community) with the freedom to share her time with those who needed her. She considers herself committed to single life in much the same way a vowed religious is committed to his or her religious life. And she told the Initiative staff that she is very happy.

A Priest's Story: The Missionary Life

A young priest in Milwaukee, Wisconsin, shared his vocational journey with a member of the Initiative staff:

> First of all, let it be said, this wasn't my fault! I wasn't planning on priesthood, nor was I one of those kids who "played" priest when they were young. When I was twenty-two, a friend told me about some missionaries in Kenya. I visited them; it was going to be a vacation, nothing more. Three months turned into three years.
>
> On the one hand, the reasons to stay were too many to count; the missionary life with the Missionary Community of St. Paul the Apostle was something that I had always dreamed of but never knew existed. The Turkana tribespeople that we worked with were an inspiration in their faith and trust of God. They are a nomadic tribe in Kenya who live lives of survival in a semi-arid land. But . . . God began to speak through the events of a missionary life and through . . . people who had dedicated their lives to serve others, to serve the poorest of the poor. God was calling me to do the same, calling me to a beautiful life, but I was so afraid to say yes. . . .
>
> It was through the dramatic and the ordinary events of everyday life that God began to call. I didn't want to say yes, but I couldn't say no. God seduces us in ways we least expect; God interrupts our lives and demands responses. God took me to Africa and told me, "Now try to ignore me and ignore my call." I couldn't. Some years of

study later I am now a six-month-old priest. God wasn't wrong; it is a beautiful life.

CONCLUSION

Discernment never happens in a vacuum. The parish's presence in the life of a young adult—through homilies, mentors, prayer opportunities, and so forth—supports the young adult in *discerning* life choices rather than simply deciding them. And vocational discernment also does not happen in a vacuum. It arises in the context of the community's relationship with the potential priest, sister, brother, married person, or single person. The community's affirmation can only take place in a setting that invites and supports the development of gifts and the sharing of talents. Through the grace of God, the Church will continue to grow in its ability to provide young adults with such settings.

THE CAMPUS CONNECTION

During their college years, young men and women make important life decisions. Typically these decisions revolve around careers, relationships, and vocations. Many students come to college very focused on career goals. Other young men and women enter college uncertain about a career and use their college experience to resolve their uncertainty. Still other students enter college with a career goal in mind but alter their goal after taking some courses in that field or being exposed to other fields of study. During this process, young adults turn to others, such as academic advisors, counselors, and peers, for guidance or companionship.

However, career choice is only one of the decisions that a young adult must make. The choice of vocation encompasses much more than career, and the process of discernment is much more complex. Engaging in this process requires committed Christians to answer some very personal questions: "Why did God create me?" "What is God calling me to do?" "What is my mission in life?" While seeking answers to these questions, young adults once again need others to whom they can turn for guidance and companionship. Campus ministers have the opportunity to fill this role for students while they are discerning their vocation in life. Here are some real-life examples of ways to guide students in discernment:

- One of the most popular vocation discernment programs is the Busy Student Retreat.[29] This directed retreat for students occurs on campus during the week, usually over a span of four or five days. During each day of the retreat, students commit half an hour of their free time to meeting with their spiritual director and dedicate another half-hour to personal prayer. The retreat's spiritual directors are vocation directors from local religious communities. During the retreat, spiritual directors assist students with learning different forms of prayer as well as with discerning God's will for their life. Some campuses include a communal prayer experience or liturgy each day as part of the retreat. Campuses can also invite participants and spiritual directors to enjoy a meal together, to enhance the

---

29   For details about conducting a Busy Student Retreat, see "Retreats," in *Young Adult Works*, Binder 4, 8B.3-8B.21.

experience of community. One of the great benefits of the Busy Student Retreat is that it begins the discernment process for many students.

- St. Augustine Church and Catholic Student Center in Gainesville, Florida, serves the University of Florida and Santa Fe Community College. Campus ministers at the Center instituted a program called Vocation Discernment Ministry. Students who form the Vocation Discernment Ministry group have met regularly on the second and fourth Tuesday of each month. On the second Tuesday, participants gather to pray, reflect on Scripture, and develop their listening and discernment skills. Speakers—married couples, priests, religious women and men, lay ministers, seminarians, secular or associate members of religious communities, and others— share their discernment stories. On the fourth Tuesday in this program, participants gather for Taizé Prayer and quiet time before the Blessed Sacrament. Over the years, the students who have participated in the Vocation Discernment Ministry group have come to appreciate that the term "vocation" does not exclusively mean "religious vocation." They know that every baptized person is called by Jesus Christ and has a vocation. They have researched the charisms that founders of religious orders have instilled in their communities. They have come to recognize that they have numerous avenues available for them to serve as disciples of Jesus Christ. The student community has also assumed the supportive role of praying for those students who are in a discernment process.

- Cornell University's Catholic community has sponsored discussion groups on church careers and vocational discernment. Several times a semester, on Saturday afternoon, the group meets for dinner together at the priest's house. The group provides a supportive environment for students to discuss various options open to them for service to Christ and the Church. Every few years, Cornell's campus ministers have also sponsored an all-day Church Careers and Vocations Fair, where representatives from almost every possible vocation in the Church have given workshops on their calls. The fair has usually included a keynote speaker.

- St. Mary's Church and Catholic Campus Ministry serves students attending the University of Miami in Ohio. Each year, this parish has sponsored a Vocation Weekend, inviting vocation directors of men's and women's religious orders to speak at the weekend Masses. Following the Masses, students can meet and talk with the vocation directors at receptions or socials. Each year, the archdiocesan vocation director has invited every student registered with St. Mary's Campus Ministry to this event. As interest has grown, a group has formed for men and women considering a vocation to religious life or non-ordained ministry.

By helping to raise students' awareness of the numerous ways in which a person can serve the people of God, campus ministers can provide a tremendous benefit to their students. Helping young adults appreciate that they have been called by Jesus Christ for a special purpose in this life, and walking with them as they discern their mission, may very well be the greatest service campus ministers can render.

CHAPTER FIVE

Community Life
and Pastoral Care

How can parishes welcome young adults, invite them into the community of the Church, and meet their pastoral needs? This chapter explores diverse ways to invite young adults into and then engage them in parish life. The chapter also shares simple strategies for connecting with young adults and programs that offer them a genuine experience of community in the context of their own cultures.

Today's hectic world demands much of young adults. They get pulled in many different directions by the media, careers, friends, family, romantic relationships, and other social needs. They cope with terrorism, war, depression, suicide, violence, eating disorders, unemployment, and debt. In all of these situations, the Church has an excellent opportunity to provide young adults with a faithful foundation—better yet, a *home* (see 1 Tm 6:19).

For example, at the first meeting of a young adult Bible study group in one parish, a few members spoke freely during the faith-sharing segment. Most, however, appeared shy or reserved, and few of the attendees knew each other. So the group decided to go to the local pub for fellowship after each week's Bible study. Over the following weeks, everyone became acquainted. Informal conversations covered sports, jobs, high school experiences, and mutual hobbies. Participants made friends and established a foundation for community. In a few months, all were more comfortable with sharing their thoughts, often private, about daily struggles, personal experiences, and their common faith.

Another parish community instituted a monthly Newcomers' Night. Once a month before Bible study, people would gather at a local restaurant. All, especially newcomers, were invited to share a meal, meet the leaders, ask questions, and join in friendly conversation. These events helped new parishioners to make friends and relax in a comfortable atmosphere. Many of the first participants in Newcomers' Night became regular members of the Bible study, sharing their faith and helping to expand the ministry.

The concepts of community life and pastoral care focus on providing a spiritual home for young adults within the Catholic Church: a place where they are appreciated, supported, and invited to contribute—and, most of all, a place where they belong. The Catholic bishops of the United States, in their pastoral plan *Sons and Daughters of the Light*, speak clearly about the Church's call to provide young adults with community life and pastoral care: "we, as members of the Church, must actively invite and welcome young adults into the life of the Church"[1] to fulfill young adults' longing for community and participation. "Pastoral care for young adults requires that parishes be a *home* for young adults where they are personally touched in their faith journey. . . . [To accomplish this,] parish leaders need an awareness of the life patterns, transience, and mobility of young adults."[2]

Parishes that are responsive to young adults remember that *young adults are the present, not just the future, of the Church*. And parishes have many options for treating them as such—for welcoming, inviting, and encouraging young adults with the ultimate goal of building, in the words of St. Augustine, the "City of God."

CHALLENGES

As *Sons and Daughters of the Light* describes, many young adults feel "unwelcome and alone—strangers in the house of God."[3] At times, young adults do seem to be noticed less than other demographic groups in the Church.[4] Parish communities are challenged to build a home where young adults are connected to the Church: in the spiritual, social, and service dimensions of their lives. Parishes are called to be responsive to young adults, to invite young adults to shift from "going to church" to "belonging to a parish." Parishes that accomplish this shift will build a rock-solid foundation for the future of families, parish communities, and the greater Church.

On this journey toward stronger community life with its young adults, the Catholic parish encounters many challenges:

- Competition from popular culture and its promotion of secular life

---

1   United States Conference of Catholic Bishops (USCCB), *Sons and Daughters of the Light: A Pastoral Plan for Ministry with Young Adults* (Washington, DC: USCCB, 1996), 2.
2   *Sons and Daughters of the Light*, 27.
3   *Sons and Daughters of the Light*, v.
4   See *Sons and Daughters of the Light*, 38.

- Demanding jobs or careers of today's young adults
- Other religions and denominations that provide many activities appealing to young adults
- Resources needed for young adult ministry
- Development of peer leaders
- Challenges of being responsive to young adults

The Church will be able to meet these challenges when parish communities make young adults a priority.

BEST PRACTICES

Parish leaders have many practical opportunities to welcome, invite, and encourage young adults to become part of the parish community. Below are seven areas to consider when working in pastoral care with young adults. Many are self-explanatory; the key is to be creative and effective.

1. Gain Perspective

Can your parish see the world through the eyes of a young adult? If so, what do you see? What priorities, needs, talents, and desires do you identify? To learn more about what issues are important to young adults, sit down with young adults in your own parish and listen to their stories. Read current articles about today's young adults and the issues that are challenging them. Review issues discussed in Chapter 1, "Creating a Young Adult–Responsive Church," as well as the Center for Ministry Development's booklet *Becoming a Young Adult Responsive Church*.[5]

2. Assess What You Can Offer

Assess what your parish community has to offer young adults. A lively liturgy? Engaging adult faith formation? A gym or available meeting rooms? A nearby coffee shop? A parish picnic or welcoming committee? When building a community that is responsive to young adults, build on your strengths. What programs and activities are available in your community to help young adults grow in the spiritual, social, and service dimensions of their lives? The profile

---

5   See Ron Bagley, CJM, John Roberto, and Joan Weber, *Becoming a Young Adult Responsive Church* (Naugatuck, CT: Center for Ministry Development [CMD], 1997).

and assessment tool in *Becoming a Young Adult Responsive Church*[6] can help you to determine your strengths and weaknesses in reaching out to young adults.

3. Welcome and Get Acquainted

Reach out and welcome young adults through one or more of the following strategies:

- *Personally greet young adults.* The simplest ways often work best. Reach out before or after Mass, or contact them by phone.
- *Make contact with young adults when they move into the area.* Consider adding a brochure to the chamber of commerce's welcome packet or to the parish's registration packet.[7] Post a newsletter at nearby apartment complexes, self-service laundries, or coffee shops to explain the activities and ministries of the parish and invite young adults to "come and see."
- *Offer fun events to draw newcomers.* For example, try having a picnic for young adults, perhaps after the late Sunday Mass. Ask for volunteers to help grill the food. Provide music, board games, soccer, or volleyball. Start off with group prayer, and then let the fellowship begin. This is an excellent opportunity for making friends, doing subtle evangelization, and brainstorming future events.
- *Communicate by listening rather than talking.* Start a conversation, but spend most of the time listening.[8] Find things in common to talk about. A helpful tip (when meeting anyone, not just young adults) is to learn one interesting aspect about that person, such as a hobby or a favorite sports team, leaving the door open for future discussions. Discover the person's background. Is he or she new to the area and perhaps searching for a support network? Learn young adults' individual and collective strengths, needs, and goals.
- *Hold a town-hall meeting that includes food, mingling, and conversation.* Town-hall meetings can accomplish several goals. They connect young adults with other young adults; they can help parish leaders determine which young adults are potential leaders; and

---

6   See *Becoming a Young Adult Responsive Church*, 23-26.
7   See "Strategy Six: Market to Young Adults," in *Young Adult Works*, ed. Ronald Bagley, CJM, John Roberto, Susan Stark, and Joan Weber (Naugatuck, CT: CMD, 1997), Binder 2, 6.41-6.45.
8   See "Strategy Five: Make One-to-One Contacts," in *Young Adult Works*, Binder 2, 6.36.

they can inform organizers about young adults' needs and interests in order to guide future ministry efforts.

- *Conduct a survey or census.* Content is key. Structure the survey so as to learn the demographics and desires of the group, get general feedback, and ask for referrals for other prospective members. Be sure that the census is easy to complete, and distribute it widely (e.g., sent by mail and e-mail, placed in the pews and on the parish Web site, inserted in the bulletin). Advertise often, and allow for easy return (e.g., via collection basket, pre-addressed envelope, fax, e-mail, or Web site). Finally, be sure to request feedback from inactive members and from non-members. Their demographics and needs are equally important, and they may pass the word along to interested friends.

4. Invite—Sincerely and Comfortably

As the bishops assert in *Sons and Daughters of the Light*, "young adults will participate when they perceive that the invitation is authentic and that their participation is constructive."[9]

- *Personal invitations are the most effective and preferred method—whether issued after Mass or over the phone.* Issuing a positive invitation, one that offers the person a wonderful opportunity, is always more effective than putting someone on the spot or trying to guilt him or her into coming. Give enough information to make a decision, but no more.[10] Add a warm, friendly feel to your message. Ask the person to just give it a try—no strings attached.
- *Reach young adults in their comfort zone.* Use mailings, bulletin announcements, e-mail, online postings, and local advertisements. Again, invite them just to think about coming—don't demand an automatic yes. Remember that word-of-mouth referrals are a primary reason people attend events. Use friends and family members as messengers. Since 29 percent of young adults consider a parent their best friend,[11] church-going parents are excellent messengers.

---

9   *Sons and Daughters of the Light*, 34.
10   See "Strategy Six: Market to Young Adults," in *Young Adult Works*, Binder 2, 6.44.
11   See "A Socio-Cultural View of Young Adults," in *Young Adult Works*, Binder 1, 1.23.

- *Pulpit announcements* are very effective, especially when made by young adults. People pay attention when someone new is speaking.

5. Communicate Often

Stay in touch with young adults. Make sure that contact continues beyond the initial invitation. Consider the following strategies.

- *Assign contact people.* Often, the young adult ministry leader or welcoming chairperson assumes this role, but consider having many individuals share the task. Designating contact people is a helpful way to welcome all newcomers and to keep a unified presence with the community. Contact people can also ensure that questions and requests are directed to the correct person.
- *Return e-mails and phone calls promptly and pleasantly.* It takes a lot of courage for some young adults to request information about a parish's resources. A prompt and pleasant reply reaffirms their interest and makes their first visit more comfortable.
- *Develop and maintain a Web site.* Web sites are an easy and inexpensive way to post information—and young adults are likely to use online resources. Ensure that your parish Web site has an event calendar or a page for young adults. Posting your information can allow it to reach a broader audience.
- *Start an e-mail group or a blog.* Many companies (for example, Yahoo!, Gmail, and *coollist.com*) offer free services for running e-mail groups. People can sign up or remove themselves from the list as they wish. An e-mail list makes it very easy to send out e-newsletters, calendars, and even last-minute reminders and invitations: just send the information to the group's single e-mail address, and the service redirects the e-mail to everyone in the group. Creating a Catholic blog also gives young adults opportunities to reflect on and share their faith individually, without committing to attend a particular event.
- *Remind young adults about upcoming events.* Don't nag—just renew the invitation.
- *Set up an e-zine (short for "electronic magazine").* An e-zine can serve as an inexpensive, convenient point of contact with young

adults in the community and a way to remind them about what their parish home has to offer. Its content can inform them about upcoming parish events, connect them with regional happenings, and guide them toward scriptural and spiritual Web sites.

- *Create a podcast or an online video.* Get a group of young adults together to interview their peers about what they look for from the Church and about how your parish fulfills their hunger for intimacy with Jesus and for living out their call to discipleship. Then offer the podcast through iTunes or on the parish Web site; post the video on YouTube, GodTube, and similar video-sharing sites. Think creatively!

- *Develop a regional or diocesan newsletter.* Go beyond a parish e-zine—consider joining forces with other parishes or campuses to publish (in print or online) a newsletter that includes events from multiple ministries. This service will help young adults to network with others who share their faith and who are on a similar journey.

- *Keep a guest book at events.* Offering a guest book allows interested newcomers to sign up and also provides you with their contact information—and the opportunity to invite them back personally. Also keep a "social list," a shared list that allows young adults to contact each other, get together socially, and further build friendships and community. When newcomers join your mailing list, allow them to indicate whether they would like their phone number and e-mail address shared with others on the social list.

- *Make use of free advertising.* Bulletin announcements, pulpit announcements, parish newsletters, neighborhood bulletin boards, the local newspaper's event calendar, the diocesan newspaper, free online ads, and radio public service announcements[12] can all serve to spread information about special events to welcome young adults.

- *Advertise other communities' young adult ministry activities.* If your community's young adults can fulfill a spiritual need at another parish, your efforts are still a success. You never know: they may bring back great ideas or return better able to contribute to your parish.

---

12   See "Strategy Six: Market to Young Adults," in *Young Adult Works*, Binder 2, 6.42.

6. Encourage Involvement: Offer Activities That Meet Specific Needs

Invite young adults to spiritual, social, and service events in the parish. These "three S's" form a foundation for a place where a young adult's faith can find a home. Make intergenerational activities more responsive to young adults,[13] and develop new activities to meet the particular needs of young adults. Some people may initially take to a single type of activity; but over time, a variety of offerings will challenge young adults to stretch and grow.

- *Ask all parish ministries and activities to assess their needs and offerings for young adult participants.* Encourage them to recruit young adults to join the leadership team, and make sure that parish-wide events help young adults feel included and welcomed. Consider holding a parish activity fair to promote young adults' increased involvement in parish life.

- *Offer enriching liturgies that attract young adults.* Preach homilies that include everyday examples of faith in action. Offer good liturgical music—traditional or contemporary—at Sunday Mass. Or try an outdoor experience of liturgy: "Mass with Mother Nature" or "Bible on the Beach." Assess whether Masses are offered at convenient times for young adults (such as late Sunday morning or early Sunday evening). Include young adults as ushers, lectors, and eucharistic ministers. (See Chapter 7, "Young Adults and Liturgy," for more ideas.)

- *Provide young adults with opportunities for self-improvement.* "Pastoral care" means taking care of the whole person and the person's whole being—social, economic, emotional, and spiritual. Invite young adults to current programs in the parish that support healthy, holy lives. Try offering workshops or one-on-one assistance in career planning, financial planning, budgeting, time management, relocating, and relationship building. Qualified parishioners can volunteer to teach these classes—if young adults are qualified, invite them to give presentations to their peers.

- *Offer discernment services.* Group or one-on-one discernment counseling can be offered to help young adults in their process

---

13   See the checklist in *Becoming a Young Adult Responsive Church*, 27, for questions to ask in making current programs more young adult–friendly.

of determining how God is calling them to committed single life, married life, religious life, or ordained life. Put them in touch with people who live a faithful life in each of the vocations. Offer them a Theology on Tap or other input session on what discernment is. (See Chapter 4, "Discernment and Vocation," for more ideas.)

- *Host social events to draw young adults who have moved into the area and are looking for ways to meet people.* Invite young adults to already planned intergenerational parish events (e.g., parish picnic, fall festival, Mardi Gras party). Or organize dances, trips to sporting events, holiday parties, local festivals, or summer picnics for young adults. Create social sports teams that change every week so that newcomers never feel like outsiders. Coordinate hiking trips or bike rides.

- *Engage young adults through service opportunities.* Parish service projects, such as Habitat for Humanity builds, nursing home or hospital visits, or visits with parishioners confined to their homes, have successfully involved young adults in parishes across the country. Ask young adults to lead the intergenerational community in a canned food drive or a volunteer session at a local soup kitchen.

7. Incorporate Successful Traits

Remember that other parishes have successfully piloted young adult community efforts. Learn from their wisdom and best practices, including some listed here.

- *Cater to varying levels of spirituality.* Balance the important need to help young adult parishioners grow in spirituality with the need to welcome non-Catholics, fallen-away Catholics, or newcomers. One way to accomplish this is by challenging the already involved young adult to journey with a newcomer—for example, by being an RCIA sponsor or a table leader at programs and events.

   Remember that many young adult Catholics are married to people of other denominations. Catholic young adults feel only as welcome as their spouses, so it is important to reach out to both. Make ecumenical efforts as often as possible.

- *Promote ownership.* Ownership empowers and can breed dedication. Get young adults involved in leadership by personal invitation or through a gifts-discernment process. Offer them the opportunity to lead and to plan events. Ask young adults who are already involved to scout for leadership and talent within their peer communities.

- *Give young adults space to participate when they can.* Don't pressure people to attend events. If an event becomes an obligation, it is automatically less enjoyable. Simply let people know they are always welcome. And avoid setting membership or participation requirements—the ultimate goal of ministry with young adults is to bring young adults closer to Christ. Requirements may prevent someone from working in the group to explore his or her faith and grow closer to the Lord.

- *Use nametags at events.* Many of us feel silly wearing nametags, but isn't it hard to remember everyone's name? Nametags allow newcomers to strike up a conversation.

- *Be dependable and honor commitments.* Newcomers are less likely to return if events are canceled without sufficient advance notice. If an emergency forces the last-minute cancellation of a program, provide information on why you had to cancel.

- *Network in your area and diocese.* Networking allows you to meet other young adults, share ideas, collaborate on joint events, and boost participation. In the Archdiocese of Omaha, young adults from parishes that have a viable young adult ministry gather every other month to exchange calendar dates, collaborate, and support each other. Ask the diocesan staff person in charge of young adult ministry to gather parish leaders on a regular basis.

- *Adopt a regional approach.* If your parish is part of a cluster, deanery, or vicariate, discuss using your cluster as a basis for starting a young adult ministry. While a single-parish young adult ministry often gives the best small-community atmosphere, demographics are rarely sufficient for a small or rural parish to sustain a sizable young adult ministry. Inviting neighboring parishes adds not only more members, but also more leaders, more resources, and more varied activities. Collaborating also expands the opportunity to meet people of the same faith who are on a similar journey: the approach described in *Sons and Daughters of the Light*.[14]

- *Use technology*. Young adults are tech-savvy. Sharing information and news with them electronically can be much easier, much quicker, and more effective than traditional methods. Consider developing a parish (or parish cluster) Web site where interested young adults can get more information about an event or a program before attending. Post your activities calendar on the Web site to save on postage. To strengthen the site, provide links to diocesan, scriptural, and spiritual Web sites. Conduct online surveys to find out what young adults are looking for.

- *Send e-mails to your young adult distribution list or e-mail group to invite young adults to, or remind them of, events*. Consider developing a young adult prayer network with a weekly e-mail listing of prayer intentions.

CULTURAL IMPLICATIONS

While it is impossible to cater to the individual needs of every young adult or every cultural group, a parish still must be sensitive to all. Striking a delicate balance between general consensus and specific needs can help engage as many young adults as possible in the community life of the parish. As an illustration, some Asian cultures are more apt to value qualities such as overt humility and even passivity, and some young adults from these cultures may prefer to work only behind the scenes, rather than out in front. When planning young adult activities or asking young adults to take part in events or liturgy, be sure to take into account not just their gifts and interests, but also their values. Parishes that are responsive to young adults of all cultures and backgrounds strive to accurately reflect the diversity of the group in such areas as culture, social class, education, financial status, political stance, and physical ability.

A parish will do well to remember that a young adult's quest for identity is *always* spiritual, though influenced by culture, gender, and other factors. Parishes that are responsive to young adults ask themselves, "What can the Church do to create a space that is conducive to finding that identity?" These parishes remain aware of cultural factors that can affect a person's sense of

---

14   *Sons and Daughters of the Light*, 48.

self. For example, in African culture, the "I" takes its meaning in the "we." In other words, individual identity is to be found within the context of the community.[15] This is also a common feature in African American spirituality. This principle helps young adults to see that everyone is connected. They do not belong to their families alone; they belong to their families, their parishes, and the whole Church. This essential concept for pastoral care with African American young adults can apply to all young adults as well. Parishes have an opportunity to help young adults find themselves in the context of their own culture, of the parish community, and of the whole Church.

Here are some general guidelines for bringing young adults from many backgrounds into one parish community.

- *Strive for total community involvement.* Invite young adults to become part of a wider community, and exert effort to institute parish policies that are inclusive of a wide variety of cultures. This effort also shows support for the cultures that make up the parish community and affirms positive role models for young adults.

- *Offer homilies and services that emphasize solutions and coping mechanisms for issues that impact the cultural identity of the young adults in your parish.* Days of reflection and educational programs could be offered by the parish education office or local committees on leadership within a specific culture (e.g., African American, Hispanic/Latino, or Asian American leadership).

- *Incorporate a system for parish networking.* This allows young adults to share their experiences and affirm other young adults' experiences, and it exposes the larger community to the different cultures of young adults.

- *Develop specific programs that foster community and expose cultures to one another.* Basic suggestions include a multi-parish young adult Mass or a softball game with a sister parish.

The key is to ensure that existing programs and efforts towards community life and pastoral care with young adults are tailored for the particular needs of the diverse community. No one wants to reinvent the wheel; ultimately, the goal is increased awareness and sensitivity. Cesar Chavez once said, "The goal of all education should be, without a doubt, the service of others. We cannot

---

15   Black Catholic Bishops of the United States, *What We Have Seen and Heard: Pastoral Letter on Evangelization* (Cincinnati: St. Anthony Messenger Press, 1984), 10.

seek fulfillment and forget the progress and prosperity of our community. Our ambitions should be broad enough to include the aspirations, needs and well-being of others as well as our own."[16]

Hispanics/Latinos account for more than 45 percent of all Catholics under the age of thirty in the United States.[17] Many Hispanic/Latino young adults identify with two cultures, and sometimes with neither very well. Developing cross-cultural communication skills is essential for those leaders (both Hispanic/Latinos and non-Hispanic/Latinos) who minister to Hispanic/Latino young adults.[18] The following suggestions can assist those involved in pastoral care with Hispanic/Latino young adults.

1. *Offer a cultural competency workshop or series* for area pastors, directors of adult faith formation, young adult ministry teams, deacons, and so forth. The objectives would be (a) promoting understanding of the tremendous range of historical experiences and cultural differences between Hispanic/Latino sub-groups in the area and (b) identifying unique mental health and pastoral care needs of various persons in need (e.g., how to recognize and make effective referrals with persons who have suffered domestic violence, post-traumatic stress disorder, sexual abuse, civil war, or immigration traumas). Such workshops or programs could also be offered in an ecumenical setting sponsored by an area ministerial association and be open to health care professionals, police and city officials, and others in public service.

2. *Utilize specific elements of cross-cultural training.* For example, conduct Eric Law's "Photolanguage"[19] exercise using pictures from the photo documentary of the Smithsonian exhibition *Americanos: Latino Life in the United States.*[20] Or have parishioners from different Hispanic/Latino sub-groups share their stories of family roots, immigration, struggles, and victories. Use information from resources like *Quality*

---

16   Quoted in Edward James Olmos, Lea Ybarra, and Manuel Monterrey, eds., *Americanos: Latino Life in the United States* (Boston: Little, Brown, 1999), 38 (only in Spanish; quote translated by authors).

17   See Instituto Fe y Vida Research and Resource Center, *Changing the Face of Ministry with Catholic Hispanic Youth and Young Adults* (Stockton, CA: Instituto Fe y Vida).

18   See Ken Johnson-Mondragón, "Pastoral Reality of Hispanic Youth," *En Marcha*, Winter/Spring 2004, *www.usccb.org/hispanicaffairs/enmarcha/spring04.shtml.* The article was excerpted from "Welcoming Hispanic Youth/Jóvenes in Catholic Parishes and Dioceses," in *Changing the Face of Ministry with Catholic Hispanic Youth and Young Adults.*

19   See Eric H. F. Law, *The Wolf Shall Dwell with the Lamb* (St. Louis: Chalice Press, 1993), 115-119.

20   See *Americanos.*

Health Services for Hispanics: The Cultural Competency Component.[21] Consider having a facilitator lead participants in a discussion of the implications for pastoral care.

Identify groups that need focused attention in pastoral planning.[22] Identify areas of cultural conflict for Hispanic/Latino young adults, such as attitudes toward women and how they affect young Hispanics/Latinas' choices in areas like working, dating, establishing spousal and parental roles, and pursuing post-secondary education. Consider offering similar training simultaneously for different age groups and then bringing all ages together to share, eat, and celebrate. (Recruit some area young adults—from the parish, area college service-learning classes, or a local community service center—to help with younger children so their parents can fully engage in the training.)

3. *Gather a team to plan effective pastoral care through* "promoción humana" *of Hispanic/Latino young adults in the region.*[23] Begin with data gathering and a social analysis of community assets and needs.[24] Then meet to build understanding of the data. Involve participants in reflecting on trends; encourage them to identify what is urgent and most important to them. Pray for God's spirit to accompany the team in discerning priorities to promote healing,

---

21   See National Alliance for Hispanic Health, *Quality Health Services for Hispanics: The Cultural Competency Component*, publication no. 99-21 (Washington, DC: U.S. Department of Health and Human Services, 2001).

22   Instituto Fe y Vida identifies four categories of Hispanic/Latino youth and young adults needing different ministry approaches: immigrant workers, mainstream movers, identity seekers, and gang members. See Chapter 12 of this book, "Young Adult Ministry: Hispanic/Latino Perspectives," as well as "Young, Hispanic, Catholic," *National Catholic Reporter*, January 30, 2004, 12-13.

23   Discuss with parish leaders the Latin American term "*promoción humana*," based on the teaching of Vatican II that human development is Christian development. See Second Vatican Council, *Pastoral Constitution on the Church in the Modern World (Gaudium et Spes)*, in *Vatican Council II: Volume 1: The Conciliar and Post Conciliar Documents*, ed. Austin Flannery (Northport, NY: Costello Publishing, 1996).

24   National data on Hispanics/Latinos pertaining to young adult ministry planning can be obtained from several sources, including the following: the Pew Hispanic Center, *pewhispanic.org*; the USCCB Secretariat for Cultural Diversity in the Church, Subcommittee on Hispanic Affairs, *www.usccb.org/hispanicaffairs*; Instituto Fe y Vida, *feyvida@altavista.net*; and the University of Notre Dame Institute for Latino Studies, *latinostudies.nd.edu/pubs*. Local data can be obtained from many sources: parishioners (through efforts such as surveys, interviews, and house meetings), police and city planning departments and other local government offices, service agencies, community colleges and universities, medical colleges, clinics, public-interest legal services, labor unions, immigrant rights advocates, Catholic Charities direct service and drug and alcohol treatment centers, domestic violence and homeless coalitions, the United Way, foundations, and environmental groups. Involve college students who are studying ministry, sociology, anthropology, urban planning, or public administration to help with data gathering and analysis as part of a service-learning project or internship.

reconciliation, justice, and spiritual growth. Review priorities from church documents.[25] Define what the team wants to see happen and how. Develop plans that define steps, responsible individuals, timelines, needed resources, and criteria for evaluation.

A CONCLUDING ILLUSTRATION

At Rensselaer Polytechnic Institute in Troy, New York, many students were overwhelmed by the amount of homework and the lack of social opportunities. The local pastor, Fr. Ed Kacerguis, took these students' needs to heart. He began organizing a large welcome picnic at the beginning of each school year to help promote a sense of belonging and to welcome new and old students alike to the parish. From time to time, he also invited groups of students over for a home-cooked meal. But most of all, he got to know the students, always greeting them by name and with a smile. In response, they felt a clear sense of belonging.

Young-adult–responsive parish communities take seriously the challenge to nurture the whole person of the young adult—the spiritual, the emotional, the physical, the psychological, and the social person. They also know that it is in community that young adults are nurtured in their faith. Young adults are drawn to parish communities that meet them in the context of their lives, listen to their stories, and support them on their journeys.

---

25   For example, see USCCB, *National Pastoral Plan for Hispanic Ministry* (Washington, DC: USCCB, 1987), which places priority on integral evangelization and on the preferential option for youth, women, the poor, and migrants. See also USCCB, *Encuentro and Mission: A Renewed Pastoral Framework for Hispanic Ministry* (Washington, DC: USCCB, 2002), which outlines a new phase for Hispanic ministry based on the principles of the Encuentro 2000 national intercultural gathering.

THE CAMPUS CONNECTION

Possibilities abound for relationships between parishes and college campuses. One possible relationship is found in the parish whose young people are preparing to leave home for college. Such a parish should desire that its students maintain a relationship with the Church and make a seamless transition from the parish to the campus. This type of parish can help students prepare for campus life by arranging for student parishioners who are home on break to talk with high school students about living their faith on campus. Parish leaders could recruit local campus ministers to speak with high school seniors about opportunities offered by campus ministry. The parish's youth minister can also help Catholic campus ministers by identifying the matriculating students to them. This is particularly helpful on secular campuses, whose administrations normally do not provide campus ministers with information on students. At any institution, Catholic or non-Catholic, campus ministers can issue a more personal invitation to Catholic students when they know who these students are.

Yet the home parish need not delegate all the care of students, even those who are far away, to campus ministry. Home parishes can take steps to stay connected during the time when their students are at school. For example, some parishes send a monthly or quarterly newsletter to their college students, informing them of parish events and keeping them up to date on their peers at other institutions. Holiday and birthday greetings can let students know that their parish cares about them. Many times, parishes can maintain these channels of contact at very little expense via e-mail. "Welcome Home" nights during winter and summer breaks can also help parishes sustain a viable relationship with college students.

Another type of parish-campus relationship exists between parishes located near a residential college, whose students rely on these local parishes for Mass and the sacraments during the semester. The campus minister, if there is one, may be a non-ordained religious or lay person who cannot offer the sacraments, although he or she may offer spiritual direction, activity planning, and other vital services. In other cases, a campus may only have a Catholic student organization, such as a Newman center, with little or no support from campus administration, faculty, or staff. Sometimes a campus has no visible Catholic presence whatsoever; in this type of parish-campus relationship, it is vitally important for the nearby parish to invite and welcome students. If a parish has a residential campus within its boundaries, and very few students attend Mass there, it may be because they do not feel welcome. This is regrettable for both the students and the parish.

On campus, students frequently encounter challenges to their faith, and they often debate whether to maintain the values and beliefs held by their parents. A welcoming parish community can be a tremendous support for young people during this transitional time of life. It may make the difference between a student's remaining Catholic or leaving the Church. In turn, a parish benefits from the vitality that collegians bring to its community. Although students' treasure may be limited, they often want to volunteer their time and talents in various parish ministries.

Parishes that are responsive to students at nearby campuses intentionally create a welcoming atmosphere for these students; they do not just assume that students will feel at home. Some parishes expressly welcome students from the pulpit and in the bulletin at the beginning of each semester. As finals approach, these parishes ask parishioners to pray that students may be successful in their exams and safe during their winter or summer break. Responsive parishes also host socials following Mass so that students can meet parishioners and other Catholic students. Such responsiveness to students can take effort; however, the rewards make this effort worthwhile.

Finally, one more vital aspect of the parish-campus connection is the work the campus minister does to keep students linked to parishes. Students are on campus for only a few years, so campus ministers avoid the temptation to focus their efforts exclusively on these years. Instead, they connect the students' time of learning, discerning, and preparing for life's responsibilities after graduation with learning, discerning, and preparing to live a mature Christian faith after college. In the academy, students learn the content and skills for their fields of study, discern their careers, and prepare to make contributions to society. Through campus ministry, students learn about the Catholic faith as adults, discern God's vision for their lives, continue to follow Jesus Christ actively, and prepare to lead in their faith communities. Campus ministry forms the faithful communities of the future. Before graduation, effective campus ministers equip students for a successful transition back into regular parish life.

CHAPTER SIX

Evangelization and Young Adults

How can parishes fulfill the Church's mission to bring the Good News of Jesus into the lives of today's young adults? This chapter explores many ways in which the parish community can reach out to young adults, listen to their stories, be present in times of transition, and share the joy and hope of the Catholic faith. Using real-life examples shared by young adults, the chapter offers strategies that parish leaders can use to invite young adults to evangelize their peers. It also offers some ways parish leaders can meet the faith needs of young adults.

The pastor welcomed the young couple, their wedding attendants, and some of their friends and family members to the wedding rehearsal. He put the group at ease and helped them to feel welcome in the church building by greeting them in a friendly way and showing honest joy at being with them. As he began the rehearsal, he spoke about the amazing event that would take place the next day: the celebration of the couple's love for and commitment to one another, and the celebration of the community's commitment to support them. After giving brief instructions about what to do and what not to do during the ceremony, he explained what the marriage rite's rituals and symbols mean. He challenged the group to remember and to ponder the idea that a couple, in professing their commitment to one another, also witnesses to the power of God's faithful love for his people.

At the end of the rehearsal, the group left with a renewed understanding of God's Good News for his people: undying love as witnessed through the Sacrament of Marriage. The pastor treated the wedding rehearsal as an opportunity not only to prepare all those present to participate better in the rite, but also to evangelize—to share the Good News of God's love with the young adults gathered there.

THE CHURCH'S VISION FOR EVANGELIZATION

Evangelization lies at the heart of the Church's ministry with young adults. As Pope Paul VI strongly articulates in his apostolic exhortation *On Evangelization in the Modern World* (*Evangelii Nuntiandi*), "evangelizing is in fact the grace and vocation proper to the Church, her deepest identity. She exists in order to evangelize, that is to say in order to preach and teach, to be the channel of the gift of grace, to reconcile sinners with God."[1]

The Catholic bishops of the United States, in *Go and Make Disciples: A National Plan and Strategy for Catholic Evangelization in the United States*, further develop Pope Paul's message in light of this country's culture. They articulate three goals for evangelization:

- "To bring about in all Catholics such an enthusiasm for their faith that, in living their faith in Jesus, they freely share it with others."[2]
- "To invite all people in the United States, whatever their social or cultural background, to hear the message of salvation in Jesus Christ so they may come to join us in the fullness of the Catholic faith."[3]
- "To foster gospel values in our society, promoting the dignity of the human person, the importance of the family, and the common good of our society, so that our nation may continue to be transformed by the saving power of Jesus Christ."[4]

In their pastoral plan for young adult faith formation, *Sons and Daughters of the Light*, the Catholic bishops apply these principles of evangelization directly to young adults by asserting that the first goal of ministry with young adults is "to foster the personal and communal growth and education of young adults toward a relationship with Jesus Christ leading to Christian maturity."[5]

---

1   Pope Paul VI, *On Evangelization in the Modern World* (*Evangelii Nuntiandi*) (Washington, DC: United States Conference of Catholic Bishops [USCCB], 1975), no. 14.
2   USCCB, *Go and Make Disciples: A National Plan and Strategy for Catholic Evangelization in the United States*, tenth anniversary ed. (Washington, DC: USCCB, 2002), no. 46.
3   *Go and Make Disciples*, no. 53.
4   *Go and Make Disciples*, no. 56.
5   USCCB, *Sons and Daughters of the Light: A Pastoral Plan for Ministry with Young Adults* (Washington, DC: USCCB, 1996), 28.

How do parishes provide opportunities for young adults to hear anew the call of the Gospel to be the light of Christ in today's world? How can parish communities nurture and support young adults "in communion and intimacy with Jesus Christ"?[6] How can your parish best evangelize, or share the Good News of Jesus with, young adults so that they in turn become evangelizers of their peers?

ENTHUSIASM FOR BEING CATHOLIC

Young adults who have been Catholic since infancy may have lost their excitement for being Catholic, taking it for granted, as do many older members of the faith community. In addition, today's young adults grew up in an era of frequent "Catholic-bashing." Consequently, they may have entered adulthood feeling apologetic about, rather than proud of, being Catholic.

Parishes can counteract the secular culture's negative messages about the Church by sharing the inspiring teachings and practices of the Catholic faith. Young adults may have picked up some of the things the Church is *against*; evangelization means helping them see what the Church is *for*. Many of the strategies found in other chapters of this book for sharing spiritual formation (Chapters 2 and 4), catechesis (Chapter 3), and sacramental life (Chapter 7) with young adults can contribute to young adults' appreciation of the Tradition and gospel values of their Catholic faith.

When young adults feel enthusiastic about their faith, they hunger to share that faith with others. Parishes have a largely untapped wealth of evangelists in young adults, but the Church needs to support them as they learn how to evangelize their peers.

PREPARING YOUNG ADULTS TO BE EVANGELIZERS

"You must take responsibility for your own faith!" Fr. George Kintiba, SVD, offered this challenge during the 2002 Mystagogy Symposium in the Archdiocese of Philadelphia.[7] Jacqueline Washington, a young adult in attendance, heard those words loud and clear. Her parish, St. Cyprian, had recently been consolidated with a neighboring parish, and she later recalled feeling unsure

---

6   Congregation for the Clergy, *General Directory for Catechesis* (Washington, DC: USCCB, 1997), no. 80, quoting Pope John Paul II, *Catechesi Tradendae*, no. 5.

7   Fr. George Kintiba, SVD, remarks at opening session, Mystagogy Symposium, St. Peter Claver Center for Evangelization, Archdiocese of Philadelphia, October 10, 2002.

about her place: "I had been very involved in my old parish, but this new combined parish was very different. I wasn't sure where I fit in. The new parish community, which had been given a new name, felt unwelcoming and unfamiliar."[8] Although she waited for some invitation to use her gifts and talents at the new parish, none came. She reconciled herself to this and became comfortable with the "view from the pew."

But then she discovered the Mystagogy Symposium. This ongoing speaker/dialogue series was designed, in part, by a young adult committee of the Archdiocese of Philadelphia to offer young adults an opportunity to gain a greater understanding of the Church's teachings and traditions. One of Jacqueline's friends encouraged her to go to the symposium when she expressed her frustration with her new parish community. Afterward, Jacqueline took her involvement into her own hands:

> There I was waiting for someone to do something about how I was feeling about my parish, waiting to be told what to do and where I fit in. After Mystagogy I realized I had the solution all along. I must take responsibility for my own faith. I had to seek out opportunities in the parish and faith community in which I could use my gifts and talents. That October evening, I left the St. Peter Claver Center feeling inspired, encouraged, and enlightened. More importantly, I felt empowered and affirmed. And so it happened. I didn't want to waste any more time. The very next morning, I called a friend who I knew was very involved in ministry throughout the archdiocese. I told her that I had already wasted too much time complaining and being idle. Since the following month was Black Catholic History Month, I felt that I had a perfect opportunity to organize a Mass to celebrate the contributions of Black Catholics to the Church.[9]

So in 2003, Jacqueline founded the African American Catholic Young Adult Network (AACYAN). The purpose of this network was to create a nurturing community for African American young adult Catholics and to provide opportunities for their service, faith formation, leadership, and prayer. With the support of the archdiocesan Office for Youth and Young Adults, the archdiocesan Office for Black Catholics, and the St. Peter Claver Center, AACYAN

---

8   Jacqueline Washington, interview with the authors, November 16, 2002.
9   Washington, interview.

has sponsored quarterly Masses, service opportunities, and social events. In addition, more African American Catholic young adults became enrolled in religious studies courses at the seminary and participated in their parish ministries and archdiocesan programming. The idea was not to "reinvent the wheel" but rather to empower young adults to assume leadership positions, be affirmed in their Catholic identity, and celebrate the gifts of their African American heritage.

As the story above illustrates, young adults have the conviction and creativity to evangelize in new ways, and they are particularly effective at evangelizing their peers. After all, who knows most about young adults' lives? Other young adults! So parishes that are responsive to young adults' needs invite, nurture, and challenge faith-filled young adults to witness to their peers. Such parishes identify those young adults who are already active in their faith and train them in peer ministry and in a style of authentic witness: one that does not preach or judge, but instead welcomes young adults from outside the Church into the faith community. These peer ministers engage in conversations with unchurched, ungospeled, or alienated young adults they encounter in everyday settings, from the cafeterias of their corporations or factories, to bars or sports arenas, to Internet forums and social networking sites.

Evangelization is not something faithful young adults—or, indeed, any adults—automatically know how to do well. Here are some strategies parishes might use to train and engage young adults as evangelizers:

- Hold a mini-retreat for young adults who are already involved in the parish. During the retreat, train them in specific outreach techniques, such as witnessing, hospitality, and Scripture sharing.
- Consider utilizing the benefits of apostolic movements like Christian Life Communities (CLC in English; CVX, Comunidades de Vida Cristiana, in Spanish), Neocatechumenal Way, Focolare, Cursillos de Cristiandad, Impactos de Cristiandad, and Encuentros Familiares.
- Ask the diocesan evangelization office to offer evangelization training for young adults from parishes around the diocese, and then recruit young adults from your parish to attend.
- Whenever the parish is holding an adult-education or faith-formation program, ask young adults who frequently attend such events to personally invite other young adults to join them. Ask involved

young adults to lead small groups or breakout sessions. Give them tips for witnessing that they can share with their peers.

- If the parish is participating in the Disciples in Mission[10] program—a ministry of the Paulist National Catholic Evangelization Association (PNCEA) that sends teams to dioceses to train parish staffs in evangelization and evangelizing strategies—recruit young adults to be part of the parish team.
- Invite young adults who work in the technology sector to enhance the parish Web site. If the site has no specific page for young adults, encourage them to develop one.

Young adults understand what their peers are going through on the faith journey. They also experience the struggle to be faithful people in a secular world. As an example of this struggle, at a 2004 TRACE (Teachers of Religion and Christian Ethics) Conference in Regina, Saskatchewan, Canada, young adults at the conference addressed the many choices that they make. One young woman described how she had recently chosen to attend a parish young adult function on Saturday night, instead of going to a party at the home of one of her friends. She had decided that attending the church function provided better witness, and that it would be easier for her to live her values at the church event than it would be at the social gathering. One of the older adults at the conference challenged her to re-evaluate her decision based on the challenge of the Gospel: to go where the Gospel is most needed. He suggested that for her to attend the social event and to witness to good choices and values might have been more important than to attend the church event. He challenged her to go into the world and to change it—not by avoiding it, but by bringing the Gospel to it. Indeed, both the parish and the world need the presence of faithful, Catholic young adults. Critical to evangelization is witnessing to the power of the Gospel in one's life through the choices one makes: "the Church evangelizes when she seeks to convert (see Rom 1:16; 1 Cor 1:18, 2:4), solely through the divine power of the Message she proclaims, both the personal and collective consciences of the people, the activities in which they engage, and the lives and concrete milieux which are theirs."[11]

---

10   Parishes can also contract directly with the association to receive the training manual. For information, write to PNCEA at 3031 Fourth Street NE, Washington, DC 20017, or see its Web site, *www.disciplesinmission.org*.

11   *On Evangelization in the Modern World*, no. 18.

BEING PRESENT AT TIMES OF TRANSITION

Crucial opportunities for the evangelization of young adults arise during moments of transition in their lives. When their lives are in flux, young adults are more open to new ways of looking at life. Parishes that are responsive to young adults can give them a sense of hope and a focus for their lives by bringing the Good News of Jesus into these transitional times. Amid an onslaught of new messages and experiences, the parish community can be a stable, safe haven for young adults, where Christ and his message are gently offered to them again and again.

As graduating high-school seniors transition from the parish community into other communities, parishes can reach out and evangelize while meeting students' need to stay connected to their home community. For example, a parish in Omaha gave its high-school graduates a computer mouse pad with the parish's name and contact information on it to take with them as they left to pursue education and careers. Parishioners attached messages to the gift, including encouragements to the young adults to share their faith with others just as the parish had shared faith with them.

As another option, a parish might give young adults a calendar for the first year after leaving high school. The calendar could contain significant church year events, parish schedules, seasonal prayers, reflections from older young adults about their experiences of leaving high school and moving into adulthood, and Scripture passages and questions that students can reflect on or journal about. The parish might also invite students, by mail or e-mail, to return to the parish for special events or seasons.

Parishes that know where their young adults are headed might provide them with listings of parishes they could visit in their new community. The home parish could also alert a parish in the young adult's new community to the young adult's presence and encourage that community to reach out to that individual. In general, parishes are most effective when they work together creatively to connect young adults with faith communities that notice their presence and absence and that reach out to meet their needs.

Consider other opportunities for evangelizing young adults in transition:

- Send young adults off to college or the military with a special ritual or blessing at a Sunday liturgy in August. Give a Bible, prayer book, or written blessings from the parish community to each young adult who is leaving.

- Hold a home ritual or home blessing in young adults' first apartments or residence halls.
- When young adults are taking final exams for school, or tests required for promotions at work or in the military, send them postcards or care packages from the parish. Include a prayer or words of encouragement to remind them of Jesus' unconditional love for them.
- Offer a session for young couples thinking about getting engaged. (The Archdiocese of Philadelphia, for example, began offering this program when young adults reported that no help was available in discerning this huge step in their lives.)
- Honor young adults who have received recognition, awards, or promotions at work. Send a congratulatory e-mail, and insert an announcement in the parish bulletin.

As mentioned in Chapter 1, "Creating a Young Adult–Responsive Church," young adult–responsive parishes seize two key opportunities to evangelize young adults. The first involves going to places where young adults spend time already—gyms, coffee shops, colleges and universities, factories and corporations, concerts and theaters, online settings—and being present to them. This is often called the "ministry of presence." The second way for effective parishes to evangelize young adults is through "entry points": moments when young adults come to the parish—for Sunday Masses, gatherings, sacramental celebrations, and events organized by the parish or the broader Catholic community. Both opportunities—through ministry of presence and through entry points—are discussed further in the next sections.

REACHING OUT TO YOUNG ADULTS

In *Sons and Daughters of the Light*, the bishops describe evangelizing outreach: "to identify places where young adults gather and to connect them personally with the Church by listening to their concerns, hopes, and dreams and by welcoming them into a community of faith."[12] The challenge to reach out to young adults in their daily circumstances and routines requires the parish community first to become aware of the young adults already in its midst. The young adult–responsive community asks itself the following questions: Who

---

12   *Sons and Daughters of the Light*, 33.

are the young adults at local coffee shops or restaurants that we visit? Who are the young adults we encounter at the gym or at our workplaces? Might we have more intentional contact and make more deliberate attempts to build relationships with the young adults in our families? How can we reach out to young adults in local universities and community colleges? Do we encounter young adults who are teaching in schools, working in retail, harvesting crops in the fields, or providing tech support?

When reaching out to young adults in the context of their lives, it is important to keep their cultural identities in mind. Here are some considerations for outreach to young adults of diverse cultures:

- *Image.* Pay careful attention to how the Church is presented in marketing materials. Do the people who are depicted represent a culturally diverse Church? The key is to show the diversity among Catholics and to make all feel welcome in Catholic settings.
- *Personal Invitation.* This can be done through mailings, e-mails, home visits, face-to-face encounters, or programs of hospitality.
- *Awareness Training.* Provide opportunities for education and for the raising of cultural awareness among current community members. Knowing the history, values, and culture of the African American, Hispanic/Latino, Asian and Pacific Island, Native American, and other Catholic communities can lead to new perspectives and more naturally inclusive evangelization efforts.

Rather than bombarding people with information about Jesus and the Good News, effective evangelization introduces people to Jesus through healthy human interactions with members of his Body, the Church. In particular, effective evangelization with young adults pays sincere attention to the circumstances of their lives. Parish communities that are responsive to young adults listen to young adults' stories and note the presence of God in their lives—wherever they happen to be on the faith journey.

Bringing the Good News Through Media and Technology

One of the key places to encounter young adults is online. If the message of the Incarnation is that God chose to set up his tent among us, consider the potential of spreading God's message among young adults on the Internet. One great advantage of creating a Web site is not only that it will be found by those who do not yet know about the parish community, but that it will serve as a touchstone for those who are already aware of the parish community. It provides a vital tool for staying in touch with a population that can be difficult to reach.

Consider the variety of elements that might make your Web site attractive to young adults:

- A virtual tour of the parish (e.g., personnel, places, programs, and history)
- Spiritual reflections from other young adults (perhaps provided through a blog, widget, RSS feed, or other social networking technology), perhaps for the daily Scriptures or the daily readings of the Lenten, Advent, and Easter seasons
- Chat rooms dedicated to discussions on faith and daily life, morality, or social justice
- Links to other selected sites: e.g., for movies, music, prayers, saints of the day,[13] blogs, online videos, podcasts
- A calendar of events and activities, with a section for special announcements
- A regular feature article on a young adult from the parish, describing his or her accomplishments, interests, and faith journey
- A thought for the day, with pertinent links
- An e-mail point of contact for those who wish to raise questions about faith
- A posting of the readings for each upcoming Sunday, with space for young adults to post their thoughts and reflections about the Gospel (which the pastor may want to skim as he prepares his homily)

Another use for online resources pertains to spiritual direction. Many young adults are comfortable using the Internet to make regular and intense contact with their peers, friends, even mentors. Why not use e-mail as a means to connect young adults with spiritual directors? For example, retired religious with access to computers and capability in spiritual direction would be excellent guides for young adults who seek guidance as they sift through the challenges of being disciples in today's world. The spiritual directors might

---

13   For a "saint of the day" Web resource, see *www.americancatholic.org/features/saintofDay*.

be located miles or states away from their directees, but through the Internet, they can connect with young adults anywhere. Consider the possibilities for young adults away at college or in the military.

On a simpler level, a parish can designate e-mail mentors to pray and journey with young adults as they transition from the parish to other communities. The population of senior citizens in Catholic parishes, for example, is an untapped resource of people who have—and take—the time to pray for others. Partnering them with busy young adults for online prayer is a win-win situation. It helps the older adult to feel needed, and it reassures the frazzled young adult that someone is storming heaven on his or her behalf.

In all this, effective parish leaders follow the model of evangelization provided by Our Lord. Jesus did not wait for people to come to him. Instead, he reached out to them, and he spoke to them in ways that they understood. Fr. Paul Dressler, OFM Cap., of St. John the Evangelist Parish in Philadelphia, Pennsylvania, follows this example by speaking with young adults in ways that connect well with them. His Friday Night Flicks program gathers young adults to view and discuss current films. The discussion usually begins with the challenges facing the characters and shifts to similar situations facing many young adults. Through guided viewing and group discussion, young adult participants focus on what they have learned and what they practice as Catholics, and they consider ways in which their own values and beliefs could have affected the characters in the film and perhaps changed the outcomes. Such programs are successful because they help young adults connect to peers, the parish, Jesus Christ, and the mission of the Church in the world—all at once.

Entry Points for Evangelizing Young Adults

Young adults make contact with parish communities on a variety of occasions. These entry points include sacramental preparation (when they seek the Sacrament of Marriage or the Baptism of their children), as well as family funerals, weddings and anniversaries, Sunday liturgies, and seasonal liturgies like Ash Wednesday and Easter Sunday. The way a parish welcomes young adults at all of these events may determine the extent to which they feel a sense of connectedness and belonging in that parish.

Does your parish have resources to give young adults that provide brief overviews of what will occur at various liturgies? Consider providing laminated cards that explain the key symbols of the celebration and the key teachings of the Church expressed in the prayers and Scripture for the rite. For example, at some weddings in Catholic parishes, many young adults attend who are not regular church-goers and who have difficulty following the liturgy's responses and gestures. Their experience might be much richer if they were given some resource that informs them not just about how to participate in the rite but also about its content, meaning, and connection to real life. At funerals, too, the parish can provide resources for young adult participants and others to better understand what is going on. Why is a pall placed on the coffin? What do Catholics believe about life after death? Why does the priest wear white?

Before, during, and after such profound events, responsive parishes extend hospitality to the many guests. As one example, a parish may have volunteers wear nametags as they welcome arriving guests. Providing hospitality—doing everything possible to extend the inclusive welcome that Jesus constantly showed in the Gospels—is a vital way to make contact with young adults at entry points.

Another entry point, sometimes neglected, is the registration process. For many Catholics, registering in a parish simply means filling out a form and receiving a box of collection envelopes. Yet registration is a prime opportunity for parishes to practice evangelization and welcome. For example, one parish in Baltimore, Maryland, never conducts registration in the parish office. People can only register on Sunday in the context of the liturgy. The entire community acknowledges new members during the liturgy and welcomes them into the parish. Everyone claps in celebration of the gifts that the new members bring to the faith community, and after the liturgy, the newcomers register and are invited to a brunch. This reflects what young adults mean when they say they want the Church to give them a sense of community and belonging.

Baptismal preparation is yet another excellent opportunity to help young adult parents establish new relationships and connections to members of the parish community. Many parishes spend much of the baptismal preparation time working on the cognitive understanding and implications of the theology of Baptism—and not enough time immersing the families into the living relationships of the community. Since relationships with others and with God also keep people connected to community, effective parishes make relationships a high priority. In conversation with a staff member for Ministry with Young Adults: A National Catholic Initiative ("the Initiative"), one family with three children shared their experience with baptismal preparation and celebrations in three different parish communities. In none of the three communities had the baptismal preparation process enabled them to connect meaningfully with any of the other households participating in the preparation, or with any members of the parish at large. Responsive parishes answer, and practice the answers to, the following questions: What can our parish community do to offer the hospitality that we profess to be part of our ethos? How can we connect young adults with each other in the process?

BEING AN INCLUSIVE COMMUNITY OF FAITH

Parishes that are responsive to young adults from all cultures and circumstances ensure that these young adults are not merely a decorative addition to the parish, but are full participants in and contributors to its life. These parishes clearly acknowledge that, without full inclusion of all groups present in the parish's local community, the parish is incomplete. Responsive parishes take young adults under the wings of the Church and nurture them during their spiritual formation, education, and training. Only with formation can young adults enter into the sacramental and liturgical cycle of the Church as fully included and active participants, not simply passive recipients. This kind of evangelization speaks best to young adults, who hunger for inclusion and community. This evangelization transforms the active life of the parish so that it truly reflects the diversity of the Church.

Parishes that are responsive to young adults of all cultures both know and preach that God speaks through the good qualities of all personalities, colors, languages, cultures, practices, and traditions. Without any one group, the Church is *incomplete* and thus longs for fullness. By reaching out to and including all the various peoples created by God, the Church is strengthened and can, in turn, strengthen the secular community.

As an example, the fastest-growing cultural group within the Catholic Church in the United States is Hispanics/Latinos. The evangelization of young adults in this culture is a task not for a few, but for all Catholics. Hispanic/Latino ministry, according to the bishops of the United States, "must be seen as an integral part of the life and mission of the Church in this country. We must be relentless in seeking ways to promote and facilitate the full incorporation of Hispanic Catholics into the life of the Church and its mission."[14] This is a challenge because so many diverse groups exist within the overall Hispanic/Latino

---

14   USCCB, *Encuentro and Mission: A Renewed Pastoral Framework for Hispanic Ministry* (Washington, DC: USCCB, 2002), no. 60.

community. Many of its young adults are alienated from the Church or do not participate in parish programs; too few are touched by Catholic educational institutions. Insufficient numbers of bilingual Catholic ministers and ministries are available to reach them.

Grounded in an experience of an evangelizing, missionary Christian community, effective parish leaders can reach out and develop relationships with more young adults of all cultures. As this chapter has already noted, Jesus went out among the people and spoke to them in ways they understood. In caring for young adults of all cultures—caring that includes cultural awareness, sensitivity, and ideally fluency in languages other than English—responsive parishes imitate Jesus' example. They let young adults know of God's care and desire for their fullness of life. Effective parishes inspire young adults of all cultures to take responsibility for their faith, to be agents of Good News and a saving grace for others, and to work toward the transformation of sinful structures. These parishes invite young adults to participate and lead within small church communities (see Chapter 10, "Forming Faith Communities of Young Adults," for more on this topic), and they facilitate the sharing and strengthening of young adults' gifts in that setting. In the critique and evangelization of culture, Our Lady of Guadalupe—the evangelizer of the Americas—stands as the model for all Catholics.[15]

BREAKING OPEN THE WORD

Young adults who shared their experiences of faith during the Initiative's listening sessions expressed a strong desire to learn Sacred Scripture. The Church has a tremendous opportunity to bring the Good News of Jesus into the lives of young adults by connecting them with the Word in many ways: through Bible study, through small faith-sharing groups that use a lectionary-based resource, or through the *lectio divina*. Some African American communities have had success with revivals that break open the Word through dynamic preaching and music.

Campus ministries and parishes across the country have also had success in using daily online resources on the Word. A parish that seeks to connect young adults with the daily readings might direct them to the podcast of the daily readings from the New American Bible at *www.usccb.org/nab*; it could also

---

15   See Virgilio Elizondo, *La Morenita: Evangelizadora de las Americas* (Liguori, MO: Liguori Publications, 1981), and Virgilio Elizondo, *Guadalupe: Mother of the New Creation* (Maryknoll, NY: Orbis Books, 1997).

circulate meditations based on the Scripture of the day. Whatever the method, when young adults develop a familiarity with Scripture in light of Tradition, they simultaneously experience evangelization themselves and become better equipped to evangelize their peers.

FOSTERING GOSPEL VALUES

Go and Make Disciples challenges the Church to foster gospel values in society.[16] *Sons and Daughters of the Light* challenges parishes to connect young adults with the Church's mission to transform the world.[17] When the people of God— young adults included—take ownership of this transformation, they reach the fullness of evangelization. Young adults are uniquely suited to this task. They are idealistic enough to believe they can do it and experienced enough to know how to do it.

Chapter 9 of this book, "Justice and Service with Young Adults," includes many strategies for putting young adults in touch with the Catholic Church's social teachings and its call to advocacy and service. These parts of Catholic identity often prompt young adults' decisions to make a difference in the world.

Go and Make Disciples also challenges parishes to provide opportunities for adults to explore issues of spirituality in the workplace.[18] Consider the following suggestions of some ways to accomplish this goal:

- Go to factories or corporations or farms (those employing migrant workers) during the noon hour, invite young adult workers to bring their lunches, and offer them the opportunity to discuss work-related issues through the lens of their Catholic faith. To attract more attendees, consider providing beverages and desserts.
- In the parish, invite young adults to evening sessions on topics related to faith and work.[19]

---

16   See *Go and Make Disciples*, no. 117.
17   See *Sons and Daughters of the Light*, 36.
18   See *Go and Make Disciples*, no. 123.
19   The Center for Ministry Development's binder resource *Young Adult Works* includes four fully developed sessions on the topic of faith and work. The sessions are aimed at young adults and entitled "A Christian Interpretation of Work," "Faith and Work," "Values in the Workplace," and "Work and Life." See "Faith and Work," in *Young Adult Works*, ed. Ronald Bagley, CJM, John Roberto, Susan Stark, and Joan Weber (Naugatuck, CT: Center for Ministry Development, 1997), Binder 5, 9.1-9.52.

- Link young adults to older adults in the parish who are working in a similar career. The older adults can serve as mentors, sharing how they have lived their Catholic values in their particular career.

Connecting young adults with the Church's commitment to families and family life is yet another way to live out the Church's call to transform society. The Center for Ministry Development's binder series *Young Adult Works* offers strategies and programs for helping young adults negotiate the transition from being adolescents to being adults within their own families.[20] Chapter 11 of this book, "Young Adults and Families," also looks at young adults through the lens of the family life cycle.

CONCLUSION

Each Catholic has a responsibility to spread the Good News, to share the faith, and to transform the world. Evangelization is both a call and a response. It is the call of Jesus reverberating down the centuries: "go into the whole world and proclaim the gospel to every creature" (Mk 16:15). How does your parish community call young adults to be witnesses and to evangelize others? How does your parish connect them to experiences in which they can meet other young adults who are excited and passionate about their faith? How do you provide support and mentors to help them carry the Gospel to their peers? How do you inspire them to transform the world?

Many, many opportunities exist for the Church to embrace the diversity of its members and to evangelize those who have left the Church, who feel alienated, or who are otherwise disconnected. Some opportunities have been overlooked or underestimated, while others have been attempted without success, perhaps because of limited resources or timing. But just as the sower scatters the seeds so as to ensure that some fall on good soil, parishes that are responsive to young adults' need for evangelization continue to seek ways to evangelize, through word and deed, all of God's people: "some seed fell on rich soil, and produced fruit, a hundred or sixty or thirtyfold" (Mt 13:8).

---

20   See "Family," in *Young Adult Works*, Binder 5, 10.1-10.35.

THE CAMPUS CONNECTION

Evangelizing on a college campus, like forming faith communities, requires a welcoming atmosphere. Campus ministers need to create an atmosphere where Catholic students enjoy coming together and sharing their lives with one another. Establishing a Catholic community on campus, informing students about this vibrant community, and welcoming them when they arrive are all vital elements of a foundation for effective evangelization. More direct efforts toward evangelization can build on this foundation.

On most secular college campuses, student organizations need official recognition from the administration and the student government. Any Catholic student group should complete the requirements to be recognized as a legitimate student organization. In this way, the group gains access to resources and channels of communication that only school-approved groups may use. For example, on some campuses, only recognized student organizations receive funding and the ability to use college facilities and vehicles. Some colleges list the organization and its contact information in their publications and on their Web sites. Only recognized student organizations are permitted to post flyers or notices on some campuses. Having access to such resources to further Catholic evangelization is well worth the effort to go through a brief administrative process.

After this initial set-up step, Catholic campus ministers can begin to publicize the presence of the Catholic student organization on campus. Find the central location (e.g., college green or quadrangle, student union, cafeteria) where student groups recruit members and advertise their activities. The student leaders of campus ministry should use this location as frequently as possible to promote membership and encourage participation in their activities. Ultimately, the best evangelizers on a campus are the students themselves. When Catholic students become excited about their faith and worship, they are easily motivated to invite fellow students to join them in Catholic programs and activities.

Still, even the most zealous students may feel awkward about welcoming new students and may tend to remain with their friends in social gatherings. The following ten steps may help Catholic students to greet and welcome other students who are new to the campus ministry setting.

1. Smile.
2. Don't be shy; walk toward the new student.
3. Be the first to speak.
4. Extend your hand in friendship.
5. Be *other*-focused: show interest in the person.
6. Don't ask yes-or-no questions.
7. Find common ground for conversation.
8. Repeat the student's name at least once during the conversation. This will make him or her feel welcome and will help you to remember.
9. Make connections by introducing the new student to others.
10. Say goodbye. It is just as important as saying hello.

Social programs can provide comfortable settings where Catholic students feel free to invite their non-Catholic friends to join. For example, the Newman Center at the University of Pennsylvania hosts a regular student dinner that attracts fifty to eighty students, including graduate students, each week. The purpose of the dinner is to create a fun atmosphere where students enjoy being together. The only overt religious expression is a prayer offered by one student before the meal. The parish priests, one or two seminarians, and occasionally a religious sister will come to dinner. The experience of community is exhilarating. Students frequently invite their non-Catholic roommates and friends. The Newman staff knows that the non-Catholics feel welcome because they return on a regular basis. Also, a few students arrive early each week to assist in preparing the meal. Occasionally, the non-Catholic students ask their peers or the campus ministers questions about the Church. The dinner affords students the opportunity to explore questions of faith in a comfortable setting—a vital part of evangelization.

Community service projects sponsored by campus ministry can also support evangelization. Many students, regardless of their religious background, are generous with their time and talent, and they desire to make a commitment for the good of the community or neighborhood. Programs of outreach to senior citizens in assisted or nursing care facilities, mentoring programs with children attending local schools, and construction programs such as Habitat for Humanity are just a few examples of community service projects popular with college students. These activities become

great instruments of evangelization when prayer and theological reflection are incorporated into the experience. Student leaders of campus ministry could choose a project that will attract their peers. They could then
recruit student volunteers to participate by distributing flyers and notices
on campus as well as by making personal invitations.

At the beginning of the service project, when the students gather to
receive instructions for the day, one or two students might offer a prayer.
In this setting, less is more. A simple invocation, requesting God's blessing
for the success of the project and protection for the participants, will generally suffice. When the project ends, encourage participants to share their
reflections on the experience. Consider asking questions such as "What did
you learn?", "How did you make a difference?", "Where did you observe
evil?", "Where did you experience grace?", and "How did this experience
change you?" These and similar questions can transform a simple service
project into a memorable experience that influences students' lives.

At the end of the discussion, campus ministers might offer the opportunity to pray. Student leaders could initiate the prayer—for example, by
thanking God for the opportunity to serve and asking him to intercede for
their peers and for those they helped—but every participant should be
welcomed to join in vocally. In such ways, community service projects with
reflection and prayer can become evangelizing moments for both Catholic and non-Catholic students.

Catholic students can also evangelize by participating in interfaith
committees and activities on campus. Many times, people of different faith
traditions have misconceptions about Catholics (and vice versa). Working
together on various projects establishes relationships and trust. It creates
opportunities for dialogue where Catholics and non-Catholics can explore
their similarities and differences. These occasions can challenge Catholic
students to better understand what they believe and why they believe it.
Sometimes, seeking answers for their non-Catholic friends provides the
necessary motivation for Catholics to participate in the religious education
program offered by campus ministry.

At one college, the Catholic campus ministry group has hosted an
interfaith fund-raising dinner for the local soup kitchen. The students
named the event the "Empty Bowls Dinner" to remind participants that
there are those in their community whose bowls are empty and who are
dependent on others for food. A simple meal of soup, salad, and bread

reminds attendees of the fare the homeless receive at a soup kitchen. Finally, various student groups for performing arts provide entertainment. These have included gospel singers, a Jewish choral group, musicians, and drama or comedy groups. In this way, the Catholic campus ministry group has sponsored an interfaith event in which students of varied religious backgrounds have enjoyed participating. These students have gained a better appreciation for the Catholic student organization on campus and for its mission. Also, an important community service has benefited.

This event is just one of many ways campus ministry can blend all the foundational elements of effective Catholic evangelization: fostering a greater faith commitment among practicing Catholics, reconnecting Catholic students who have been estranged from the Church, and welcoming non-Catholic students who are searching for God and meaning in their lives. Reflect on all the ideas provided above, and imagine how you can lay this solid foundation on your campus.

CHAPTER SEVEN
Young Adults and Liturgy

How can parishes provide the most life-giving experience of the Church's eucharistic worship to young adults? This chapter explores what young adults are looking for in liturgy—from a welcoming community to relevant homilies to an engaging environment to encounter with Christ. The chapter also describes opportunities for connecting young adults with other sacraments and with other forms of Catholic worship.

As young adult–responsive parishes seek ways to connect young adults with the liturgy and sacraments that nourish their faith, they remain aware that generations born after the 1960s have a deep spiritual hunger. Indeed, the Catholic bishops of the United States, in their pastoral plan *Sons and Daughters of the Light*, recognized "developing a spiritual life" as one of the primary tasks of young adulthood.[1] While some young adults today may have "a wariness toward organized religion,"[2] most seek to strengthen their faith, and many continually express a yearning for a deeper relationship with the Creator of the universe. Their reaction against the excessive rationalism of modernism finds expression in their intuitive attraction to the symbolic and mystical. The Catholic Church is well positioned to satisfy the spiritual hungers of today's young adults. The Catholic liturgical life and sacramental system can be rich sources of spiritual growth for them. The challenge for parishes is to celebrate these liturgies well.

Of all the points of contact between the Church and young adults, the one with the greatest potential for engaging them is the eucharistic liturgy. Young adults come to liturgy—some daily, some every Sunday, and still others occasionally. But they do come: for Christmas and Easter, for Ash Wednesday, for funeral Masses and anniversaries and weddings. Parishes that are responsive to the spiritual needs of young adults live out the Church's belief that the celebration of the Eucharist is the "source and summit" of Catholic life. They do this by providing their young adults, indeed all of their people, with good liturgical experiences.

---

1   United States Conference of Catholic Bishops (USCCB), *Sons and Daughters of the Light: A Pastoral Plan for Ministry with Young Adults* (Washington, DC: USCCB, 1996), 13-15.

2   *Sons and Daughters of the Light*, 13.

Many have asked what type of liturgy will meet the spiritual needs of today's young adults. Good news—Ministry with Young Adults: A National Catholic Initiative ("the Initiative") found that the things young adults say they seek from the liturgy are the same things that most Catholics indicate they desire:

- They want to feel *welcome* when the community gathers.
- They want *good music* through which they can express their faith.
- They look for a *high quality of preaching* that connects the Gospel to their everyday lives.
- They seek parishes where the *assembly actively participates and enjoys celebrating* together.

In other words, parishes and campus ministries that already provide quality liturgy have made a good start in meeting the needs of young adults. These efforts are only enhanced through young adult leadership and liturgical catechesis to address the interests and concerns they bring.

Young-adult–responsive parishes also take cultural realities into consideration when preparing liturgies. When planning worship with a particular cultural group, liturgists need to be aware of the artistic dimensions of the liturgy, the manner in which the environment for worship is prepared, and the way in which these relate to the spiritual content of liturgical prayer. Through the incorporation of words, music, and meaningful cultural religious expressions, responsive parishes can demonstrate a consistent, conscious effort and a sincere desire to acknowledge the cultural backgrounds of young adults in the Catholic liturgy.

YOUNG ADULTS AS LITURGICAL MINISTERS

Before considering how to prepare for celebrations of the liturgy that encourage the participation of young adults, parishes first need to identify how many young adults are involved in liturgical leadership. Are young adults on the liturgy committee? Are they welcomed or personally invited to join? Does the committee meet at times that are accessible to young adults? Are young adults' opinions valued? In other words, one way to ensure that young adults have the richest experience possible in the eucharistic liturgy is to invite them to be members of the liturgy committee. Young adults seek significant roles in church life, and they have much to contribute to liturgical celebration, such as helping to decorate the church for Lent/Easter and Advent/Christmas, selecting music for liturgies, giving the homilist input, or especially serving as liturgical ministers.

Young adults particularly appreciate liturgies and feel welcome in a parish community when they see parishioners their own age involved in liturgical ministries. *Sons and Daughters of the Light* encourages worshiping communities to "invite young adults to be liturgical ministers, and provide the necessary training."[3] This involvement not only serves as another sign of welcome, but also gives participating young adults the faith formation and ministry training that will help them become confident and competent members of the parish. *Sons and Daughters of the Light* goes on to remind pastoral leaders to "be flexible and respect [young adults'] time availability when developing criteria for participation in liturgical ministries."[4] Consider how many lectors, ministers of hospitality (greeters, ushers), cantors, choir members, instrumentalists, servers or acolytes, and extraordinary ministers of Holy Communion in your parish are young adults. Are your parish's young adults—including singles who might come alone to Mass—invited to present the gifts?

One example of young adult leadership in liturgy happened at the traditional pre-dawn prayer service for the Feast of Our Lady of Guadalupe, Mañanitas a la Virgen, at St. Agnes Church in Omaha, Nebraska. An overwhelming number of young adults have participated in this celebration with sincerity, fervor, leadership, and depth of faith. At one Mañanitas service, four young adults played instruments in the music group, a young man and woman sang solos, six young adults brought symbolic offerings and offered prayers for all areas of life (e.g., relationships, sports, sickness), and one proclaimed a Scripture reading. Young adults were key ministers to the standing-room-only crowd.

Seeing liturgical ministers from their own cultures is also important to all young adults who come to worship. For example, Bishop Ricardo Ramirez of Las Cruces, New Mexico, stresses the priority that effective parishes give to the formation of liturgical ministers in the Hispanic/Latino community, which in 2000 made up more than 35 percent of all Catholics in the United States:[5] "If we are going to have an impact on the liturgical life of this country from the Hispanic perspective, then we must be alert and anxious to contribute to the

---

3   *Sons and Daughters of the Light*, 35.
4   *Sons and Daughters of the Light*, 35.
5   See *www.usccb.org/hispanicaffairs* and the U.S. Census Bureau.

formation of liturgical ministers. Every one of them."[6] Bishop Ramirez calls for training in the skills to implement good liturgy, but also for the training of "professional liturgical thinkers" who possess a deeply theological and cultural understanding of Hispanic/Latino religious tradition and liturgical needs.[7] He also emphasizes that those involved in liturgy need to know Spanish.[8] These principles, which any parish can adapt as appropriate for its community, become even more important for helping young adults, of any culture, to feel like the parish understands their needs and welcomes their presence.

Young-adult leadership in parish liturgies is not merely important—there is no excuse for omitting it. Young adults may be more likely to respond to a personal invitation than to a bulletin announcement when you recruit liturgical ministers, but their participation is worth the extra outreach.

ENGAGING LITURGY

An Illustration

St. Joseph's University Parish in Buffalo, New York, is a marvelously blended community of people from many races, cultures, and backgrounds. The parish, which is located near a large state university campus, also mixes a fairly typical congregation of all ages with the community of university students. The parish has not designated a specific Mass time for students;[9] they are free to choose any of the five Sunday Masses, although many gravitate to the 11:30 a.m. and 8:00 p.m. Masses.[10] Because St. Joseph's provides well-prepared celebrations of the liturgy, it attracts not only a large number of students, but also people from across the city and nearby suburbs, including many young adults who are not in college.

What attracts young adults to St. Joseph's? Homilies connect the Gospel to the real-life issues they face. The music—which is high in quality and

---

6   Bishop Ricardo Ramirez, "Envisioning Hispanic Liturgy: Challenges for the Instituto at the Beginning of the Millennium" (presentation to Instituto de Liturgia Hispana Board Meeting), February 23, 2001, 8, *www.dioceseoflascruces.org/root/bishop/PDF/speeches/bp_sp_08.pdf.*

7   "Envisioning Hispanic Liturgy," 8.

8   See "Envisioning Hispanic Liturgy," 9.

9   In *Sons and Daughters of the Light,* the bishops of the United States urge parishes to "remember that worship in most parishes is intergenerational, gathering in single persons, students, and married couples with or without children" (35).

10   Certain times may prove more convenient for young adults. Where parents with children, for example, may prefer a morning Mass, single young adults may look for a Sunday evening Mass. A parish with a significant number of young adults might consider scheduling Masses accordingly.

engaging in selections—lifts them up. People are happy to be there and are welcoming toward newcomers. St. Joseph's provides a genuine experience of Catholic worship.

Welcome and Hospitality

Hospitality helps people know they are welcome in the community. How can parishes make young adults feel welcome? Some parishes have begun a ministry of hospitality, including greeters and ushers who pay attention to new faces entering the worship space. They give particular attention to single adults who come to Mass alone. Besides offering a friendly smile and a warm welcome, they introduce these people to other members of the congregation. They know that if some kind of bond is forged, young adults will return.

As one example, St. Leo's Parish in Omaha, Nebraska, started inviting young adults who attend the last morning Mass on Sundays to sit together in a designated part of the church. A survey conducted in the Archdiocese of Omaha had revealed that the biggest reason given by young adults for not attending Sunday Mass was "I didn't have anyone to go with." So St. Leo's young adult ministry team decided to eliminate that problem by inviting young adults to sit together. The young adults began going out for brunch to continue the celebration after the liturgy; they now have a standing reservation at a local restaurant, and many young adults flock to the liturgy and the post-liturgy meal.

Many parishes place greeters at the church doors, but some have taken an extra step to welcome newcomers by having the pastoral staff arrive at church well before Mass begins. They look for new faces, eagerly introduce themselves, welcome newcomers, learn something about the newcomers' backgrounds, and share something about the parish that might connect with the newcomers' own experiences. Many parishes, in the opening announcements, also extend a special word of welcome to all visitors. While these strategies can be effective with every age group, they work particularly with young adults, who respond well to face-to-face interaction and invitation.

Welcome and hospitality are key to inviting young adults of every culture to the table of the Eucharist. For example, in the 2002 document *Encuentro and Mission*, the bishops of the United States elevate the importance of liturgy and community prayer as priorities for ministry with Hispanic/Latino

Catholics.[11] The bishops strongly emphasize the need for parishes to become experts at "transforming hospitality." This hospitality was the central theme of the convention Encuentro 2000, sponsored by the United States Conference of Catholic Bishops. The principle of hospitality applies across cultures. "As members of one family of God, we are called to encounter the living Jesus Christ by authentically receiving and reflecting his gracious hospitality in and through one another, as the way to conversion, communion, and solidarity."[12]

A community can especially show good hospitality to new parents by demonstrating respect for the needs of their children. Parishes that are responsive to the needs of young adult parents provide child care for very small children, allowing parents to worship without distraction. Including older children in the worship tells the parents that their presence is welcome. Offering a Liturgy of the Word for Children[13] and helping children participate in the liturgy in other ways all indicate to young adult parents that they are a part of the community. A Liturgy of the Word for Children is also called a "children's dismissal" when parish catechists hold a separate session for children to learn more about the Gospel. The session often includes a brief talk by the catechist, followed by dialogue in which the children participate. This dialogue opens up the readings for children and allows them to understand more fully.

While leadership and ministry are key to welcoming young adults, hospitality is the responsibility of the entire assembly. Effective parishes not only provide special ministries but instill a hospitable attitude in every member of the parish. Even if greeters at the entrance provide a warm welcome, the mood can cool quickly if other parishioners seem distant or disengaged. Encourage all the members of the assembly to extend welcome to one another. Some people are very private and might consider it irreverent or intrusive to greet someone who enters their pew, so establish ways for all parishioners to show warmth and attention to others without risk of disrupting their own or another's prayer. For example, in St. Bonaventure's Parish in West Seneca, New York, the lector finishes the announcements before Mass by inviting all to stand, introduce themselves to those around them, and offer a word of welcome before the gathering song—a strategy that works well for the community. As time has passed,

11   See USCCB, *Encuentro and Mission: A Renewed Pastoral Framework for Hispanic Ministry* (Washington, DC: USCCB, 2002), nos. 28, 34.

12   USCCB, *Many Faces in God's House: A Catholic Vision for the Third Millennium* (Washington, DC: USCCB, 1999), 2.

13   See *Directory for Masses with Children*, in *Masses with Children*, Liturgy Documentary Series 12 (Washington, DC: USCCB, 1996), nos. 24, 28, 240, and 245. This document is also available in *The Liturgy Documents: A Parish Resource*, 4th ed., vol. 1 (Chicago: Liturgy Training Publications, 2004).

many parishioners at St. Bonaventure's have become more eager to welcome others spontaneously, without being invited to do so.

In effective parishes, hospitality continues after Mass, when members of the congregation are given an opportunity to socialize. Many parishes and campus ministries offer coffee, doughnuts, or other refreshments after the liturgy. One parish in New Jersey has offered cheese and crackers on Saturday night and pastries and coffee on Sunday morning. Other refreshments popular with young adults include latte, cappuccino, and biscotti. But special preparation is for naught if young adults come over for refreshments after Mass and are then ignored. At young adult–responsive parishes, members of the welcoming committee and parishioners in general always watch for new faces or people who seem to be alone. They make an effort to meet those people, introduce them to other members of the community, and get to know them better. This welcoming spirit is perhaps most vital at key liturgical celebrations attended by many young adults—Christmas, Easter, Ash Wednesday, and so on. At these times, the parish community has a tremendous opportunity for welcoming young adults; on holidays, the young adult–responsive parish might give out a welcome packet or at least an invitation to return the following Sunday. Some faith communities also follow up a Sunday encounter with young adults by telephoning them during the week to ask if they plan to attend Mass the following Sunday and to offer a ride. That is going the extra mile in the name of hospitality.

Good Music

Music has the power to evangelize. It can draw people into the mystery of Christ and into the community of the Church. It is both a crucial element of worship and an opportunity to invite young adults into the life of the faith community. Well-prepared music can make possible "full, conscious, and active participation" in the liturgy, as called for by the Second Vatican Council.[14]

Young adults especially appreciate a variety of styles and expressions of music in worship. Parishes that are responsive to young adults' musical tastes know that young adults do not automatically prefer rock music—or folk music, or traditional compositions, or any other style. Young adults' tastes vary widely and may range across many genres. At some times, young

---

14   Second Vatican Council, *Constitution on the Sacred Liturgy* (*Sacrosanctum Concilium*), in *Vatican Council II: Volume 1: The Conciliar and Post Conciliar Documents*, ed. Austin Flannery (Northport, NY: Costello Publishing, 1996), no. 14.

adults—indeed, people of all ages—are uplifted by an upbeat and lively song of praise. At other times, the solemnity and reflective mood of a chant from Taizé express their faith well. Many contemporary and traditional hymns and songs can engage young adults in worship.

Many parishes have discovered that selections from diverse genres of liturgical music are most likely to engage young adults. Music directors who are responsive to young adults' diverse tastes might have music ministers lead the congregation in a rousing African spiritual and then follow up with plainsong or Gregorian chant. They might use bilingual songs to remind young adults of the universality and diversity of the Catholic community. They could choose compositions in which the assembly sings a simple repeated phrase, while the choir adds harmony and richness. And they may include selections from the wide range of contemporary and traditional Catholic hymns that appear in every congregation's repertoire. Whatever role music plays in young adult–responsive parishes, it must be easy enough to sing—aesthetically pleasing, yet within the ability of the average congregation. People are willing and eager to join in when they know how to sing the music.

Personal preferences notwithstanding, young adults can pray with a variety of musical styles, as long as the music is well done and reverent. The eclectic tastes of today's young adults permit them to appreciate a wide variety of musical styles and idioms. But in an age of technological sophistication, every effort should be made to ensure the music is of high quality—a key feature of faith communities, Catholic and non-Catholic alike, that excel in attracting young adults.

In addition, the music provided by a broad range of musical instruments enhances the congregational singing at a celebration. Consider this an excellent opportunity to invite young adults with musical talent to offer their gifts. Inviting young adults to add their voices to the choir or to play instruments as a part of the music ministry helps to instill stewardship of gifts as well as encourage active participation.

A variety of musical styles and instruments also provides the opportunity to vary the moods and atmosphere for different seasons or parts of the celebration. That variety, as well as the aesthetic appeal, will draw young adults into a prayerful celebration. It is also important that those who select the music are conscious of the needs of the various ages and cultures that make up the congregation.

Young-adult–responsive parishes involve young adults in music ministry. When they are involved, young adults can help the parish choose music that speaks to the hearts of their peers and draws them deeper into communion with Christ.

Good Preaching

The demand for quality preaching has been voiced in all circles of the Church today. Catholics have highlighted the need for good homilies in many national surveys and opinion polls in the last thirty-five years. Many Catholics, including young adults, may measure the caliber of a liturgical celebration largely by the quality of the homily. They seek churches where the homilist can explain the Scriptures and help the listeners apply the Good News to their daily lives.

This need highlights an important point for those who want to reach young adults through their preaching. Young adults want a homily that is rooted in the Scripture readings of the day and enlightened by the Tradition of the Church. They also want a homily that outlines some practical application of the Scriptures to their everyday lives. In light of the practicality that characterizes post–Vatican II generations, young adults understandably appreciate the challenge to put their faith into practice.

Homilists often use illustrations, stories, or anecdotes to introduce the topic or highlight an important point. In a parish that is responsive to young adults, these illustrations address or reflect young adults' experiences and challenges. For example, many young adults are single, so the priests at a young adult–responsive parish might use stories in their homilies that are relevant to the lifestyles of single Catholics today. While many homilists have frequent contact with young adults and can readily come up with pertinent illustrations, others do not have immediate contact with young adults. A useful resource for homilists and liturgy planners that relies on the work of the Initiative is *Connecting Young Adults with the Word*.[15] In addition to historical and cultural background on the gospel reading for every Sunday and holy day, this three-volume resource gives reflections written by young adults to illustrate the theme of each day's gospel reading. The resource also offers suggestions for developing a homily that speaks to the experiences of young adults.

---

15   Published in three volumes, one for each cycle of the lectionary: Ron Bagley, CJM, ed., *Connecting Young Adults with the Word* (Naugatuck, CT: Center for Ministry Development [CMD], 1997-1999).

For example, on the Feast of the Ascension in Cycle A, the Gospel is Matthew 28:16-20—often referred to as "the Great Commission" because it describes how Jesus sends the disciples out to be missionaries who spread the Good News. For that feast, *Connecting Young Adults with the Word* offers the following story written by a young adult just out of college. Using a story such as this helps connect young adults to the life of the Church:

> Paul [the young adult] never thought of himself as a missionary, although his grandmother always reminded him that his namesake was one of the Church's first great missionaries. When he was in his senior year of college, he began asking himself what he would do after graduation. Would he go to graduate school? Would he look for a job? Would he take some time off? One idea kept coming back to him: a year or two of volunteer service. He told himself if he didn't do it now, he might never be able to again.
>
> After some soul-searching, writing for information and a lot of conversations with friends, Paul decided he wanted to sign up for the Jesuit Volunteer Corps. After he was accepted, he was sent to work with children in Appalachia. In addition to tutoring them in the basics like math and reading, he was also asked by the local priest to teach them religion. Paul had always had a strong faith, but he still found it a challenge to explain the important aspects of the Catholic faith to others. He struggled to come up with good answers to their many questions. Looking back on the experience, Paul sees how his own faith became stronger in the process of trying to share it with others.[16]

Examples from contemporary media may also help young adults connect with the message of the Scriptures. In the end, though, well-posed questions or some new insight into the Scriptures will challenge young adults to live differently as a result of having met Jesus in the Word. Young adults do not want a watered-down Gospel. Most are looking for real spiritual food. A good homilist can provide this food for the entire assembly.

---

16   *Connecting Young Adults with the Word: Cycle A* (1998), 69.

Active Participation of the Assembly

Young adults appreciate and will seek out communities where the assembly participates actively, with a lively spirit and joyful faith expressed in word and gesture. They look for people who are happy to attend Mass, who look forward to being together to celebrate their faith.

When parishioners radiate a contagious excitement and energy, liturgy can be a moving experience. After a warm welcome and gracious hospitality, it does not take long to discover that the young adult–friendly congregation is eager to celebrate the liturgy with enthusiasm. A young adult–responsive parish is a beautiful example of the "full, conscious, and active participation" that the Second Vatican Council envisioned. In song, word, and gesture, the congregation is fully engaged. Not only is the music good, but the presider and other ministers lead the congregation in an engaging way. On certain occasions, gesture, drama, and other artistic expressions might be woven appropriately into the celebration.

Have you ever been in a church that actually fills up from the front to the back, one where the only empty seats—if any—are in the back of the church? Have you worshiped in a parish where very rarely does anyone leave before the Mass has ended? Something unusual happens in a parish that puts its time and talent into the liturgy. It is a sign of the vitality and eagerness of the congregation. Communities like this exhibit a lively faith that attracts young adults.

The environment in which the community worships can also engage young adults. Today's young adults are visually oriented, accustomed to having all of their senses engaged. Attention to the environment helps to establish the mood for the liturgical feast or season (e.g., joyous during Easter, stark or solemn during Lent) and appeals to the senses of the congregation. The Catholic liturgy offers so many ways to engage the senses: it employs candles, incense, holy water, and oil as sacramentals to make present the realities being symbolized. Meanwhile, flowers, banners, statues, colors, and other visual elements help to draw attention to the ceremony's meaning. This sensory approach appeals to the current generation of young adults.

Another way to actively involve young adults in the liturgy is through special blessings and other rituals. The Book of Blessings[17] provides parishes with an abundance of blessings to mark significant events in the life of the community and its members. Blessings for students, for engaged couples,

---

17   See Book of Blessings (Collegeville, MN: Liturgical Press, 1989).

for couples before childbirth, for pilgrims, and for a new home may be particularly relevant for young adults. To ritualize these moments at home, the revised *Catholic Household Blessings and Prayers*[18] offers special blessings that families can use to make the connection between the faith and the lives of their young adults. Some parishes also offer prayers in the parish setting, such as a blessing and sendoff for students going away to college. St. Joseph's University Parish, mentioned earlier in this chapter, blesses the students as they leave college and move on.[19] Parishes that are eager to include young adults will look for such ways to recognize and bless the milestones of their lives.

TEACHING ABOUT THE LITURGY

Catholic young adults who have come of age after the reforms of the Second Vatican Council have learned the liturgy primarily through experience. But some form of liturgical catechesis can also serve an important role: to help young adults fully appreciate the meaning of the gestures, symbols, and texts used in Sunday worship. A teaching session by a priest or someone else who is knowledgeable about the eucharistic liturgy can effectively explain the pattern and prayer responses in the Mass. Catechists could also use media or online resources to guide young adults toward a richer understanding of the reasons behind the forms of Catholic liturgy.

During the Initiative listening sessions, a campus minister related the following story. A student at the University of Dayton had approached the chaplain after Mass one Sunday to ask why Catholics fan themselves during the liturgy. The priest was perplexed by the question until he realized the young man was referring to the gesture of making three small crosses on oneself before the Gospel—no one had ever told him the words that accompany the gesture. So instead of reflecting on bringing the Word of God into his mind, on his lips, and into his heart, the student had thought the chapel was just getting hot. The Church has an ever-present opportunity to help connect the rituals of the faith with the lived experiences of young adults.

Young adults from a variety of cultural backgrounds may have specific needs in learning the meaning of the Eucharist and eucharistic symbols. As an illustration, *Mestizo Worship*, by Fr. Virgilio Elizondo and Timothy Matovina, and *Misa, Mesa y Musa*, edited by Fr. Kenneth Davis, offer helpful descriptions

---

18   See USCCB, *Catholic Household Blessings and Prayers*, rev. ed. (Washington, DC: USCCB, 2007).
19   Parish leaders could consult *Connecting Young Adults with the Word* for more ideas like this one.

of symbols and traditions treasured in Hispanic/Latino liturgies and how to understand, affirm, incorporate, and draw out their meaning for a fuller expression of faith.[20] These books present an inspiring invitation to what they call an "integrative approach" to liturgical ministry, forging a dynamic "*mestizaje*" (i.e., the coming-together of cultures, giving way to a new common identity) between the rich Catholic liturgical tradition and the Hispanic/Latino community's treasured expressions of faith. Likewise, other cultural groups within the Church will have rich and valuable contributions to make.

CELEBRATING THE REAL PRESENCE

Young adults—like all members of the faith community—should be formed to believe in the Real Presence of Jesus in the Eucharist. The Initiative found that the reason some young adults said the eucharistic bread and wine were symbols of Jesus, rather than his actual Body and Blood, was due to a lack of catechesis about the Eucharist, not to substantive disagreement with church teachings.

Parishes have the opportunity to provide catechetical sessions on topics like the Real Presence. If such sessions are offered to the entire adult community, extend special invitations to young adults so that they feel welcome. Parish leaders who wish to target young adults might make the Real Presence the topic for a Theology on Tap[21] evening or some other gathering of young adults. *Young Adult Works*, from the Center for Ministry Development, includes several complete catechetical sessions about Christology and sacramental theology. Young-adult leaders can guide their peers through these sessions, all of which are praxis-based,[22] and invite young adults to ponder the Gospel in relation to their own experiences.

In addition to the liturgy itself and liturgical catechesis, eucharistic adoration can help young adults enter more deeply into the mystery of the Real Presence. Many young adults of today find adoration of the Blessed Sacrament to be a particularly powerful practice in their spiritual journeys.

---

20   See Virgilio P. Elizondo and Timothy M. Matovina, *Mestizo Worship: A Pastoral Approach to Liturgical Ministry* (Collegeville, MN: Liturgical Press, 1998); Kenneth G. Davis, OFM Conv., ed., *Misa, Mesa y Musa: Liturgy in the U.S. Hispanic Church* (Schiller Park, IL: World Library Publications, 1991), 51.

21   For information on bringing Theology on Tap to your area, see *renewtot.org*. For additional information, including how to order the *Theology-on-Tap Manual*, see *www.yamchicago.org* or write to the Young Adult Ministry Office, Archdiocese of Chicago, 711 W. Monroe Street, Chicago, IL 60661.

22   "Praxis" refers to a methodology that begins with reflection on faith through the life experience of the learner and then motivates the learner to act as a result of that reflection.

PARTICIPATION IN THE SACRAMENTS

The sacraments are one of the major ways that Catholics pray together. In addition to promoting participation in the liturgy of the Eucharist, parish communities that are responsive to young adults seek to promote their active participation in the sacramental life of the community.

Sacraments of Initiation

Many young adults will be involved in different roles in participating in the Sacraments of Initiation: Baptism, Eucharist, and Confirmation. Some young adults will be preparing for initiation; others will sponsor their friends or family members. Young-adult parents may be involved in providing for Baptism, First Communion, or Confirmation for their children. Other young adults will attend when family members and friends receive sacraments, even if they themselves do not participate in a parish on a regular basis. Each of these roles presents an opportunity for a parish to connect young adults with community life and participation in sacraments in a new, meaningful, and welcoming way.

Communities can seize these opportunities in a variety of ways. As a starting point, they might reach out intentionally to young adults and invite them to consider participating in Christian initiation. Catechists can follow up on this invitation and welcome by addressing young adults' needs within the initiation process in practical ways. Communities can also reach out to young adults who did not experience Confirmation during childhood or adolescence. Parishes might provide special programs to prepare young adults for Confirmation, using times that fit their hectic schedules and catechetical methods that match their learning styles. (See Chapter 3, "Catechesis and Young Adult Ministry," for a more detailed discussion of catechetical methods.) Those responsible for the Rite of Christian Initiation of Adults (RCIA) in the parish will be most effective when they use programs suitable for young adults. The content of such programs is clear and well founded; the methodology is engaging and experiential.

Dialogue, discussion, and question-and-answer sessions are important to young adults preparing to receive sacraments. They seek the opportunity to receive direct and honest answers to their questions. They deserve liturgical catechesis that connects the sacraments to their daily lives. Parishes that are responsive to young adults' spiritual needs look ahead to engaging them in the community as neophytes after the Easter Vigil—for example, by involving them in small faith-sharing groups, or by inviting them to act as liturgical ministers at Mass. Ultimately, in a parish that is responsive to young adults, each sacramental celebration is planned with young adult participants in mind, and planners give special consideration to young adults who have been away from active church participation.

As an example, San Jose Parish in Jacksonville, Florida, recruits young adults to serve as sponsors to other young adults who join the RCIA process. These sponsors pray, learn, and grow in faith with their candidates or catechumens as they prepare to celebrate the rites together. The Diocese of Youngstown, as well as many other dioceses, holds an annual Confirmation of Adults so that young adult participants can prepare for and celebrate the sacrament with other adults. This gives young adults the opportunity to meet others who, though they may be of different generations, are experiencing the same stages on the faith journey.

Sacraments at the Service of Communion

As young adults grapple with life choices and vocational discernment, parish communities can provide catechesis about the Sacraments at the Service of Communion: Marriage and Holy Orders. Parish leaders might bring in speakers who can witness to their lives as married people or as priests and deacons. As young adults engage in community life and form relationships with other Catholics who live out married or ordained vocations, the informal friendships and witness of these Catholics' lives will provide a lived explanation of these sacraments. (For more ideas about fostering vocational discernment with young adults, see Chapter 4, "Discernment and Vocations.")

Sacraments of Healing

Parishes can also help young adults to experience the Sacraments of Healing by guiding them as they receive the Sacrament of Penance and Reconciliation and by providing for those who need the Sacrament of Anointing of the Sick. Many young adults hesitate to take advantage of the peace and grace of Reconciliation; parishes can help them overcome their hesitation by preparing them to participate, by inviting the young adult community to join a wider parish celebration of the Sacrament of Penance, or by offering a Reconciliation service specifically for young adults.

Written materials on the Sacrament of Penance and Reconciliation, including the Act of Contrition and a guide for the examination of conscience, can help all young adults enter into the experience more deeply, especially those who have been away from the sacrament for a time. They can participate with less anxiety if they have a refresher on the meaning and practice of the sacrament. As one example, the United States Conference of Catholic Bishops has published a pamphlet titled *Celebrating the Sacrament of Penance*[23] that helps participants enter into the sacrament. Another resource is "How to Celebrate the Sacrament of Reconciliation Today," a *Catholic Update* (a series of four-page summaries of Catholic teaching, including imprimaturs).[24] It, too, provides concise Catholic teaching on the sacrament and how to participate in it.

Young adults should also be aware of the power of the Sacrament of Anointing of the Sick. Those who are experiencing serious illness or who are undergoing major surgery can contact a priest to receive this sacrament. The parish might provide the contact information and make this possibility known to young adults. Young adults who are overcoming drug addictions and other dangerous patterns in their life may also wish to experience the peace of this sacrament.[25]

With all of the sacraments, the Church has an opportunity for liturgical catechesis through the actual rites and symbols. Immersing young adults in the words of the rite and engaging them with the symbols of each sacrament can help them see the connection between the sacraments and their everyday lives.

OTHER LITURGICAL OPPORTUNITIES

Liturgical experiences other than the Mass and celebrations of the sacraments offer tremendous potential for connecting with young adults. Many young adults today are drawn to the Liturgy of the Hours, while adoration of the Blessed Sacrament attracts others. Seder meals and other non-eucharistic experiences can engage young adults as well. Parishes that support young adults on their faith journeys will ask them which of these experiences appeal to them and then work together with young adults to provide them.

Bishop Ramirez calls attention to the fertile ground where popular rituals surrounding rites of passage are brought together with liturgy. He points to an example from the Hispanic/Latino community—the success of the celebration

---

23   See USCCB, *Celebrating the Sacrament of Penance: Questions and Answers* (Washington, DC: USCCB, 2003).

24   See Thomas Richstatter, OFM, "How to Celebrate the Sacrament of Reconciliation Today," *Catholic Update*, catalog no. C0800 (Cincinnati: St. Anthony Messenger Press, 2000).

25   For a fuller explanation of the Sacrament of Anointing of the Sick, as well as guidance for the use of the Sacrament, see Kathleen Hughes, "Pastoral Care of the Sick," in *Saying Amen: A Mystagogy of Sacrament* (Chicago: Liturgy Training Publications, 1999), Chapter 8.

of *quinceañeras* (fifteenth-birthday celebrations for young women)—and he says that more can be done to incorporate popular rituals of birth, young men's coming of age, marriage, and death, and also to recognize the advantage of the Hispanic/Latino Catholic tradition of *padrinos* and *compadres*.[26] A *padrino/compadre* serves as a godparent or sponsor to a child and also develops a strong relationship with the child's parents, so that the *padrino/compadre* serves as a mentor throughout the life of the child and "walks with" the parents as an extended family.

Bishop Ramirez also recommends looking for creative ways to incorporate various cultures' Holy Week and Advent traditions and the many traditions of pilgrimages, patronal feasts, processions, and novenas. In a special way he urges all Catholics to continue to find ways to celebrate the treasured Feast of Our Lady of Guadalupe across the Western Hemisphere.

CONCLUSION

Even if young adults are underrepresented in liturgical assemblies, Sunday liturgy is the most frequent opportunity the parish community has to connect with them. *Sons and Daughters of the Light* challenges Catholics to connect young adults with Jesus and the Church,[27] and the liturgy is a significant opportunity for helping young adults forge these bonds. Parishes and campus ministries that celebrate liturgy well—with genuine welcome, good music, dynamic preaching, and active participation—will be successful in attracting young adults and connecting them with the Church. Indeed, the entire faith community will be enriched, because young adults want the same thing that all Catholics want from liturgy: a closeness to and relationship with Jesus Christ.

---

26   See "Envisioning Hispanic Liturgy," 4, 7.
27   See *Sons and Daughters of the Light*, 28, 33.

THE CAMPUS CONNECTION

One of the best ways to help all students feel welcome at the table is to include their peers as participants in liturgical ministries. Yet frequently, students do not respond to a parish's usual avenue of recruitment: an announcement in the parish bulletin. Announcements and encouragement from the pulpit may help a little. However, if a parish is serious about including students as liturgical ministers, the best method of recruitment is personal invitation. Of course, a priest or other parish minister can extend the invitation to a student as he or she is leaving the church following Mass. Perhaps a better opportunity, though, would come during a social or some other similar occasion—especially if food is served (students love to eat). Then those charged with parish ministries can personally invite students to volunteer and participate.

An annual "one-shot" training will probably not yield many student volunteers. Rather, campus ministry leaders, or leaders of nearby parishes who want to recruit students for liturgical ministry, need to schedule and conduct liturgical training in a manner sensitive to the lifestyle of students. This means offering a variety of training opportunities at a variety of times. Students frequently have classes or work schedules that conflict with evening events during the week. A helpful alternative is to schedule training around the weekend Mass that is most frequented by students. One parish found that most students were available on Sunday afternoons or evenings. Another parish was so interested in having students participate in liturgical ministries that it arranged training by appointment. Campus ministers can also respond to the rhythms of university life by recruiting at the beginning of each semester. A student's schedule might have been too hectic to allow for participation during the fall semester, but the spring semester may be more relaxed—or vice versa. When campus ministers are sensitive to students' scheduling concerns, the rewards include not only more students participating in liturgical ministries, but a greater number of students attending Mass and getting involved in the total life of the faith community.

Participation in liturgical ministries such as music ministry can have a tremendous impact on the spiritual life of a student. For example, the Newman Catholic Student Center at the University of Iowa in Iowa City has transformed its choir, the Newman Singers, into more than just a choir.

Through the integration of music, prayer, and service, the Newman Singers have accepted the mission of spreading the Gospel. Not only do they sing for Sunday liturgies, but through their summer internship program, they travel for eight weeks around the United States. During that time, they present concerts, sing for liturgies, and participate in service projects such as summer camps for children, building projects, and soup kitchens. The Newman Singers also engage in their own spiritual journeys through daily prayer, small group discussion, and activities. Many who have witnessed their outreach, including the Catholic Campus Ministry Association, have acknowledged the quality of their liturgical and inspirational music. Learn more about the Newman Singers by visiting *www.newmansingers.com.*

Young adults respond very positively to liturgy or worship that is done well. Education about Catholic liturgy will bring young adults to a better understanding of—and a stronger desire to participate in—liturgy's structure and form, its function in the worshiping community, and the steps involved in planning and implementing it. Fr. Roc O'Connor, SJ, a pastoral and liturgical minister for campus ministry at Creighton University, has created resources—available on the Web—that move students beyond an intangible experience to an educated knowledge of liturgy. Available topics include "Introduction to a Method of Liturgical Planning," "Liturgy Planning for the Church Year," and "An Existentialist Approach to Liturgy." The last topic focuses on the relationship that liturgy establishes between the worshiping community and the action and presence of the Triune God. These, as well as other topics, are great resources for those educating students about liturgy. Students can also use the resources to educate themselves.[28]

When students are well catechized and well prepared to participate in liturgy, when they feel welcome to participate in a reverent celebration, and when they have a rich sense of the liturgy as the central place for meeting God in their lives, they will be eager to come and worship. Catholic campus ministers have an unparalleled opportunity to offer all these things to students—and, through them, to give students opportunities to grow closer to God.

---

28   For more on Creighton's liturgical resources, see *www.creighton.edu/~rocsj.*

CHAPTER EIGHT

Leadership Development

How can parishes involve young adults in leadership in the Church? Using Jesus as a model, this chapter explores ways to recruit and train young adults for leadership. The chapter draws on insights into leadership development from the business world as well as particular examples of leadership formation from diverse cultural perspectives.

Ministry with young adults looks very different from parish to parish, from diocese to diocese, and from campus to campus. But one concept on which all faith communities seem to agree is the importance of leadership *by* young adults in ministry *with* young adults. People in their twenties and thirties often have the maturity, wisdom, energy, passion, and understanding needed to minister effectively to their peers. They have great leadership abilities and even greater potential. Parishes that are responsive to the needs and capabilities of young adults invite these talented young leaders into leadership and ministry. Within the broad structures of the parish and campus community, effective leaders of faith communities empower young adults to serve in a variety of capacities. They open up opportunities for young adults to join them in their task.

JESUS' MODEL OF LEADERSHIP

The Gospels tell a leadership story. Two thousand years ago, Judaism faced major crises. The Roman occupiers were hostile toward Jewish teachings. Followers of the faith were often shunned and persecuted. Many well-intentioned religious leaders became preoccupied with preserving their power base and seemed more intent on following the letter of the law than the spirit of it. Things needed to change if the people of God were to fulfill their mission. Providentially, God intervened. The Second Person of the Trinity became incarnate. When his time for ministry began, he gathered a motley group of fishermen, tax collectors, and other Jews and proclaimed the Reign of God. Two thousand years later, Christians are still following his lead. Jesus had a mastery of leadership development. He spent three years working to build on his disciples' leadership abilities. He instructed, trained, mentored, and prayed with them, empowering them to carry on his ministry. He had a profound ability to call forth the best in others. No matter whom he met—Martha, Mary, a tax collector, a blind man, a Pharisee—he found a way of connecting with all, challenging their views of the world, and helping them to live more fruitful and faithful lives. And when Jesus invited people into leadership, he trained and equipped them for that work before putting them in charge.

THE CHURCH'S RESPONSE

The Church, the country, and the world need Catholic leaders now more than ever. Just as Jesus called and trained the apostles, the Church continues to call and train young adult leaders. The Catholic bishops of the United States state this clearly in their pastoral plan *Sons and Daughters of the Light*: "if the Church is to continue to regenerate and renew its members, the training of young adults is key. Young men and women already provide valuable service in the Church. Parishes and campuses should provide them with leadership training, especially for core members of the young adult commission and parish staff."[1] Pope John Paul II reinforces this concept in his apostolic exhortation *The Church in America* (*Ecclesia in America*): "America needs lay Christians able to assume roles of leadership in society. It is urgent to train men and women who, in keeping with their vocation, can influence public life, and direct it to the common good."[2]

Those engaged in leadership within the Church are called to follow Jesus' model by training, mentoring, and empowering young adults (and all Christians) for leadership in the world and the Church. Before inviting young adults into leadership within the Church, effective parish leaders prepare to provide the skills and information young adults need to succeed within leadership positions. So where can young adult leaders be found, and how can parishes and other faith communities engage them in carrying out the mission of Jesus Christ and the Catholic Church?

---

1   United States Conference of Catholic Bishops (USCCB), *Sons and Daughters of the Light: A Pastoral Plan for Ministry with Young Adults* (Washington, DC: USCCB, 1996), 41.
2   Pope John Paul II, *The Church in America* (*Ecclesia in America*) (Washington, DC: USCCB, 1999), no. 44.

YOUNG ADULT LEADERSHIP

Young adults are *adults*—an important point to remember when talking about young adults and leadership. Young adults are teachers, doctors, farmers, fire-fighters, CEOs, nurses, construction workers, missionaries, scholars, musicians, and politicians. Young adults are single, married, divorced, or widowed; some have children, and some do not; some have answered a call to religious or ordained life. Young adults are leaders in their families, workplaces, and communities. The Church needs their leadership as much as that of any other age group.

Leadership for Life, a leadership book for Catholic young adults, defines "leadership" as "the shared activity through which a group and its members work together to achieve their goals in a given situation."[3] Young adults want to make meaningful contributions to a worthwhile cause. What cause is more worthwhile than the Reign of God and eternal life in heaven? To engage young adults more fully in this cause, effective parish leaders make intentional efforts to invite them into leadership and participation within the faith community.

INVITING YOUNG ADULTS INTO LEADERSHIP

Jesus went out and called the apostles by name. He knew that the way to involve people in his mission was to ask them to participate. The same simple solution works today. If a parish community would like more young adults involved in leadership roles, it simply needs to ask them. Personal invitation has proven time and again to be the single biggest predictor of a person's willingness to be involved in a project.

Consider an example from the corporate world. In direct-response marketing, a successful ad placed in the Sunday newspaper for a $50 product would produce a 0.006 percent response rate—that is, only six out of every thousand readers would purchase the product in response to the ad. A successful personal direct-mail campaign for the same product would generate a 2 to 4 percent response rate. An even more personal telemarketing campaign could produce a 25 to 30 percent response rate. But a face-to-face sales pitch, delivered to valued customers in a retail store setting, would result in a 60 to 75 percent response rate.

3   Michael Poulin, Lori Spanbauer, Joan Weber, and Jennifer Willems, *Leadership for Life: Discovering Your Gifts for Christian Leadership* (Naugatuck, CT: Center for Ministry Development [CMD], 1997), 10.

So when a community is looking for leaders, especially among young adults, it must consider the medium used to reach them. If a very successful ad is run in the parish bulletin, a 0.006 percent response rate can be expected—probably meaning that the same few people who sign up for everything will sign up for this, too. On the other hand, if a community follows Jesus' model and makes face-to-face invitations (for example, by approaching young adults after Mass on Sunday and asking for their help), more than two-thirds are likely to accept the call.

How else can parishes invite young adults into leadership? One way is to ask them to fill out a "Catholic résumé,"[4] a document that lists the various gifts and talents they bring to the Catholic community as well as their experiences of parish leadership (e.g., liturgical minister, retreat leader, or speaker) and areas of expertise (e.g., musician, computer expert, graphic artist). It is important to remember that many young adults hold major leadership positions in their careers, or were leaders within youth ministry or campus ministry earlier in their lives, and they are ready for significant leadership in their parishes. Young adults reported to Ministry with Young Adults: A National Catholic Initiative ("the Initiative") interviewers that they want not to be passive recipients in the pews but rather to be involved in church life in meaningful ways.

A parish in Omaha, Nebraska, that was involved in the Initiative came up with a unique way to invite young adults into leadership. Young-adult leaders in the parish hosted a potluck dinner every six months to which potential leaders were invited. The hosts shared the opportunities available throughout the parish, along with the time, talent, and training needed to be effective in each position. The leaders didn't wait until there was a vacancy in leadership to have the dinner, because they didn't want to ask young adults to lead merely because there was no other choice. They believed the community was blessed with gifted young adults, and they wanted to have a viable talent pool of people ready to serve whenever a need arose.

Parishes can invite parishioners to recommend young adults to be leaders and then encourage them to extend an invitation to those they identify.

---

4   The idea of a Catholic résumé surfaced in Ministry with Young Adults: A National Catholic Initiative when campus ministers from the University of Iowa in Iowa City reported that they invite graduating seniors to fill out a Catholic résumé alongside their professional résumé. For a description and template of the résumé, see "Strategy Twelve: Make the Campus to Parish Connection," in *Young Adult Works*, ed. Ronald Bagley, CJM, John Roberto, Susan Stark, and Joan Weber (Naugatuck, CT: CMD, 1997), Binder 2, 6.115-6.122.

This could be a modified version of the "Called by Name" program that many dioceses use to identify potential candidates for the priesthood.

Another strategy to recruit young adult leaders involves writing a job description for each leadership position for which the parish seeks a young adult and then sharing it with potential candidates. The job description should give the young adults all the information they need to make a good, holy decision about whether to apply, including the time commitment, talents needed to be effective in the position, and any training that will be provided. Also important to young adults are the benefits—practical and spiritual—of responding to the invitation, so these should be clearly articulated in the job description. Informing the candidates for leadership that they will build skills they can use in other areas of their lives (e.g., running a meeting, teaching a class) may encourage them to say "yes" to the request.

Inviting Culturally Diverse Leadership

A vital element of inviting young adults into leadership is being conscious of the cultural diversity within the parish community. A young adult–responsive parish needs to strategically invite young adults from each culture in its community to be part of its leadership team in all aspects of parish life, including ministry with young adults. A parish can enlist the aid of diocesan offices for African American Catholics, Hispanic/Latino Catholics, Asian and Pacific Islander Catholics, Native American Catholics, and other cultural groups for ideas on effective recruitment techniques within a given culture. A young adult–responsive parish also takes into consideration cultural attitudes toward leadership when it invites young adults of a given culture into leadership.

Some young adults are more likely to respond to the invitation when they see their peers meaningfully involved and trained well. For example, a parish that seeks to develop young adult leaders in its African American community can start by assessing whether African Americans are prominently included in the parish's leadership: from qualified lay leadership (e.g., on the parish council, or as liturgical ministers) to ordained leadership (e.g., in the diaconate or priesthood). The parish can also inquire into whether its diocese offers programs that promote leadership within the African American Catholic community; some parishes even make funds available to send young adults to those programs.

Hispanic/Latino young adult Catholics today face a special challenge, because they are entering adulthood just as Hispanics/Latinos are becoming a majority in the Church in the United States. (Hispanic/Latino young adults, for example, make up more than 50 percent of Catholics in the United States today under the age of twenty-five.[5]) The authors of *La Juventud Hispana y la Respuesta Pastoral de la Iglesia* see Hispanic/Latino young adult Catholics as young prophets renewing the Church and renewing society.[6] Like the prophet Jeremiah, they aren't asking for this mission, but the Spirit is calling and empowering them to stir the Church to resist false values of materialism, ritualism, machismo, and elitism, and to embrace instead the values of the Reign of God.[7] Pastoral leaders such as Fr. Allan Deck, SJ, and Lydia Menocal affirm that the Hispanic/Latino experience with *mestizaje*—having suffered exclusion and yet kept the faith—well prepares young Hispanic/Latino Catholics to be compassionate agents of a welcoming, vibrant, culturally diverse Church that empowers all to live the mission of Jesus in the world.[8] Will Hispanic/Latino young adults step up to the challenge to honor, embrace, and bridge the cultural, racial, and linguistic differences[9] and lead the Church in this increasingly globalized world? And will the Church personally invite them into leadership so that they can do so?

Effective parishes ensure that leaders from all the cultures in their faith communities—clergy, religious, and lay—are visible and well trained and are provided opportunities for leadership. Parishes are most responsive to young adults of all cultures when they invite these young adults to use their gifts and to take their rightful places as leaders in the Church.

A Real-Life Example of Personal Invitation

Personal invitation is integral to getting young adults involved in parish life and leadership, and within ministry to their peers. One example of the power of the personal invitation occurred at St. Katharine of Siena Parish in Wayne, Pennsylvania.[10] At the parish's Time and Talent fair, young adult volunteer Christine Smith offered to staff a table for young adults. Paul Lavallee (a co-

---

5   See *www.usccb.org/hispanicaffairs* and the U.S. Census Bureau.

6   See Alejandro Aguilera-Titus, Carlos Carrillo, Pedro Castex, Carmen Cervantes, Juan Diaz-Vilar, SJ, and Juan Huitrado, MCCJ, *Profetas de Esperanza*, vol. 1, *La Juventud Hispana y la Respuesta Pastoral de la Iglesia* (Winona, MN: St. Mary's Press, 1994), 21.

7   See *Profetas de Esperanza*, 22.

8   See Araceli M. Cantero, "Hispanos para Servir a Todos: NCCHM Invita a los Católicos a Raíces y Alas 2002 para Dialogar con la Sociedad," *La Voz Católica* 49, no. 11 (November 2001), *www.vozcatolica. org/46/servir.htm*.

9   See USCCB, *Encuentro and Mission: A Renewed Pastoral Framework for Hispanic Ministry* (Washington, DC: USCCB, 2002), no. 57.

10   Paul Lavallee, interview with the authors.

author of Chapter 5 of this book) was a recent college graduate at the time and was interested in getting to know others in the community. When he saw the sign for the young adult table, he struck up a conversation with Christine. The next day, Christine called Paul to say that she had been accepted to graduate school and was leaving the area. She asked if he would get young adult ministry started by contacting the people who had signed up.

Paul called the other young adults and organized a meeting of six young adults and the pastor to discuss options. They agreed to start a weekly Bible study and faith-sharing group. The pastor offered them a meeting room at the parish, and the Young Adults of St. Katharine's and St. Isaac's (abbreviated "Yaski") began. The original six agreed to meet weekly for Bible study even if everyone could not attend. Some weeks, only two or three could make it, but they persisted and invited others to join them, and the numbers gradually increased during the first year. Suddenly ten young adults were attending, and then fifteen or twenty. It all happened because Christine asked Paul, and then Paul and the core team members personally invited others to attend.

YOUNG ADULTS FOLLOW PEER LEADERS

Like anyone, young adults are hesitant to get involved in a church activity as the only representative of their age group. They want to make sure that others of their age will be in attendance—both for the "safety in numbers" and for the assurance that the particular activity is attractive to other young adults, indicating that they too might enjoy it. One of the best ways to make a ministry attractive to young adults is to have other young adults in leadership positions in the community. Effective campus ministries invite students to assume roles of leadership. Parishes that want to involve more young married couples will invite young married couples into leadership roles. A parish, cluster, or diocese that wants more cultural diversity will invite persons from a broad variety of cultures to join the leadership teams for those structures. In general, if a community values young adults' presence and desires their leadership, it will soon find out that many young adults are like Thomas the Apostle—they need to see it in order to believe it.

Some Catholic groups are already training and inviting younger, more diverse leaders to participate in leadership teams and initiatives. For example, in 2001, the Catholic Leadership Institute (CLI) identified as a strategic priority the need to develop a more effective response to the fastest-growing segment of the Church in the United States: Hispanic/Latino Catholics. While this sounded good on paper, CLI knew that, to fulfill this priority, it needed to make changes to its mostly Caucasian and African American team of facilitators. So the group obtained a grant to launch a pilot program for fifty Hispanic/Latino young adults and hired Miriam Espadas to coordinate the program. Miriam brought to the program a passion for the initiative and personal knowledge of the Hispanic/Latino community—both of which were critical to the program's success. The two-year pilot program concluded in November 2004 and has made a huge difference in the Hispanic/Latino Catholic community and the Catholic Leadership Institute. As a result of Miriam's leadership, CLI now has six bilingual facilitators and can offer leadership programs in Spanish or English throughout the United States. More importantly, the young adults who have participated in this training have stepped into leadership roles at the parish and diocesan level, thereby bringing another generation of leaders to the Church.

If young adults attract other young adults into leadership, how do you get the first group of young adults involved to attract their peers? Every age group has a small percentage of natural leaders who are willing to set new directions and forge new paths. These are the young adults whom current parish leaders should seek to include when initiating something new. Also, keep in mind that thirty-year-old married young adults with three children may not think of themselves as "young," but their participation during liturgy, on committees, or as catechists may help empower a twenty-five-year-old to participate in parish life more fully.

EMPOWERING THE NEXT GENERATION: TRAINING

Great leaders realize that the mission is more important than any individual. They realize that their time on this earth is limited. They want to look back at the organizations they used to lead and see that the organizations became even stronger after they left. Great leaders are therefore always training others to be leaders and grooming their successors.

Jesus was a great leader. He knew that after his death, he would soon ascend to heaven, so he instructed, trained, and empowered the Apostles to carry on the mission for him after his death. He identified Peter as his successor and the head of the Church and entrusted the care of the Church to him. Great Catholic leaders, whether conscious of doing so or not, follow

Christ's example: planning to make a significant contribution while serving, but always keeping an eye on the long-term mission. As the bishops have stated, strong Catholic leaders commit time and resources to the training of future leaders.

Parishes that are responsive to young adults offer the training that young adults, or any leaders, need in order to be effective in leadership roles in the community. They think creatively about how to provide training to busy, often over-committed young adults. Consider the following strategies for young adult–responsive leadership training:

- Start by having the young adults get in touch with their own baptismal call to leadership and service. Unpack the meaning of words like "Baptism" and "ministry" with them. A good strategy to link leadership with faith is to have each trainee write a personal mission statement for his or her life.[11]

- Invite young adults interested in a leadership position in the parish to shadow a parishioner who currently holds that position. Shadowing and mentoring give a real picture of the time and talent needed to do the ministry well while teaching how it is done. Yaski, the young adult group described earlier in this chapter, practices mentoring. All committee chairs assume responsibility for grooming their successors. Current Yaski leaders are motivated to involve others in the work so that they can learn how others handle responsibility and can mentor new members in leadership.

- Try training outside a group setting. Offer print and online resources. For example, a young adult who is recruited to be a catechist for the high school religious education/youth ministry program could be directed to Scripture, the *Catechism of the Catholic Church*, and documents from the USCCB for church teaching on the topic he or she is being asked to teach. Online resources can provide contemporary context for discussing issues with high-school–aged youth.

- Provide group training sessions. Many ministries already build training sessions into their usual work; but to appeal to young

---

11   See *Leadership for Life*, 112-120, which takes young adults through a step-by-step reflection process for creating their own mission statements.

adults, consider including spiritual enrichment in the process. Also, consider providing "transferable skills" training (e.g., time management), so that young adults know their learning will be beneficial to them in the future and in other leadership roles. Finally, incorporate social time to allow young adults to make connections with other members of the faith community.

- Train in the context of a leadership retreat. Again, provide a mix of spiritual formation and practical leadership skills. For example, consider the leadership qualities that Jesus exemplified (e.g., having a vision for the future, being a person of integrity) and encourage the retreatants to pursue Christlike standards in their own leadership. Discuss practical leadership skills like communication, conflict resolution, delegation, and pastoral planning through the lens of Christianity.

- Take advantage of diocesan leadership training as a resource for young adult leaders. In the Archdiocese of Philadelphia, the Leadership Experiential Adventure Program (LEAP) retreat has been offered by the Catholic Leadership Institute (CLI).[12] Core leaders can develop a better appreciation for their individual and collective gifts through this powerful experience.

- Look into existing resources. The Center for Ministry Development offers extensive experience and resources for training young adult ministry teams in parishes around the nation. The Center's two-weekend training program, Making the Connection, seeks to implement the bishops' pastoral plan for young adult ministry, *Sons and Daughters of the Light*.

Cultural Considerations in Training

Just as the young adult–responsive parish is sensitive to cultural needs when *inviting* young adults into leadership, effective parish leaders remain aware of specific cultural considerations when *training* young adults for leadership. Eric Law states convincingly that a culturally diverse church "can no longer train leaders ethnocentrically."[13] But sensitivity to the diverse interests of vari-

---

12   See *www.catholicleaders.org* for information on CLI. The special "Campus Connection" section at the end of this chapter describes the LEAP program in greater detail.

13   Eric H. F. Law, *The Wolf Shall Dwell with the Lamb* (St. Louis, MO: Chalice Press, 1993), 35. Law asserts that young adult ministry needs to train leaders to analyze power structures and move from mono-cultural leadership to multicultural leadership.

ous cultures within a parish community remains important to recruiting and training the parish's leaders, including young adults.

For example, the Archdiocese of Philadelphia offers a pastoral ministry certificate program with a concentration in ministry to African American Catholics. This initiative promotes leaders' awareness of and sensitivity to pastoral issues among African Americans. Additionally, the archdiocese encourages annual forums that foster networking, dialogue, and leadership about African American Catholic interests.

Strong efforts are currently being made to support the networking and formation of Hispanic/Latino young adult Catholic leaders on a national level under the guidance of La Red, the National Catholic Network de Pastoral Juvenil Hispana.[14] For example, the first Encuentro Nacional de Pastoral Juvenil Hispana (or National Hispanic Youth and Young Adult Ministry Encounter)— a national symposium of Hispanic/Latino youth and young adults and those in ministry with them—was held at the University of Notre Dame in 2006. Gatherings like these help dioceses and parishes to assess their effectiveness in involving Hispanic/Latino young adults in ministry in the Church, and they prompt planning and dedication of energy toward this ministry for the service of the Church and society.

Many organizations also offer resources for training Hispanic/Latino young adult leaders. The South East Pastoral Institute, which has conducted workshops on *pastoral juvenil hispana* since the late 1970s, also offers a leadership formation process, La Pascua Juvenil, that has produced a bilingual young adult ministry book on varying themes of faith and life each year since 1983.[15] Another organization, Instituto Fe y Vida,[16] is responding to the urgent need to direct resources specifically into Hispanic/Latino youth and young adult ministry formation.[17] Instituto offers a model called Prophets of Hope for the evangelization and faith formation of Hispanic/Latino youth and young adults in small faith communities. The model can also be used to train youth and young adult ministers in theological and pastoral vision, social sciences, and practical skills for animating small communities.[18] In collaboration with St. Mary's Press, Instituto Fe y Vida has published several volumes in the

---

14   For more information on La Red, visit *www.laredpjh.org.*

15   For more information on this organization, contact South East Pastoral Institute, 7700 SW 56th Street, Miami, FL 33155, (305) 279-2333, *sepimiami@aol.com.*

16   For more information on this organization, contact Instituto Fe y Vida, 1737 West Benjamin Holt Drive, Stockton, CA 95207, (209) 478-5357, *feyvida@altavista.net.*

17   See "Young, Hispanic, Catholic," *The National Catholic Reporter,* January 30, 2004, 12-13.

18   See *Profetas de Esperanza,* 180.

Prophets of Hope series, each in English and in Spanish. Instituto also consults with dioceses and offers courses around the country to train diocesan teams.[19]

Other national organizations offer similar experiences of leadership training within the context of specific cultures. For the particular cultural groups represented in your parish, look into similar programs and models that may be available for cultivating leadership in young adults.

THE OPPORTUNITY TODAY

In *Sons and Daughters of the Light*, the bishops laid out a plan to connect young adults with Jesus Christ, the Church, the mission of the Church, and a peer community. Young adults are looking for all four of these connections in their lives. In turn, the Church is looking for the energy, faith, ideas, and leadership of its young adults. All who are involved in work with young adults at the campus, parish, cluster, and diocesan levels have the opportunity to serve as bridge builders between young adults and the Church. Without these bridge builders, young adults often experience a disconnect between the life of the Church and their own daily lives.

In their book *The Leadership Challenge*, writers and researchers James Kouzes and Barry Posner point out that organizations need to develop a sense of trust among those involved. Kouzes and Posner challenge all leaders: "they must demonstrate their trust *in* others before asking for trust *from* others."[20] Current parish leaders and older adults need to trust the leadership, fidelity, and talents of young adults. When they "trust first," they can confidently make room for young leaders on their parish pastoral councils and key committees (e.g., finance, liturgy, social concerns). All can call young adults by name and ask them to assume roles of leadership in parish communities. Each community can invest the necessary time and resources to train young adults so that they have the confidence and courage to assume those roles. When they do, great things can happen.

---

19   In the summer of 2003, Instituto Fe y Vida offered three opportunities for intense formation in *pastoral juvenil hispana* and Christian leadership for pastoral ministers and for young adult leaders with two years of pastoral experience. At St. Mary's College in Leavenworth, Kansas, they held (1) a one-week intensive symposium on evangelization and faith formation of Hispanic/Latino youth and young adults, (2) a seminar on the issues of sexuality and spirituality for Hispanic/Latino young adults, and (3) the first of three courses in a pastoral-theological certification program for advisors and adult leaders in youth and young adult ministry. For information on Instituto Fe y Vida's current summer programs, see *feyvida.org/programs/summer.html*.

20   James M. Kouzes and Barry Z. Posner, *The Leadership Challenge: How to Get Extraordinary Things Done in Organizations* (San Francisco: Jossey-Bass, 1995), 167.

When Yaski, the young adult group mentioned earlier in this chapter, first formed, each leader took it upon him- or herself to invite other young adults to join the group, and soon the ministry grew: from twenty or thirty people a week to forty, then sixty and seventy. Instead of one or two small faith-sharing groups, four or five ran simultaneously. Young adults began attending from all over the region, and soon several hundred young adults were on the mailing list. The team made it standard practice for Yaski to send all current and future team members through a leadership training program. This guaranteed Yaski a pool of qualified leaders with the skills and confidence to fulfill the core team role.

None of the original core team members are involved in Yaski today. At this writing, the organization has undergone several complete changes in core team leadership and is stronger than ever. And an even more interesting outcome of this investment in leadership training is what happened to those former members. More than half moved into other leadership roles in their parishes and dioceses: as pastoral council members, stewardship committee members, evangelization coordinators, religious education teachers, service coordinators, lectors, and extraordinary ministers of Holy Communion, to name a few. The Church has a whole new generation of Catholic leaders who, in keeping with their vocation, are influencing parish and public life and directing it to the common good.

The Catholic Church today is dealing with major challenges and transitions. As he did two thousand years ago, God has sent gifted people—many of them young adults—to lead Catholic communities in dealing with these challenges and in helping his people grow closer to him. The challenge and opportunity for parish leaders is to recognize these young adults and to invite them to do what God created them to do.

THE CAMPUS CONNECTION

One of the purposes of higher education is to prepare the future leaders of society. This includes the future leaders of the Catholic Church. At Catholic colleges and at secular institutions, campus ministers have long considered it a priority to nurture the development of well-trained, faith-filled leaders for both the secular and religious spheres. As we progress into the third millennium of Christianity, committed Catholic Christians are needed for leadership positions at the parish, diocesan, and national levels of the Church. Today, Catholic campus ministries have an unparalleled opportunity to form and train leaders who not only lead on campus, but who will eventually lead within a parish community.

Campuses have employed a variety of models in training students to be leaders. Most models include theological education, leadership skills training, and mentoring of students in leadership positions. The Catholic Campus Ministry Association has recognized one such model for its exemplary quality: the Christian Leadership Program at Corpus Christi University Parish at the University of Toledo. The goal of the Christian Leadership Program is to prepare leaders for the Church and society who are solidly grounded in Catholic tradition.

The Christian Leadership Program offers theological education, leadership training, and spiritual formation over a four-year period. Each year a committee selects twelve students who receive scholarship assistance for their participation. The students are required to take special classes and to assume leadership positions. During the first year, students must meet certain requirements to continue in the program, including being active in the parish, participating in at least one parish-sponsored retreat and lecture, and completing a credit course in contemporary theology. In the second year of the program, students learn how to use the Bible, the documents of Vatican II, and the *Catechism of the Catholic Church* to respond to contemporary issues. Later in the year, they learn leadership skills from experts in the field. The third- and fourth-year students assume leadership positions and write theological reflection papers on their activities. The campus ministry staff helps the Christian Leadership Program to build the skills of these future leaders in a variety of ways. They help students learn to be leaders through peer ministry programs, invite graduating students to serve for a year as ministry assistants, and encourage students to take leadership positions in student government and other groups on campus.

Similarly, the Institute for Catholic Leadership at Southwest Missouri State University seeks to enhance students' knowledge of the Catholic faith as well as their ability to articulate their faith to their peers. The goal of the Institute is to train leaders not only for campus ministry but for future leadership in parishes. Students who participate in the Institute attend monthly sessions on a variety of theological topics such as spirituality, human sexuality, social justice, and liturgy. Institute participants are expected to write monthly reflection papers on the topics. Student interns are chosen by the Institute staff based on the quality of their participation in the Institute, and they receive scholarship assistance.

The Newman Center at the University of Pennsylvania uses a weekend retreat as its leadership training for student leaders. Penn students have participated in the Leaders Experiential Adventure Program (LEAP) of the Catholic Leadership Institute in Philadelphia for a number of years. LEAP affects students on many levels. It is a retreat experience that powerfully and effectively focuses on all the dimensions of Christian leadership. During the retreat weekend, students consider, discuss, and act on their relationship with Jesus Christ. They focus on the importance of a faith community on campus. They learn to discern and commit to their personal mission as well as to the mission of the Catholic community on campus. They identify their leadership skills and learn to work together effectively as members of the Church. By the conclusion of the program, the student leaders recognize that they are empowered to be disciples of Jesus Christ, and they appreciate all the grace and responsibility that discipleship implies. The staff at the Newman Center believes that the LEAP Weekend has had an incredible impact on its ministry program. As more students have participated in the LEAP training, many more have also become active in the Newman Center on the Penn campus.

Throughout the country, examples abound of peer ministers providing strong and powerful leadership on college campuses. These young adults serve as student leaders of retreat teams (for their peers and younger youth), as leaders of service programs (especially alternative spring break programs), and in a variety of other campus ministry programs.

One of the challenges for the Catholic Church is to connect these leaders back to a parish community once they graduate from college. Too often, young adults with strong leadership skills and a healthy spiritual life find it difficult to enter into a new parish community. This can happen because the young adults do not make themselves known to the parish community by registering, volunteering to help, or sharing their gifts. Sometimes, a parish community also neglects to welcome or invite the participation of young adults. Over time, these talented young adults find other avenues for their leadership, and the parish community loses a great gift. To prevent this loss, campus ministers can follow some of the suggestions found in Chapter 5, "Community Life and Pastoral Care," to help graduating students connect with communities off campus where they can continue to develop as leaders.

CHAPTER NINE

Justice and Service with Young Adults

How can parishes engage young adults in the works of justice and service that the Church promotes? Through the stories of young adults, this chapter focuses on inviting young adults into service, engaging them in understanding Catholic social teaching, and challenging them to be a voice for the voiceless. The chapter also explores opportunities for inviting young adults to embrace a spirituality of justice and offers ideas for lifestyle changes that can help young adults— and all parishioners—show solidarity with the poor and vulnerable.

Young adults become effective agents of God's mercy, compassion, and justice when they are educated and empowered to live their baptismal call. The authors of *Profetas de Esperanza* recommend that the Church embrace the energy of all young people.[1] When they are well equipped and well guided, young adults have the creativity and commitment to transform society according to the ideals of the Reign of God. They can passionately affirm Dr. Martin Luther King Jr.'s message in his 1963 letter from the Birmingham jail: "injustice anywhere is a threat to justice everywhere. . . . [and] whatever affects one directly, affects all indirectly."[2]

In the Church today, young adults constitute a greatly underserved population. Yet their gifts and perspectives can contribute to the full expression of the Church's understanding of social justice. Young adults can connect parish communities with persons who might otherwise be difficult to reach, and they can share the Good News in fresh, new ways. As the first generations to grow up amidst widespread diversity and a sense of the world as a "global village," young adults can help older Catholics to see intolerance, greed, racism, and other social problems through a new lens. At the same time, because young adults tend to have great idealism and passion, they are often less settled in

1   See Alejandro Aguilera-Titus, Carlos Carrillo, Pedro Castex, Carmen Cervantes, Juan Diaz-Vilar, SJ, and
      Juan Huitrado, MCCJ, *Profetas de Esperanza*, vol. 1, *La Juventud Hispana y la Respuesta Pastoral de la Iglesia*
      (Winona, MN: St. Mary's Press, 1994), 22.
2   Martin Luther King Jr., "Letter from a Birmingham Jail," April 16, 1963, *www.thekingcenter.org/prog/non/
      Letter.pdf*.

their own views or life choices than are older adults and may have yet to commit to vocation, career choices, family life, or home ownership. Thus, they are also ripe for reflecting, with the Church's help, on how Jesus calls them to live their own lives so as to build the right relationships as modeled throughout the Gospels.

To invite and retain young adults' participation in social-justice activities, parishes need to reach out to young adults, offer education and reflection on social justice, and then provide chances to develop leadership skills for acting on the information. Many parish and diocesan young adult ministries do include an outreach component but offer little opportunity for reflection or education on Catholic social teaching. Others encourage service or giving but do not participate in or provide many programs that address the root causes of injustice. Parishes that are responsive to young adults' desire for service offer opportunities that include justice education, action, and advocacy. Their programs incorporate perspectives on international as well as domestic peace and justice.

Parishes that take seriously this challenge to include young adults in social justice work would do well to review the work of Ministry with Young Adults: A National Catholic Initiative ("the Initiative"), particularly the compiled list of ten elements that young adults look to the Church to provide (see Chapter 1 of this book, "Creating a Young Adult–Responsive Church").[3] The young adult–responsive parish can provide two of the critical elements on the list by connecting young adults with the justice tradition of the Catholic Church: (1) inspiration, and (2) opportunities for leadership and service. In the listening sessions of the Initiative, many young adults identified living the gospel call to service as the key conversion experience in their lives. The challenge of Catholic social teaching and of Catholic Tradition can inspire and embolden today's young adults, who reject the temptation of cynicism and jaded tolerance toward the world's injustices.

---

3   See Ron Bagley, CJM, John Roberto, and Joan Weber, *Becoming a Young Adult Responsive Church* (Naugatuck, CT: Center for Ministry Development [CMD], 1997), 12.

INSPIRING YOUNG ADULTS THROUGH
THE CHURCH'S VISION OF JUSTICE

To invite young adults to pursue justice, parishes need to connect them with the Catholic vision of justice: a vision that involves working with the poor (not just for them), addressing long-term issues of injustice, and building intentional relationships with the disadvantaged and vulnerable. In their pastoral plan for young adult formation, *Sons and Daughters of the Light*, the Catholic bishops of the United States call Catholic leaders "to invite young adults, through healthy relationships, work, and studies, to embrace the mission of Christ to promote the building of the kingdom of God in the world today, thereby bringing about the transformation of society."[4] The bishops ask Catholic parishes, organizations, and movements to join them "in connecting young adults with the church . . . [and to] welcome young adults and allow them adequate opportunities to participate and lead."[5]

In light of the bishops' vision, the young adult–responsive parish provides education for justice that links love of God with love of neighbor through an approach rooted in Catholic social teaching, Scripture, and Tradition. Effective education for justice is transformative, changing the hearts and attitudes of those it reaches; it leads to action that addresses both immediate needs and long-term social problems.

The Vital Role of the Parish in Formation for Justice

Many young adults live their commitments to charity and justice outside the parish community because they do not see the parish as a community that provides ongoing formation: that will not only continually challenge them to deepen their faith but will also connect them to more young adults in order to build community. Nor do they perceive the parish to be a community that invites and welcomes them to lead.

Social-justice leaders in the parish can play a crucial role in encouraging young adults to see the parish as a place to acquire the ongoing formation and critical reflection skills necessary to take effective, faithful action in their own lives and communities. Parishes that want to connect young adults with justice can begin with two great resources on parish social ministry issued by

---

4   United States Conference of Catholic Bishops (USCCB), *Sons and Daughters of the Light: A Pastoral Plan for Ministry with Young Adults* (Washington, DC: USCCB, 1996), 36.

5   *Sons and Daughters of the Light*, 49.

the Catholic bishops of the United States: *Communities of Salt and Light: Reflections on the Social Mission of the Parish* and its accompanying *Parish Resource Manual*.[6] Many of the suggestions in the *Parish Resource Manual* particularly appeal to young adults: such as connecting the homily with ways to live justice in daily life, offering brief explanations of Catholic social teaching in the Sunday bulletin, and generally finding ways to weave justice into the fabric of parish life, so that the Catholic community truly "walks its talk" about justice and service.

Responsive parishes know that young adults bring an appreciation for community and authentic relationships to their encounters with justice. These parishes provide young adults with time to get to know others, to celebrate together, and to enter into the context of community in which the Catholic social mission can be conveyed.

In addition, many young adult Catholics value and seek intergenerational, inclusive communities where many cultures are represented. If those in parish leadership all come from the same culture and are middle-aged or retirement-aged only, young adults will continue to perceive parish leaders as people who do not share their daily experiences, who may not understand their backgrounds, and who therefore may not welcome their participation. Parishes that are responsive to young adults instead tap into many different cultural traditions for prayer, worship, and leadership to engage young adults more deeply in the universality of the Church.

Connecting Service and Faith Through Catholic Social Teaching

Capturing the hearts of young adults includes linking love of God with love of neighbor in the context of Church Tradition and the body of Catholic social teaching. According to research reported in *Young Adult Catholics*, "while young adult Catholics rank social justice high in what they regard as essential to their faith, the relationship between social justice and a specifically Catholic identity remains unclear" to them.[7] Young adults may have learned to care for people in poverty or may be concerned with protecting human life, but they may not grasp Catholic social teaching as a body of wisdom

---

6   See USCCB, *Communities of Salt and Light: Reflections on the Social Mission of the Parish* (Washington, DC: USCCB, 1994); USCCB, *Communities of Salt and Light: Parish Resource Manual* (Washington, DC: USCCB, 1994).

7   Dean R. Hoge, William D. Dinges, Mary Johnson, SND DeN, and Juan L. Gonzales Jr., *Young Adult Catholics: Religion in the Culture of Choice* (Notre Dame, IN: University of Notre Dame Press, 2001), 27.

or as a tool for real-life application. Furthermore, although "social justice is perceived by most young-adult Catholics as a necessary part of their faith . . . few are involved, and few have knowledge or understanding of the tradition in this regard. . . . 53 percent of young adult Catholics think that the Church should stick to religion and not be involved in economic or political issues."[8] Later in *Young Adult Catholics*, the authors suggest that "if the relationship between social justice and a specifically Catholic identity were more immediate to young adult Catholics, their perspective might be more concerned with structural approaches, aggregate effects, power, and institutional systems."[9]

The social teachings of the Catholic Church, grounded in the Scriptures, and the Tradition of these teachings as lived out in the Body of Christ, help young adults to make the connection between social justice and a Catholic identity. Catholic social teaching gives young adults a "road map" for how to look at the signs of the times and use their faith to reflect and act on them. From Pope Leo XIII's 1891 encyclical *Rerum Novarum* (with its commentary on capitalism and the condition of labor),[10] to the USCCB's quadrennial statement on faithful citizenship (with its teaching about the political issues that face contemporary voters in the United States),[11] to Pope Benedict XVI's 2009 encyclical *Caritas in Veritate* (on the principle of charity in love as a guide to social justice)[12]—young adults can be assured of the Church's guidance in dealing with complex issues. The Church speaks through these resources, calling young adults, and all Catholics, to live their faith by acting on behalf of and in solidarity with those who are poor and vulnerable.

Parishes that are responsive to young adult Catholics' hunger to learn more about this Tradition seek to connect young adults with ways to live in keeping with Catholic social teaching—especially in matters that affect their everyday choices (e.g., purchasing habits, environmental impact, sharing of resources). This connection can be seen in the reflections of Nora O'Brien, a former intern for the Catholic Campaign for Human Development (CCHD) of the United States Conference of Catholic Bishops (USCCB): "I enjoyed learning about the difference between justice and charity work . . . [and] about

---

8   *Young Adult Catholics*, 166.
9   *Young Adult Catholics*, 224.
10   See Pope Leo XIII, *On Capital and Labor* (*Rerum Novarum*) (1891), www.vatican.va/holy_father/leo_xiii/encyclicals/documents/hf_l-xiii_enc_15051891_rerum-novarum_en.html.
11   The USCCB issues a faithful citizenship statement every four years, just before each U.S. presidential election season, to help voters discern the impact of Catholic social teaching on political issues; see *FaithfulCitizenship.org* for more information.
12   See Pope Benedict XVI, *Charity in Love* (*Caritas in Veritate*) (Washington, DC: USCCB, 2009).

Catholic social teaching. Although the values discussed in the [CCHD] material seem intuitive, I had never linked them directly to Catholicism before. Knowing that the Church is so devoted to social justice has deepened my faith."[13]

One way parishes can increase young adults' awareness of the relationship between the Church's social mission and the Church's teachings is to offer resources that young adult small faith-sharing groups can use in order to focus on the social teachings of the Church—or resources for parishes to start such groups, if they do not already exist. Since faith-sharing groups appeal to young adults (especially if they are flexible in location, size, and schedule) and can be led by young adults, Catholic social teaching can be shared very effectively through such groups. The binder series *Young Adult Works*,[14] from the Center for Ministry Development (CMD), includes several fully developed sessions for young adults on justice issues. Using the pastoral circle process,[15] the sessions engage young adults in each issue, invite them to analyze the issue, guide their reflection on the issue from a perspective of faith, and encourage them to choose a course of action they can pursue to eliminate the injustice. The sessions assume that the group leaders are young adults, and the resource provides all information, methods, and handouts needed to set the leaders up for success. Scripture and Catholic social teachings are embedded in each of these sessions. Other organizations, including CCHD and the Ministry Center for Catholic Community in Seattle, Washington, also offer faith-sharing booklets and other resources that focus on Catholic social principles and teachings.

One strategy that emphasizes the importance of formation in Catholic social teaching is to organize a JustFaith small group in the parish. A program for all adults, JustFaith[16] is a conversion-based process that seeks to help participants integrate personal spirituality and social ministry. For thirty weeks, JustFaith groups meet weekly, using books, videos, lecture, discussion, prayer, retreats, and hands-on experiences to educate and form themselves in the rich, remarkable justice tradition of the Church. The program aims to empower participants to develop a passion for justice and to express this passion in concrete acts of social ministry.

---

13   Nora O'Brien, *CCHD Intern Final Report* (unpublished report, 2003).
14   See *Young Adult Works*, ed. Ronald Bagley, CJM, John Roberto, Susan Stark, and Joan Weber (Naugatuck, CT: CMD, 1997).
15   The pastoral circle process follows four steps: involve, explore, reflect, and act. See *www.youngneighbors. org/features.cfm?i=3* for a brief explanation of this process.
16   Contact JustFaith Ministries directly by visiting *www.justfaith.org* or calling (502) 429-0865.

Fostering a Spirituality of Justice

Helping young adults to connect their passion for justice with their Catholic identity is one step toward fostering a spirituality of justice. Fr. Ron Rolheiser, in his book *The Holy Longing*, describes social justice as one of the four non-negotiable pillars of a balanced spirituality.[17] He also points out that "in the Christian scriptures, one out of every ten lines deals directly with the physically poor and the call from God for us to respond to them."[18] Young adults respond to this message with passion. The Church has the opportunity to help young adults understand that justice really is a virtue—a good habit—that is essential to being a disciple of Jesus.

As young adults explore jobs and career, start families, and develop community, many yearn to see profound meaning in their lives. Referring to his friends who were on the corporate track, a young man from Philadelphia who was interviewed for this chapter said, "Many did everything right. They might even have a steady paycheck now, and yet they are not happy, not fulfilled." Social ministers, he said, "can capitalize on their hunger for meaning . . . and attract them by sharing how engaging in social justice provides meaning— the meaning of the mission of Jesus Christ—and how satisfying it is to get outside yourself."[19]

Parish social ministers can be catalysts for young adults to consider a spirituality of giving or faithful stewardship. Parishes can reach out to and engage young adults who hunger for meaning by offering an evening of reflection on *Stewardship and Young Adults: An Invitation to Help Change the World*, a statement of the USCCB.[20] The questions at the end of *Stewardship and Young Adults* can prompt in-depth conversations among young adults regarding the way they share their time, talent, and treasure as people of faith.

"*Carpe diem*" (the Latin phrase meaning "seize the day") is a great principle for parishes to follow when engaging young adults in justice. Many parishes have been successful in gathering young adults spontaneously to discuss particular justice issues when they appear in the news. For example, get young adults together to talk about morally defensible war when armed conflict breaks out, or to discuss capital punishment when that issue arises in current events. Such informal gatherings can help young adults to probe their

---

17   Ronald Rolheiser, *The Holy Longing* (New York: Doubleday, 1999), 53, 167.
18   *The Holy Longing*, 64.
19   Interview with the authors (Washington, DC, December 12, 2003).
20   See USCCB, *Stewardship and Young Adults: An Invitation to Help Change the World* (Washington, DC: USCCB, 2004).

own positions on the issues in light of the Gospel and the Church's teachings. In this way, young adults can address global issues of injustice, not only national and local ones.

Still another way in which effective parishes connect young adults with the Church's spirituality of justice is to take time in liturgy and community events to commemorate saints and martyrs whose lives and witness embody the Church's social teachings and inspire young adult parishioners to live prophetically in the world today. This can also serve to recognize and honor the Catholic history of various cultures represented in the community. For example, if older Hispanic/Latino parishioners remember encounters with heroic figures like Archbishop Oscar Romero or Fr. Miguel Pro, perhaps they could pass on these vital community memories to young adults by sharing the stories. An example of such sharing took place in a commemorative celebration at Creighton University on the anniversary of Archbishop Romero's death, March 24. In addition to personal testimony, the event also included a liturgy, meal, and presentation of the film *Romero*. This idea could be adapted for events exploring the work of the groups of martyrs in Nagasaki (St. Paul Miki and followers) or Uganda (St. Charles Lwanga and companions)—while they are no longer in living memory, their examples still nourish the Catholic identity of many.

ENCOURAGING YOUNG ADULTS
TO LIVE JUST LIVES

Young adults are as diverse as all of society. Some are desperately poor, while others struggle with unemployment or underemployment. Many other young adults work in well-paying jobs. Most are facing new life decisions and can easily become absorbed by who and what society thinks they should be—instead of who and what God is calling them to be. Parishes that are responsive to young adults help them to see that spirituality of justice includes making the decisions of everyday life in the light of faith.

For example, decisions about purchasing clothes have global ramifications. Consider inviting speakers from a sweatshop awareness campaign to educate young adults about the conditions in which their purchases were created, whom their purchases affect, and what they can do to positively enhance the work environment and uphold the dignity of workers.

Parish leaders might similarly present personal use of the Earth's resources—like water, electricity, natural gas, and fuel—as an issue of justice. Leaders of discussion groups might encourage young adults to monitor how much water they use (for example, while showering or brushing teeth), to re-evaluate where and how often they drive, and to think of other ways they can reduce their consumption.

Responsible stewardship of finances is yet another lifestyle consideration in which the Church can interest young adults. Many young adults are already making decisions about how to invest their money in stocks, bonds, and retirement plans. Others are more concerned with budgeting from month to month or even week to week. A program that appeals to all parishioners, but especially young adults, might offer practical ideas and skills for how to spend, save, and invest in ways that reflect gospel values and the Church's social teachings on economics.

When interviewed about justice and stewardship, a young woman in Philadelphia commented, "Young adults are at an age where you want all the good things in life, don't want to question your lifestyle, and yet this is the time when you are forming the lifestyle that will determine the rest of your life." In addition to encouraging young adults to critique their own lifestyles and habits, parishes might work to increase young adults' understanding that individuals have many options for committing acts of charity and justice that go far beyond their checkbooks.

Career Challenges

Young adults have grown up in a society where one of the decisive career-discernment questions is, "How much does this job pay?" Imagine the transformation that could take place if parishes invited young adults to ask the following countercultural questions about their professional lives in the light of justice and faith:

- What gifts and talents do I have to help change the world and make it better for everyone?
- What does the world need me to do?
- What would Jesus do if he were me?

Effective parish leaders help young adults to become people of justice in any career and at any pay rate. Many lawyers who make a good living also do

pro bono work; doctors and nurses volunteer their time and talent by offering free medical treatment in developing countries. Effective leaders celebrate
young adults who share their gifts in this way. They also provide resources for
linking such service with young adults' Catholic faith.

Many young adults have been "ruined for life"—as the Jesuit Volunteer
Corps so aptly puts it—by committing to a year or two of dedicated service
with the poor and marginalized. As a result, these young adults no longer buy
into advertising that tells them the way to happiness is through material pos-
sessions. Parishes can support such commitment and conversion by display-
ing copies of *Connections* and *Response*[21] (booklets from the Catholic Network
of Volunteer Service that list one- or two-year service opportunities sponsored
by religious communities and other faith-based organizations) in the parish
library. Or leaders could simply give copies to each young adult who is searching for a meaningful way to live out his or her commitment to justice.

PROVEN STRATEGIES FOR RECRUITING
YOUNG ADULTS FOR SERVICE

Effective parishes go beyond providing young adults with formation in Catholic social teaching. Parishes that are responsive to young adults' desire for
service include young adults as an integral part of the parish's social ministry committee and as leaders in its social justice activities. Towards this end,
responsive parish leaders consider why young adult participation and leadership is so important, how to identify and recruit interested young adult leaders, and how to retain the interest and involvement of young adults in the
parish's social ministry.

The binder series *Young Adult Works* offers many resources that young
adults and those who minister with them can use to foster meaningful calls to
service. The "Justice and Service" section[22] has a template that young adults
can use to create and implement service projects, ensuring a solid and successful service experience. This resource also includes a "Young Adult Guide
to Service"[23] that can be personalized, modified, copied, and distributed to
young adults (both those who do and those who do not attend group programs in the parish) to help them connect justice and service to everyday

21   For more information on these publications, visit the Catholic Network of Volunteer Service at
      www.cnvs.org.
22   See "Justice and Service," in *Young Adult Works*, Binder 5, 11.19-11.20.
23   See "Young Adult Guide to Service," in *Young Adult Works*, Binder 5, 1-35.

life. The guide asks tough questions that put young adults in touch with their motives for service and develop their awareness of the broader dimensions of being people of justice in the world.

Engaging young adults in social-justice efforts can increase their success and expand the leadership pool for justice ministry. But parishes that are responsive to young adults go above and beyond when inviting more young adults to participate. In Virginia Beach, Virginia, for example, facilitators of a JustFaith group saw concrete results when they reached out to and personally invited young adults.[24] In an interview, the facilitators recalled one young adult who was searching for answers and who found in JustFaith a community with which she connected and in which she could explore Catholic social teaching and its application to her life. JustFaith provided an opportunity for her to delve deeper into Catholic social teaching and its relevance to her justice efforts. Other social-justice leaders might ask how this JustFaith group was able to recruit Catholics in their twenties and thirties to join this intense nine-month formation program, when many leaders sometimes struggle to get young adults just to show up for a visit to the soup kitchen or to write a form letter to their congressperson. In this case, the key to success was the leaders' intentional invitations to young adults, which grew from the recognition that the community would be enhanced by the young adults' gifts and perspectives.

Social-justice leaders can also engage young adults through intentional recruitment strategies. For example, a young adult who helped CCHD to plan Brake the Cycle events[25] in Chicago, Illinois, described in an e-mail interview how she became involved. Her story identifies strategies that others have found effective time and again: offering young adults a personal invitation from a supportive community, and involving them in the accomplishment of specific common goals.

> I did not seek out CCHD. I was asked to attend a meeting (and I made [my friend] come with me). Once we were there, we were so impressed with everyone that we wanted to be a part of it. When [the CCHD director] and other committee members asked us for our help, we tried as best we could. They gave us tasks, asked for our

---

24   See Marisol Hugo, Victor Hugo, and Gina Kelley, phone interview with the authors (December 16, 2003).

25   The Catholic Campaign for Human Development (CCHD) hosted a bicycle journey across the United States in summer 2003. Two dozen volunteer cyclists, one-third of whom were young adults, traveled to dioceses and parishes throughout the United States to raise awareness about poverty in the United States and to engage Catholics in CCHD's mission of breaking the cycle of poverty in America.

input, and offered any help they could. A lot of young people we know have the desire to be involved. They just get a little lazy when it actually comes down to it (myself included). Clear and direct pleas for involvement (and pressure to follow up) will get results. Ask for help, and then be ready to answer the question, "What do you want me to do?"[26]

The next subsections provide other concrete ideas that help parishes to identify prospective young adults to recruit and to determine how best to recruit them.

Whom to Invite

- Approach and invite current young adult leaders in parish and diocesan young adult ministries, and ask them to identify other young adults who have shown an interest in service and justice.
- Ask older adult leaders to invite their young adult children.
- Identify former long-term volunteers from programs such as Jesuit Volunteer Corps (*www.jesuitvolunteers.org*) or Mercy Volunteer Corps (*www.mercyvolunteers.org*) in your parish to take leadership roles in new justice initiatives.
- Identify Catholic college alumni and former participants of Newman centers who live in your parish and who have the leadership skills needed to organize justice and service projects. Strong commitments to justice that begin during the college years often continue after graduation. Some young adults seek post-graduate volunteer work, choose professions in the Church, or work for other non-profit organizations so that they can stay close to the pivotal and formative experience of their college years. These young adults can and should be tapped for leadership in the parish's social mission.
- Connect with ministries that serve particular cultural groups in order to identify and invite young adult Catholics from a range of backgrounds. Remember that many young adults in the United States, particularly immigrants, have personally experienced injustice. These young adults may have a clearer vision and more immediate awareness of what is needed in social-justice work,

---

26   Response to e-mail survey (December 16, 2003).

since they themselves or their friends and families may be part of underserved populations.

Effective social-justice leaders are aware of the various forms of oppression and discrimination that many immigrant groups have experienced—for example, widespread neglect by fellow Catholics; exploitative immigrant-worker programs; ongoing struggles to gain access to safe work, just wages, and quality education that respects culture and language; and fights to fend off predatory lending and other unscrupulous and discriminatory practices in housing, employment, the justice system, health care, and social services. Pastoral work today is most effective when it not only ministers to those who are suffering but invites and empowers them to be agents of God's justice in their own communities.

Young adults who have a personal stake in a social justice issue can become powerful leaders for that cause, especially when they or their families or communities have experienced injustice. As an example, a college student from Cleveland, Ohio, whose mother is from El Salvador and whose father is Native American, expressed interest in Creighton University's El Salvador Immersion. She was not able to travel at that time, so instead she participated in a low-cost service trip to a Native American reservation over spring break. She chose a reservation where she would have an opportunity to learn more about native culture and spirituality. She became active both in the Native American Student Association and in the Latino Student Association. The following year she was invited to lead a spring-break service trip, which required her to commit to several months of attending formation and organizational meetings, taking responsibility on committees, and leading all aspects of her group's trip, from finances to reflection. She discovered that she had many skills for service, justice, community, and reflection. In her senior year, she chose to coordinate a trip that allowed her to use her knowledge of Spanish and learn from Hispanic/Latino immigrants of the Pilsen neighborhood in Chicago. In addition to leadership in the spring-break service trips, she became involved in the Latino Student Association's ongoing local community service of tutoring adults who are learning English at the local high school at night after working all day. She also wrote for the school newspaper, often contributing articles about justice issues.

How to Invite

Identifying likely social-justice leaders among young adults is only the first step towards recruitment. How the parish invites these leaders is equally as important.

- *Invite young adults personally.* A direct approach that is tailored to the individual and his or her gifts and interests has proven to be the most effective means of recruiting young adults. Personal invitation by a peer has proven especially effective. When surveyed for this chapter, many young adults responded that they had first become involved in social-justice work because a friend or family member invited them to participate.
- *Start small and expand.* As the director of CCHD for Chicago, social-justice leader Elena Segura has successfully convinced young adults to make long-term commitments to serve on the archdiocesan social-justice committee by first offering them experience in planning a one-time creative event.
- *Capture their imaginations.* Use movies, music, podcasts, or television as starting points for group discussions of Catholic social teaching and issues of injustice.
- *Use issues relevant to their lives.* Some issues appeal to all young adults. Others are particularly appealing to people because of a personal connection. A discussion of a developing country, for instance, is likely to attract young adults who themselves come from such a country. One young adult Filipina in the Diocese of Oakland became aware of the connection between her passion for justice and her Catholic identity when she worked to clean up the environment in the Philippines, left neglected after decades of use by the American military. She came to understand the relationships between colonialism, Catholicism, and environmentalism; after her experience, she traveled around the United States to educate Filipino American communities.

  To draw the attention of African American young adults, the United States Conference of Catholic Bishops (USCCB) proposes addressing problems relating to economic issues, such as unemployment (especially among black youth), substandard housing, homelessness, and general public assistance.[27] The bishops also recommend that communities address issues relevant to Hispanic/Latino young adults: "a commitment to social justice is one of the pillars of Hispanic ministry. This commitment should involve ongoing formation on Catholic social teaching and collaboration on advocacy and public policy issues. Issues of immigration, education, human rights, border concerns, voter registration, and dialogue with labor union leaders are all issues relevant to the Hispanic community."[28] In short, when a social-justice program aims to resolve issues that particularly affect a community or a culture, young adults who identify with that community or culture will desire to be part of the solution.

OPPORTUNITIES FOR LEADERSHIP AND SERVICE

Parish ministers can encourage young adults to apply their natural gifts in the parish's social ministries by offering formation and leadership development for young adults and by including young adults in leadership positions. In all this, it is key to recognize that young adults are hungry to be of service. Parishes do not need to try to motivate young adults—they can simply provide opportunities to serve and then personally invite the young adults to take those opportunities.

Often, young adults already possess the skills needed to develop their own service projects. They may already have participated in Habitat for Humanity builds, campaigns against hunger, and other service projects on campus or at work. The young adult–responsive parish provides a setting where young adults gather and mobilize their peers for service. For example, when one suburban parish in Omaha, Nebraska, publicized service opportunities in the parish bulletin, the young adults in the parish organized themselves and attended as a group. In Philadelphia, Pennsylvania, a young adult group known as Jack's YACs (Young Adult Catholics) at St. John the Evangelist Parish advertised service opportunities for young adults via e-mails that briefly described each activity and how to sign up for it.[29]

---

27   See USCCB, *Here I Am, Send Me: A Conference Response to the Evangelization of African Americans and the National Black Catholic Pastoral Plan* (Washington, DC: USCCB, 1990).

28   USCCB, *Encuentro and Mission: A Renewed Pastoral Framework for Hispanic Ministry* (Washington, DC: USCCB, 2002), no. 50.

29   For more information on Jack's YACs, including contact information, see *www.jacksyacs.com*.

Consider ways to build on the exciting justice work that is being done with and by young adults in Catholic colleges and universities across the country. Many young adult Catholics are first formed in the Church's social teachings through their experiences with campus ministry or service learning projects. As a result, by the time they leave college and enter parish life, many have already committed themselves to action on behalf of justice. They have also learned that being in relationship and working with those who are poor and vulnerable are at the heart of Catholic social teaching. By helping young adults to build on their existing learning and past experiences of working for justice, parishes can contribute to a more just future.

Many young adults want to experience service that accomplishes a clear, meaningful goal within the short term. In particular, some groups of immigrant young adults may wish to serve but may not be able to make long-term commitments because they are in the country on student or work visas. They have no long-term security of residence in the country, and they may not even know how long they will wish to stay. When developing service experiences for such groups, parishes need to focus on short-term opportunities in the beginning, working toward longer ones if and when groups and activities stabilize over time.

For advocacy efforts in particular, education is key. Parishes need to provide young adults with information to make educated choices about being a voice for the voiceless. Many online resources are available at the click of a mouse. Encourage young adults to take the Poverty Tour at *www.povertyusa.org*, for instance. Conduct a brief reflection, or simply offer a quote, on service and justice via e-mail or electronic message board. Pair young adult Catholics with other young adults who are addressing structural injustice in a community-based, faith-based organization.

Sometimes young adults can become overwhelmed trying to figure out the "right" answer or action. When a community of faith reaches out to young adults to solicit their assistance with a social-justice activity, effective social-ministry leaders ease young adults' fears in two main ways—by affirming that young adults are not expected to have the right answer or know everything about everything, and by not overwhelming or overloading them with information or programs. Members of Jack's YACs, the group described earlier in this section, confirmed this need in an interview: "most young adults want to do something and are concerned about people who are poor. But often they are nervous or busy. . . . they think that if they care about one thing, they will have to care about everything."[30]

Effective parishes are also aware that a large single social-justice group may not be the best answer for young adults. Different groups could work separately on small projects and come together for larger ones. Some groups could work on interests unique to particular cultural communities. These projects could not only serve to unite the specific cultural community but could also educate the larger parish community.

Finally, the effort to connect young adults with the parish's social mission can be more successful when the parish has a global perspective. For example, parishes that have a sister parish in a developing country often find that the young adult parishioners have the courage, initiative, and creativity required to develop a meaningful relationship with the sister parish, through which both parishes develop a sense of dignity and hope. Parishes that are part of a legislative network, like the one provided through Catholic Relief Services, give young adults the opportunity to affect public policy through their faith. Parishes that coordinate consistent and ongoing service projects for parishioners of all ages (e.g., taking responsibility to bring and serve the meal at a soup kitchen on a regular weekly or monthly interval) allow young adults to try out parish service and meet other parishioners without making a long-term commitment.

Partnering with Other Organizations

Parishes need not come up with social justice activities alone. Parishes and organizations can partner to make a real, lasting difference for social justice in a way that engages young adults' interest, helps them grow in a spirituality of justice, and gives them opportunities to make a real difference. Effective social-justice leaders in a parish take the time to identify and partner with agencies that serve the many cultures represented in the United States. They know that such partnerships can engage young adults from every background in the Church's work of justice and service.

Opportunities for partnership abound. NETWORK, a Catholic lobbying organization in Washington, D.C., educates people and provides resources for education as it works toward national legislation to promote justice.[31]

---

30   Members of Jack's YACs, interview with the authors (Philadelphia, PA, October 12, 2003).
31   To receive NETWORK's e-mail alerts on legislative issues before Congress, see *www.networklobby.org* and click on "Receive E-mail Updates."

The Center for Ministry Development offers a similar program specifically for young adults, entitled Young Neighbors in Advocacy, which trains young adults in lobbying Congress on issues of justice as people of faith. Some state Catholic conferences organize "Catholic lobby days," when people of all ages gather in their state capitol to advocate for the voiceless on issues that are currently before the state legislature;[32] parishes can help their young adults tap into these opportunities through publicity and related events (such as a dinner afterward to reflect on the day). Finally, parishes can engage young adults by inviting them into campaigns designed to end particular injustices. Coordinating a young adult group to attend the annual March for Life in Washington, D.C., is a prime example; others include participation in sweat-shop campaigns, hunger drives, petitions to end the death penalty, and voter registration efforts.

Parishes might consider partnerships with other organizations spe-cifically to involve young adults of all cultures in justice. For example, the issues addressed by the Urban League, NAACP, or other relevant organiza-tions may connect with African American young adult Catholics. In a concrete example of such partnership, Hispanic/Latino young adults in Omaha, Nebraska, worked together and received support from more than twenty area congregations, including Our Lady of Guadalupe Parish, to obtain soccer fields for the city's Latino Soccer League. The parish priest and pastoral min-isters of the parish attended the meetings of clergy and leaders of the church-based community organization Omaha Together One Community (OTOC). After OTOC obtained the soccer fields, they identified packing-house wages and working conditions as the next issues needing change. With the assis-tance of the Food and Commercial Workers' Union (UFCW) and the support of many church members from around the country, they learned how to orga-nize workplace committees. After two years, they successfully voted in unions and negotiated improved pay and working conditions in three meat-packing plants in Omaha for the first time in more than twenty years.[33]

Today's young adults are especially aware of how policies of the United States government can affect the international community—a social con-sciousness that parishes can tap into, especially through collaboration with

---

32   For more information on the work of state Catholic conferences, visit the National Association of State Catholic Conference Directors (NASCCD) online at *www.nasccd.org*.

33   The bishops of the United States recommend that parishes and dioceses work to educate Hispanic/Latino Catholics about, and involve them in, public policy issues and community organizing. See *Encuentro and Mission*, no. 57.

organizations that work on these issues. Having grown up in a globally aware world, young adults are attracted to evenings of reflection or workshops on the international effects of the nation's choices. The Fair Trade Coffee Program of Catholic Relief Services (CRS) is one great resource for engaging young adults in social ministry.[34] Through the program, young adults can host a coffeehouse evening where fair-trade coffee—coffee for which struggling small-scale farmers earn a fair price for their crops—is served during a discussion of fair-trade issues. Young adults might also promote and sell fair-trade coffee at their parish or in their workplace. Catholic Relief Services has several similar campaigns through which young adults can advocate for the poor and marginalized in the world.[35]

Being Advocates for Social Change in the Long Term

One of the greatest challenges in educating about social justice is the tendency to focus on the short term. Many young adults (as well as older adults) tend to be active in serving the immediate needs of the poor and vulnerable—one time, for one day—but often do not know how to respond to long-term social issues. Justice-oriented solutions require a long process and may not be realized for years to come. Parish leaders who are responsive to young adults' hunger and thirst for justice remind them that they stand on the shoulders of great leaders such as Cesar Chavez, Martin Luther King Jr., and Dorothy Day, all of whom patiently did their part to build a more just world.

Leaders can bridge the short and long terms by pairing a charity-oriented, short-term action with a long-term justice-oriented action or with an opportunity for education and reflection. For example, after coordinating a project in which young adults serve food to the homeless, invite the volunteers to spend time with an empowered low-income leader who is addressing the long-term problem of affordable housing in the community. Include time for writing persuasive letters to the appropriate elected official regarding affordable housing policies. These opportunities enable young adults to build relationships across cultural and economic boundaries.

---

34   For resources, see *www.crsfairtrade.org/coffee*. The CRS Fair Trade Coffee Program aims to assist small-scale farmers by directly marketing fair-trade coffee to more than 65 million Catholics in the United States.

35   See *www.crs.org/act* to check out the various campaigns, advocacy, and fair trade programs in which young adults can participate.

Recruiting Young Adults to Be Justice Mentors

Young adults have reached a stage in life that teenagers dream of reaching. Consequently, they make great mentors for youth—particularly in the arena of justice. Inviting young adults to chaperone a youth service trip, for example, is a win-win for a parish: the youth get great chaperones with whom they can identify, and young adults undergo a transformative experience.

A member of the Initiative staff shared the following story. A woman in her early twenties volunteered to chaperone teenagers from her parish who were attending Young Neighbors in Action, a national Catholic youth service week that combines direct service with justice education. The group traveled to a large metropolitan community to serve the poor. This woman entered into the experience with her whole being—even more than the youth did. She had the passion, the maturity, and the openness to take in the suffering of others, to listen to the Gospel and the social teachings of the Church, and to stand in solidarity with those who are voiceless. She inspired not only the youth but also the program leaders, who were reminded of their own passion for changing the world when they were younger.

CONCLUSION

Sarah Stolfa, a young adult who cycled with the CCHD Brake the Cycle of Poverty Bike Tour, had no idea how an invitation to ride her bike for poverty awareness would change her life and her faith in dramatic ways. Later, she said, "If you give once, you receive a hundred times over. I just agreed to go ride my bike . . . which led me back to my faith. I got to use my talents to do a great photo project," and that "led to trips where I can present my photo project." She also married another cyclist from the trip.[36]

Parishes that are responsive to young adults' desires for a more just world invite young adults into active participation in justice ministry. They provide opportunities for faith-filled reflection, leadership formation, and concrete action within the context of community. Consider how your parish and community can combine these strategies and apply them to your circumstances. Embrace the vision of a community acting in solidarity, and remain open to the guidance of grace in exciting new ways. The task is large and

---

36   Sarah Stolfa, interview with the authors (Washington, DC, December 12, 2003).

takes much reflection, planning, evaluation, and celebration, but when young adults' gifts and perspectives are included, Catholic social ministries will grow and be strengthened. One never knows where an invitation to live out the faith will lead.

THE CAMPUS CONNECTION

Guiding college students to appreciate the Church's rich social tradition can be a challenge. It can also provide the most profound faith experience many young adults will have during their college years. Many college campuses already offer a wealth of programs that create an interface between service and learning. The Church on campus—through campus ministry, a center or curriculum for justice and service, a Newman center, or a local parish—can not only join in these efforts but enhance them with prayer and reflection.

In the basic model of this effort, students learn the social teachings of the Catholic Church by experiencing service and by praying about and reflecting on their experiences under the guidance of campus-ministry leaders. Actual service projects may vary from community to community. Some campus ministries offer ongoing programs for tutoring local students, volunteering at local soup kitchens and senior centers, or participating in local advocacy efforts on pro-life, environmental, or labor issues. For example, during a $25 million capital campaign, the St. Thomas More Catholic Center at Yale University dedicated a portion of the new building to hospitality toward the poor in their midst, in the form of a weekly soup kitchen.

Many students are drawn to alternative programs that take them off campus, sometimes out of the country, during their winter and spring breaks. These opportunities give them a concentrated experience of service. One such opportunity is the Social Justice/Guatemala Immersion Program of the St. Philip Neri Newman Center at the University of Tulsa. This trip includes both educational and service immersion components. The educational component consists of six weeks of study on the themes expressed in the Church's teachings on social justice. The topics covered include the dignity of the human person, community and the common good, the option for the poor, and the dignity of work. The course also includes information about the historical and political situation in Guatemala and the life of Fr. Stanley Rother, a missionary priest from Oklahoma who was murdered while stationed there.

The immersion component of this program reinforces with concrete examples the topics discussed in the classes. While in Guatemala, the students participate in a house-building program sponsored by the local parish. The students work alongside the people of the village and have the opportunity to interact with them on a personal level. They talk with them, learn from them, and come to appreciate them more deeply than they could as mere visitors. In the town, the students work with children in the parish school, meet the parish staff, and tour the various ministries that the parish provides to its congregation. In this context, the Church's social-justice teachings come to life. The principle of solidarity is transformed from a concept to a reality for students who work shoulder to shoulder with local construction workers, parish staffers, teachers, and day laborers. Personally witnessing poverty and experiencing the disparity in the social classes brings home the importance of human dignity and the Church's special consideration for the poor. After this experience, students in the program often realize how much they take for granted their opportunities for decent health care, proper education, and proper employment. They begin to recognize the overwhelming impact such opportunities could have on the lives of people who are not so fortunate.

Participating in the faith life of Guatemalan parishes also allows the group to experience the universality of the Church. This experience has had a profound effect on students who have never left the United States before. The trip organizers make a conscious effort to provide time for prayer and reflection on each day of the trip, in order to help each person process the day's experiences. As a result, students feel the effects of their journey long after their return home. Several students who have participated in the trip have gone on to volunteer for national and international missionary programs following college. Also, students who traveled on the Guatemala trip have increased their participation in the St. Philip Neri Newman Center. Some have even continued to participate in these ministries after they have graduated and moved into local parishes.

At Iowa State University, St. Thomas Aquinas Church and Catholic Student Center generally takes a more local approach in exposing students to the Catholic Church's perspectives on justice and service. Interested students are invited to join the Service and Justice Team, which is led by a peer minister. The Service and Justice Team takes responsibility for planning and executing a variety of service projects with fellow students. At the beginning of each semester, the team participates in an overnight in-service, which includes theological reflection, social analysis, prayer, training, and planning for specific projects. The team plans service activities for the upcoming year, such as providing meals at a shelter, visiting a nursing home, volunteering at a Boys and Girls Club, building with Habitat for Humanity, assisting with religious education, and tutoring in ESL programs; each project also includes a reflection led by one of the Team members. At the overnight in-service, the Service and Justice Team also plans upcoming educational experiences (e.g., movies on justice, a fast and liturgy to educate about hunger, and a sleep-out on campus in cardboard boxes to raise awareness of homelessness). The Service Team also collaborates with the parish's Charity, Justice and Peace Commission (*www.staparish.net/cjp*). Taken as a whole, this model involves students in service and justice projects and in reflection on Catholic social teaching. It also provides enhanced training and education for the members of the Service and Justice Team.

In addition to providing direct service to the poor, some students participate in advocacy efforts to change political policy, thus addressing social-justice concerns on a systemic level. LeMoyne College, a Jesuit college in Syracuse, New York, has sent busloads of students to Georgia each November to commemorate the anniversary of the murder of six Jesuits from El Salvador in 1989. They have joined other communities from across the country to call for an end to the Western Hemisphere Institute for Security Cooperation (formerly the School of the Americas) in Georgia, where the soldiers who killed the Jesuits were trained by United States forces. In a larger protest, thousands of college students march in Washington, D.C., each January on the anniversary of *Roe v. Wade* to speak out in defense of the rights of the unborn. These examples show how students and pastoral ministers can seize opportunities to put their faith into action.

Inviting young adults into service and social-justice efforts on college campuses and into advanced study will help them work for justice in an increasingly globalized economy and world. Effective campus-ministry leaders do not presume that all students understand or identify with the oppressed communities in the area of their college or university. They recognize the need to learn students' individual backgrounds, interests, and skills in order to awaken students to their calling to justice. Leaders then provide students with opportunities to experience service and solidarity, as well as opportunities to integrate their experiences intellectually and spiritually. As students begin to ask questions and make connections when reflecting on experiences of injustice, effective campus ministers invite them into leadership teams where they will continue to learn, become aware of their strengths and weaknesses, acquire the skills and processes of collaborative leadership, and begin advocating for and with oppressed groups.

CHAPTER TEN

Forming Faith Communities of Young Adults

How can parishes give young adults the sense of community and belonging within the Church for which they yearn? This chapter suggests many ways to form small church communities or small faith-sharing communities of young adults. Using real-life examples from successful young adult groups, this chapter explores the many foundations on which faith sharing can be built—topical interests, cultural background, stage of life—and offers strategies for creating small communities within the larger parish community.

S mall faith-sharing groups and small church communities, in which young adults walk the spiritual journey together, have proven to be an effective way to form young adults in the Catholic faith. The research of Ministry with Young Adults: A National Catholic Initiative ("the Initiative") identified this easy yet powerful strategy as one of the most compelling for young adults and parish leaders alike. More and more, the Church is seeing the positive results of small faith-sharing groups, both intergenerational and age-specific.

THE NEED FOR COMMUNITY

Faith, like spirituality, is a divine perspective on life and an expression of a personal relationship with God based on that perspective. The Letter to the Hebrews (11:1) describes faith as "the realization of what is hoped for and evidence of things not seen." Faith is powerful, but it is also intangible; it can be elusive in solitude and fortified in community.

At the very beginning of Christianity, the followers of Christ gathered in small groups in homes to celebrate and strengthen their faith. Today's young adults seek this same sense of belonging to a community—which is one of the reasons why they keep attending church services and why they will travel great distances to a particular parish that welcomes them. Effective parishes provide opportunities for young adults to come together to see God from the context of their lives, from their own cultures and experiences, and to reach out to him through all that surrounds them.

Small faith-sharing communities provide support for questioning and reaching, while they ground faith in the context of members' experiences. Fr. Bernard J. Lee, SM, in *The Catholic Experience of Small Christian Communities*,[1] identified reasons for why anyone joins small church communities, including social support, the chance to meet new friends, spirituality, and the opportunity to learn more about God and religion. Compare these reasons to three items on the Initiative's top-ten list of what young adults seek from the Church: a sense of community and belonging, spiritual growth and enrichment, and religious education. Clearly, small faith-sharing groups meet some of young adults' top needs. (See Chapter 1 of this book, "Creating a Young Adult–Responsive Church," for the rest of the list.)

As one illustration, the parish community at St. Dominic Church in San Francisco, California, has gathered in small groups to reflect on the Sunday Gospel during Advent and Lent. Seeing a need to form small church communities for its young adult population, the parish specifically invited young adult parishioners to be group facilitators. These group leaders were then trained in conflict resolution, communication skills, and group dynamics so that they felt comfortable in their roles. Because not all of the parish's small faith-sharing communities consisted of only young adult participants, the young adult leaders added input to keep the material responsive to every adult generation's experience.

As another example, when the young adult leadership team of St. Vincent de Paul Parish in San Francisco saw a need for greater community and connection to the Catholic faith, the team created a volunteer position charged with forming small faith-sharing communities. The bi-monthly young adult meetings that already took place were attracting more than eighty people, so the parish responded to young adults' need to gather in smaller groups in order to build personal relationships and talk about their faith in a more intimate setting.

In both examples, the parishes met the need to form small faith-sharing communities for young adults, and they did so within the larger goal of building stronger connections among their parishioners. As the Catholic bishops of the United States describe in their pastoral plan for young adult faith formation, *Sons and Daughters of the Light*,[2] the formation of small church

---

1   Bernard J. Lee, SM, *The Catholic Experience of Small Christian Communities* (New York: Paulist Press, 2000).
2   See United States Conference of Catholic Bishops (USCCB), *Sons and Daughters of the Light: A Pastoral Plan for Ministry with Young Adults* (Washington, DC: USCCB, 1996).

communities with young adults touches upon many aspects of ministry with young adults, including worship, community life, small church communities, evangelization, and committee work in parish ministries and organizations. In *Sons and Daughters of the Light*, the bishops particularly focus on providing opportunities for young adults to gather with people their own age who share their values and beliefs.

Young-adult–responsive parishes work for and with young adults to develop activities and materials that specifically target their developmental needs and that emphasize dialogue and shared communal experiences. In *Sons and Daughters of the Light*, the bishops identify particular developmental tasks of young adulthood that parishes can support: "during our [focus group] meetings, young adults spoke of many concerns, which can be grouped into four key areas: *personal identity*, *relationships*, *work*, and *spiritual life*."[3] Each of these four areas can readily be addressed through small faith-sharing groups that acknowledge the life tasks of young adults through dialogue and an experience of community.

GETTING STARTED

One easy way to start developing small faith-sharing communities is to look for already existing communities with faith as a unifying thread. Encourage existing parish (or even diocesan) groups to expand their meetings or events to include brief times for prayer and faith sharing, either before or after the event. Such groups could include parish ministries that meet regularly (committees, choir, parish council) as well as recreational groups within the parish or diocese: softball teams, worker organizations, environmental action groups, *baile folklórico*, young parents' groups, book clubs, dinner groups, support groups, or groups of professionals such as the Catholic Leadership Institute. Effective parish leaders take the opportunities already present within these communities to deepen their spiritual aspect.

Another approach is to form shorter-term small communities, perhaps in the context of parish pilgrimages, service trips, teams of young adult retreat leaders, peer ministry groups, or parish groups to work on a project with Habitat for Humanity or Amnesty International. Facilitators of these short-term experiences need to make special efforts to get to know and invite young adults, particularly from a variety of cultures. Young adults who have not had

---

3   *Sons and Daughters of the Light*, 8.

much experience with retreats or organized service, either in school or other parishes, would especially benefit from and enrich small groups greatly.

As you consider ways to develop small faith-sharing communities in your parish, reflect on the following questions to assess your parish's opportunities in this effort:

1. Does the parish have ample meeting facilities for meditation or small-group reflection and discussion? If not, does it have access to diocesan or community facilities suitable for such gatherings, perhaps at a neighboring parish? Would parishioners be willing to host small groups in their homes?

2. Does the parish offer retreats, programs, or services that foster faith sharing and cultural awareness? If these offerings are short-term, could participants be encouraged to deepen their connections with each other and the Church through longer-term faith-sharing groups?

3. Do existing parish ministries or recreational groups put Christ at the center of their discussions and actions?

4. Does the parish promote faith formation among young adults of all the cultures represented in the area?

Peers Training Peers

Some young adults have been involved in small church communities for years and are a great resource for identifying opportunities to develop small faith-sharing groups, for training future leaders for the groups, and for promoting the importance of connecting in these smaller groups with other young adults. Parishes can identify these young adults through a survey at Sunday liturgies and then gather them at a convenient time to ask for their help in organizing small church communities.

A coffee-and-doughnuts or wine-and-cheese gathering after a well-attended liturgy or on a weekday evening will entice young adults to attend a meeting. The meeting doesn't have to be elaborate. Efforts to welcome them and invite their collaboration will go a long way toward inspiring them to share their commitment and passion in this ministry. They in turn will attract new people, especially other young adults, better than any promotional tool could. And parish leaders can train them to be group leaders and organizers who will go out and invite others to develop faith-sharing opportunities.

FORMS OF FAITH-SHARING COMMUNITIES

Small faith-sharing communities within the Catholic Church have taken many forms. Parishes that seek to develop new small church communities can benefit from other parishes' successes in forming groups around common activities, interests, and life experiences.

One of the most common types of small faith-sharing communities is the Bible study group. A typical approach is for the group to study the Bible through the lectionary: reading, listening, and reflecting on each Sunday's Gospel to prepare young adults to participate more fully in the liturgy. Young adults connect more fully with the Word and with each other as they relate faith to their everyday life in this setting. After the Initiative, the Center for Ministry Development created a three-volume, lectionary-based resource for small faith-sharing groups of young adults. This resource, *Sharing God's Word Through the Year*,[4] includes real stories from young adults that tie into each Sunday's Gospel, as well as the historical and cultural background needed to fully understand the richness of each Scripture passage.

The Catholic Church is blessed to include many organizations (such as Landings, Disciples in Mission, and RENEW) that provide great resources for forming small church and faith-sharing communities. RENEW International,[5] a group that fosters spiritual renewal by supporting individuals and small communities, offers faith-sharing programs that specifically address the particular life issues and spiritual hungers of young adults. For the 2000 Jubilee Year celebration, RENEW International also provided national momentum for forming small faith-sharing communities. Many parishes sponsored small faith-sharing programs with the resources of RENEW and other organizations. These small communities continue today and have developed into lasting relationships based on shared faith. Continuing to support and acknowledge these communities encourages them to find new ways to connect more deeply with their faith.

The Ministry Center for Catholic Community in Seattle, Washington, has published a variety of six-week topical series for adult faith-sharing groups. Particularly relevant for young adults are the series addressing faith and work, Catholic social teaching, and Christian spirituality. The Ministry Center also

---

4   Ron Bagley, CJM, ed., *Sharing God's Word Through the Year* (Naugatuck, CT: Center for Ministry Development [CMD], 1997-1999).

5   To contact RENEW International, see *www.renewintl.org* or call (908) 769-5400.

publishes six-week Lent and Advent series each year, resources that young adults find meaningful and enriching during these sacred seasons.

Other good resources like *Sunday by Sunday*[6] or *Quest*[7] are geared toward all adults, not young adults exclusively. Many can be adapted effectively to connect young adults with each upcoming Sunday Gospel. Young adults can select the questions that most apply to their lives and explore them in greater depth.

The flexibility and variety of small faith-sharing groups are two of their greatest strengths. The following sections cover a sampling of other ways in which young adults can participate in faith sharing.

Kindred-Spirit Groups: Bonding Within Life Stages

During the young adult years, friendships that developed during adolescence often change. Some relationships deepen as others fade. But new bonds can be forged in much the same way as adolescent bonds: through shared experiences and stages in life.

Many young adults with small children, for example, become friends with parents of other small children through school or community activities, thereby forming small communities for support and information sharing. Parishes can encourage this process by providing opportunities for young parents to gather for discussion of faith and life issues. Groups might consist of mothers only or fathers only, or of couples together.

As another example, career-based faith-sharing groups can focus on participants' jobs, giving members the opportunity to seek together for ways to live an ethical life in their chosen careers and workplaces.

Intergenerational Faith-Sharing Groups

Although connecting young adults to a faith community of their peers is one of the goals of *Sons and Daughters of the Light*, connecting young adults with the whole Catholic community is equally important. Strong intergenerational relationships provide opportunities for engaging in dialogue on critical issues and for sharing stories of faith. Sharing faith across generations helps people of different ages and perspectives to find common ground as people of faith. Older members sometimes serve in a mentoring role because of their wisdom accumulated through years of faithful living. Young adults bring their own

---

6   *Sunday by Sunday* is published weekly by Good Ground Press; see *www.goodgroundpress.com*.
7   *Quest: A Reflection Booklet for Small Christian Communities* is published by the Archdiocese of Hartford, Connecticut; see *www.sccquest.org*.

wisdom, often inspiring older members to look at faith and life in new ways. In genuine faith sharing, the group's relationships involve mutual giving and receiving to identify and develop the unique gifts of each member. Shared responsibility for the group is a core value when forming faith communities of any kind.

Groups Created from Personal Interests

Mutual hobbies and activities can also form the foundation for developing faith-sharing groups of young adults. For example, "Knit One, Pray Too" retreat weekends connect the traditional hobby of knitting, which has become popular again, with discussions of faith in which friends interweave Scripture and prayer. As retreatants enjoy textile arts and learn a traditional skill that addresses the basic needs of clothing and warmth, they reflect on what Scripture says about meeting human needs.

Some parishes provide movie nights in which participants watch popular films and talk about themes of spiritual growth, moral values, and the struggle between good and evil in the world. Most films, even the most secular, can be analyzed for spiritual and moral themes that can then be related to church teaching and daily struggles of faith. Likewise, book clubs offer a great chance to talk about Catholic doctrine in a realistic, supportive environment—especially now, as religious topics continue to crop up in popular fiction.

Many young adults raise money for and awareness about various charitable causes by participating in races, triathlons, and marathons. These endeavors take a lot of training and are accomplished in a supportive community. This setting offers a ready-made opportunity to connect what a parishioner (or group of parishioners) is doing in the name of social justice with Scripture and Catholic faith. For example, the parish can offer prayers for these individuals and gather them before and after the event to reflect on their involvement on behalf of the sick, poor, or marginalized recipients of the funds raised. Participants might begin and end training sessions with prayer. For young adults, this brings faith to a community they have already established and opens a new connection with their parish as a supportive environment in which to share their lives.

Cross-Parish Groups

The Church encompasses communities that practice faith in primary life relationships (families, households, friendships) and in public relationships (parishes, dioceses, campus ministries). For public relationships, as more people attend parishes outside their geographical parish boundaries, or as young adults become scarce in a particular parish, participation in neighboring parishes and dioceses can connect young adults to the universal Church, while small church communities strengthen their commitment to the life of their specific parish community.

As an example of diocese-level participation, the Archdiocese of Chicago Young Adult Ministry promotes diocese-wide small faith-sharing groups at twenty-three parishes in combination with a Lenten reflection series offered at a few locations for those wanting more theological education and deeper Scripture study.

Equally important is equipping young adults to nurture and communicate the faith in their primary life relationships, including those outside the parish community. Young adults lead active lives through careers, hobbies, athletics, and service—all of which can be transformed into faith-sharing opportunities.

Communities Created and Sustained Online

Small faith-sharing communities can also be connected online. While many communities already do this successfully for young adults who are away at college, this type of faith formation need not be limited to college students. E-mail, blogs, social networking sites, and other forums for online outreach are great ways to connect parishioners, especially those young adults who prefer the Internet as a primary form of communication.

St. Bonaventure Parish in the Diocese of Buffalo, in New York, sends an e-mail to its students away at college to commemorate religious holidays. The note contains a connection to a daily prayer Web site produced by the Irish Jesuits or to a spiritual e-card. Similarly, setting up an online chat room may sound impersonal, but for young adults who travel during the week, this may be their only connection to their parish community when they are feeling isolated and homesick.

St. Dominic Parish in San Francisco, California, has a comprehensive Web site with a section for faith formation. This includes information on the parish's established programs, like Landings and RCIA, as well as suggested books, Bible study guides, spirituality, and prayer. While visitors can use many of the resources for solitary formation, the Web site also functions as a chance to encourage individuals to take leadership for forming small church communities in their parish, among their circle of friends, and at work.

Communities for Those Outside the Catholic Community

Many young adults raised in the Catholic faith undergo a period of questioning and searching for true meaning and value in their lives. Sometimes, during this period, they leave the Church or consider themselves to be outside of the Catholic faith. Many of these young adults are actively searching for a more permanent community, which they sometimes find in organized religion. Their search is a significant opportunity for the Catholic Church to invite them back specifically.

Paulist Reconciliation Ministries' Landings program and the Diocese of Buffalo's Quest program are examples of faith-sharing group structures designed to invite the fallen-away young adult Catholic back into the community of the Church. Landings is a ten-week program built around certain religious themes on which "returnee" and "welcomer" lay Catholics can build a faith community. Young adults attending these programs feel validated in their struggles with faith and know that they are not alone in the world. This short-term program responds to young adults' needs to ask questions and make commitments within a community that respects their busy lives.

Quest was developed in Buffalo after that diocese realized that the most effective programs for welcoming back fallen-away Catholics were geared toward middle-aged and senior adults—not to young adults. Quest is a cross-parish program, in which a cluster of parishes pools resources to welcome young adults to a gathering, invite them to share their stories, identify their needs, and empower them to take ownership of meeting those needs within the context of the community of faith. *Young Adult Works*,[8] a binder resource from the Center for Ministry Development, describes the step-by-step process for developing a program like Quest on the local level.

Many young adults participating in such welcoming programs will feel nurtured and appreciated by the Catholic Church for the first time in many years. However, remember that small faith-sharing communities do not need to be limited to structured programs and purchased material: "for where two or three are gathered together in my name, there am I in the midst of them" (Mt 18:20).

---

8   See *Young Adult Works*, eds. Ronald Bagley, CJM, John Roberto, Susan Stark, and Joan Weber (Naugatuck, CT: CMD, 1997), Binder 2.

One Model That Works

At Stanford University in California, young adults working in Silicon Valley have connected to the campus ministry to develop a comprehensive ministry called the Stanford Young Adult Circle. They have reached out to five parishes in the area to act as liaisons for young adults attending those particular communities—not to take the young adults out of the parish, but to provide a service. Stanford University's campus ministry provided opportunities for young adults to sign up for small faith-sharing communities via its Web site. The sign-up process was simple: the specifics were listed up front, and those who signed up were asked for a one-semester commitment. (This time period usually fits schedules well, even for young adults who are no longer students.) Campus ministry promoted the activity by appealing to young adults' needs with key phrases like "meet new people," "satisfy our hunger," and "impact our personal lives." The Web site included links to background information on "small faith-sharing communities" for those not familiar with the concept, as well as personal stories from other young adults about how an experience of small faith-sharing community changed their lives. The online registration form asked specific questions about preferred day, time, and type of group (e.g., married, single, permanent community beyond the semester, parents and children) and about whether the registrant could host in his or her home. This process has helped to reduce young adults' apprehension about taking on more responsibility for their faith by providing a comfortable, safe environment online to research options and get connected.

SMALL FAITH-SHARING COMMUNITIES AND CULTURE

Cultural sensitivity is vital within small church communities of young adults. Each culture brings its own gifts and challenges, and young adults' experiences of faith communities can mirror their experiences of society in the United States. Small church communities seem to be everywhere—a group of friends get together to discuss how they cope at work; young men spend time discussing why they would or would not consider the priesthood; people who attend parishes in the same community gather to play softball, volleyball, or basketball; or a lot of young adults come together for a "biknic" (bike ride and picnic). But how can one be a part of these smaller communities if one does not feel included in the larger community?

In Philadelphia, Pennsylvania, for example, many African American young adults were experiencing this sense of exclusion in parishes that did not have a large number of African Americans or a large number of young adults. Although the archdiocese has a thriving young adult ministry, and although many small church communities for young adults could be found throughout the archdiocese, members of the African American Catholic young adult community still felt a sense of disconnect. That sense led to the formation of the African American Catholic Young Adult Network in the Archdiocese of Philadelphia. Members of this network expressed a need to share with a group of peers who were familiar with their experiences in the Catholic Church. The network's Growing in Faith Together Reflection Series has helped its members grow in faith and thereby gain a deeper understanding of and personal relationship with Jesus Christ. While members of this group have participated in many local programs, this particular connection to a peer faith-sharing community has especially enabled them to move toward the full, conscious, and active participation in the Church called for by the Second Vatican Council.[9]

Another example of the importance of cultural sensitivity in forming faith-sharing communities comes from Asian and Pacific Island American young adults. They may feel alienated from the culture of the United States, because many Asian and Pacific Islander cultures emphasize harmony, family, and the greater good, in contrast to the individualism more typical of U.S. culture: "harmony is crucial, along with the notion that the individual must sacrifice his or her interests to serve the greater needs of the group, which may be the state, the community, or, especially, the family."[10] For Asian and Pacific Island American young adults, such alienation can multiply the loneliness already felt by many young adults of any culture. An inclusive parish with small faith-sharing groups for young adults can provide a welcome remedy, especially effective because "Catholic identity is intimately connected with family and local community" for Catholics of Asian and Pacific heritage.[11] Accordingly, the bishops of the United States have advocated that parishes encourage Asian and Pacific Island American young adults "to take part in parish youth and young adult formation and leadership programs and become actively involved

---

9   See Second Vatican Council, *Constitution on the Sacred Liturgy* (*Sacrosanctum Concilium*), in *Vatican Council II: Volume 1: The Conciliar and Post Conciliar Documents*, ed. Austin Flannery (Northport, NY: Costello Publishing, 1996), no. 14.

10   USCCB, *Asian and Pacific Presence: Harmony in Faith* (Washington, DC: USCCB, 2001), 14.

11   *Asian and Pacific Presence*, 14.

in the organization of program activities."[12] For example, the Filipino ministry in the Diocese of Arlington in Virginia adapted Theology on Tap[13] to fit the cultural preference of Filipino immigrant young adults. Theology on Tap is a program that usually brings together young adults with a speaker for theological reflection in a casual environment like a bar or pub. But because many Filipino immigrant young adults, especially women, do not customarily go out to bars or pubs, the parish instead gathered young adults in a Filipino restaurant for a buffet dinner, theological reflection, and karaoke singing. A Filipino priest provided the theological reflection, which incorporated Filipino cultural values and faith practices, delivered in a mixture of English and Tagalog.

Parishes can similarly adapt existing programs to appeal to the particular cultures present in their communities—and also to bring together young adults from a variety of heritages to build connections across cultural boundaries. When young adults of any culture find a community of support and belonging, they can, in turn, draw in more young adults from their own or other cultures.

Cultural education is an essential part of the training and formation that young adults need and constantly seek. In addition to the broad variety of small faith-sharing group ideas discussed earlier in this chapter, a parish that wants to include cultural education might form small study groups to focus on better-known heroes such as Martin Luther King Jr. or Dorothy Day, or they could introduce a variety of lesser-known heroes such as the martyrs from various countries who exemplify struggles in each respective culture. For example, Vietnam has an estimated 130,000 Vietnamese martyrs, of whom 117 were canonized in 1988;[14] other groups of martyrs who have been canonized or beatified have come from Košice (Slovak Republic), Spain, Korea, Japan, China, and Mexico, to name a few. A parish study group could also view and discuss movies, such as *Romero*, that depict experiences of faith together with experiences of culture.

Hispanic/Latino Contribution

In 1976 and 1977, hundreds of small church communities of Hispanics/ Latinos around the country met to reflect on and draw conclusions for the

12   *Asian and Pacific Presence*, 23.
13   For information on bringing Theology on Tap to your area, see *renewtot.org*. For additional information, including how to order the *Theology-on-Tap Manual*, see *www.yamchicago.org* or write to the Young Adult Ministry Office, Archdiocese of Chicago, 711 W. Monroe Street, Chicago, IL 60661.
14   See *Asian and Pacific Presence*, 11.

mission of evangelization as it relates to culture, education, political responsibility, and human rights in the Hispanic/Latino Catholic community in the United States. Young adults from this community made up a significant percentage of the participants. Their input formed a working document that was approved at the Second Encuentro Pastoral Nacional Hispano in Washington, D.C., in August 1977. The conclusions of that document—and later those of the Third Encuentro in 1985 and the United States Conference of Catholic Bishops' *National Pastoral Plan for Hispanic Ministry*—capture and direct the Church's commitment to the model of being a "community of communities" pledged to being leaven for the Reign of God on earth.[15]

The book *Evangelization of Hispanic Young People* presents a well-developed rationale and vision for this kind of development and multiplication of small communities. The book emphasizes discipleship and mission among Hispanic/Latino young adults;[16] it presents goals, a methodology, and the proposed content for the formation, ongoing evangelization, and nurturing of such small church communities. This model hinges on the formation and training of advisors who in turn become responsible for the formation and support of small-community "animators." Instituto Fe y Vida offers training in this model of ministry with Hispanic/Latino young adults,[17] and the entire Church can learn much from its efforts.

The Jesuits have also been promoting the model of small church communities (based on Ignatian spirituality and the Spiritual Exercises) among young adults for many years through their Christian Life Communities (CLC)—or Comunidades de Vida Cristiana (CVX), as they are known in Spanish. CLC/CVX includes an international association that networks small communities from sixty countries on five continents, as well as a world secretariat that hosts a Web site[18] of resources and news in Spanish, French, and English.

The South East Pastoral Institute has been fostering the growth of small communities of Hispanic/Latino young adults for more than twenty years through its La Pascua Juvenil project. The Institute gathers teams from various dioceses in the southeast region of the United States. A theme is chosen for each year, and diocesan young adult teams build on the theme to produce

---

15   See USCCB, *National Pastoral Plan for Hispanic Ministry*, in *Hispanic Ministry: Three Major Documents* (Washington, DC: USCCB, 1995).

16   See *Evangelization of Hispanic Young People* (Winona, MN: St. Mary's Press, 1995).

17   See Alejandro Aguilera-Titus, Carlos Carrillo, Pedro Castex, Carmen Cervantes, Juan Diaz-Vilar, SJ, and Juan Huitrado, MCCJ, *Profetas de Esperanza*, vol. 2, *La Juventud Hispana y la Respuesta Pastoral de la Iglesia* (Winona, MN: St. Mary's Press, 1994), Chapter 6.

18   See Christian Life Communities (CLC) and Comunidades de Vida Cristiana (CVX) at *www.cvx-clc.net*.

chapters of a book of readings, reflection questions, and songs to be used in small faith-sharing groups during Lent. These books were published exclusively in Spanish for twenty years, but now they are available in completely bilingual editions.[19]

Parish leaders can learn much about setting up faith-sharing groups for young adults who share specific cultural backgrounds by paying attention to these contributions that the Hispanic/Latino Catholic community has made to this endeavor. Many of their ideas can be adapted to develop small faith-sharing communities with young adults of other cultural backgrounds. Indeed, the Catholic bishops of the United States, in their statement *Encuentro and Mission: A Renewed Pastoral Framework for Hispanic Ministry*, set the stage for the development of small church communities with young adults of all cultures, challenging leaders to "build faith communities in which all cultures are constantly transformed by gospel values in order to be leaven for the reign of God in society."[20]

CONCLUSION

Each time members of the parish meet for any purpose, a community of faith grows when the meeting begins with prayer and reflection. As young adults are invited to be a more active and visible part of every aspect of the parish community—through parish councils, liturgy committees, finance councils, and so on—forming a community of faith can become a normal practice for all parishioners.

Small communities of faith are an integral part of parish life. *Sons and Daughters of the Light* challenges Catholic leaders to connect young adults to a peer community—but first, and most importantly, to Jesus. Through community with one another, Catholics connect with Christ. When young adults connect one-on-one with people who share similar values and interests, they establish a bond that keeps them participating in the Catholic Church and reveals the transformative power of God's love in their communities. Faith leads to hope for the future; a community of faith embodies the future as it witnesses to God's love.

---

19   For information, contact the South East Pastoral Institute at (305) 279-2333 or see *www.sepimiami.org*.
20   USCCB, *Encuentro and Mission: A Renewed Pastoral Framework for Hispanic Ministry* (Washington, DC: USCCB, 2002), no. 61.

THE CAMPUS CONNECTION

Many young adults are looking for something more from their experience of the Church. All too often, "church" seems to young adults like a crowd of people attending Mass on a Sunday. If the young adult misses Mass, people seem not to notice and not to care. This is especially true for students on a college campus. In many instances, students are new to the campus or area, and they feel strange and out of place. They may only know their roommates and perhaps one or two other students. Yet they crave a sense of belonging. They want to associate with people who know who they are—people who know their names and care about what is important to them. They are searching for an intimate, personal experience of the Church. And they want their experience of the Church to engage them. In short, many young adults—and especially college students—are searching for community.

One of the most effective ways to establish a meaningful community of faith on campus is to create small groups that enhance participants' experience of faith. The specific task of a small faith-sharing community can vary with the interest of the students. Some small faith-sharing communities will form around studying the Scriptures, either by reflecting on the upcoming Sunday's readings or studying one of the books of the Bible. Other communities might spring up around liturgical ministries, community service, or justice projects. Communities could form as student-led prayer or discussion groups, or they could develop around intellectual pursuits, such as reading and discussing church documents from the early Church until the present. And some communities develop (especially on a secular campus) when Catholic students gather together on a regular basis simply to be with other people who understand them.

At Colorado State University, in Ft. Collins, Colorado, the student choir at the Blessed John XXIII Catholic Center could be described as more of a small church community than a choir. The group, called Mass Chaos, accomplishes its specific task of providing music for liturgies on campus and in the parish with inspiring enthusiasm. The group also comes together twice a year for a weekend retreat, which is organized by students. During the retreat, students not only rehearse new music but also discuss the meanings of the songs that they are preparing. The retreat includes time for students to get to know each other and to praise God through prayer and song. The group also discusses possible service projects to work on each semester. In all these ways, Mass Chaos directs its talents to serve the Ft. Collins community.

In the past, Mass Chaos has used its gift of music to benefit the poor in the Ft. Collins area. The group recorded a CD of its favorite liturgical music and named the collection *Home Away from Home*. The proceeds from the sale of the CD were donated to the local mission of Catholic Charities. To assist that same mission, the group also created and sold a recipe book called *Mass Chaos in the Kitchen*. Mass Chaos is an example of a community whose faith leads to action and whose actions lead to faith.

Years ago, the University of Scranton, a Jesuit university in Pennsylvania, was concerned about low levels of student participation in the liturgy. Faculty and campus ministers asked themselves, "How can we create a sense of community?" In response, they established a series of retreats. Initially, student response to the retreats was disappointing. However, after a few years of perseverance, attendance at the retreats spread like wildfire. The University of Scranton now offers more than twenty-five retreats each year, with eight hundred or more students participating and with more than forty trained student leaders. The campus ministry created a manual, *Building Faith Community*, to serve as a guide to its nine most popular retreats. Although campus ministers still strive to improve existing programs and to create new models to interest students, the retreats have accomplished their goal. A genuine sense of community pervades the entire campus.

After surveying students and reflecting on *Sons and Daughters of the Light*, the campus ministry team at St. Thomas More Chapel at Yale University discerned that the young adults on campus were seeking an experience of community in addition to Sunday liturgy. The campus ministry team concluded that it could connect young adults to Jesus Christ and to one another by establishing Bible study and reflection groups. These small church communities include both peer and intergenerational groups. St. Thomas More Chapel has found that communities that include undergraduates, graduate students, and faculty provide the greatest satisfaction to participants.

These small church communities at Yale begin and end each semester with a special Mass and dinner. Each week they meet in groups of eight to twelve. During their gathering, they read the first reading and Gospel of the upcoming Sunday, as well as a commentary. They spend time reflecting on the readings and writing answers to reflection questions in their journals. Then the small church community subdivides into groups of three or four to discuss their answers. Finally, the larger group reconvenes to continue the discussion as a whole. The process allows for everyone to speak and everyone to be heard. In a segment called "Response in Action," participants make suggestions on how to act on the Scriptures, especially as they relate to social justice. Participants rotate the responsibility for facilitating the discussion as well as writing a summary of the discussion. As an interesting twist to Yale's small church community, the summaries—as well as any unanswered questions—are given to the homilist for the next Sunday. The homilist reviews the summaries and provides a response to the questions in the homily. Finally, each small church community selects one member to be on the pastoral team for the Chapel. The team meets monthly with the chaplain to maintain a pastoral connection. St. Thomas More Chapel has found that many of the participants become involved in ministry beyond the small church community.

The Catholic Student Center at the University of Maryland has similarly created community through a group that studies each Sunday's Scriptures. This small faith-sharing community is for graduate students and is called Coffee, Tea, and Prayer. Because the participants are graduate students, who stay more connected to the university between semesters, the group has been able to meet weekly year-round except on major holidays. Meetings have taken place after dinner; in keeping with the title, beverages are served as well as a homemade dessert. The formal part of the evening usually begins with prayer. Then various members read the texts aloud. After quiet reflection, the discussion follows the pattern of a graduate seminar. Participants share their personal reflections, as well as scholarly interpretations. Resources on hand include the *New American Bible*, the *Jerome Biblical Commentary*, and the *Catechism of the Catholic Church*.[21] Some participants have a background in biblical studies, while others have little or no previous experience with scriptural study. The variation can make for some interesting discussions. Wherever the discussion leads, it

---

21   See Raymond E. Brown, Joseph A. Fitzmeyer, and Roland E. Murphy, eds., *The New Jerome Biblical Commentary* (Englewood Cliffs, NJ: Prentice-Hall, 1990), and *Catechism of the Catholic Church*, 2nd ed. (Washington, DC: USCCB, 2000). For a good selection of Catholic Bibles like the *New American Bible*, visit a Catholic bookstore. To find a Catholic bookstore, go to *www.usccbpublishing.org* and click "Find a Bookstore in Your Area" under "Resources."

usually doesn't end by the close of the meeting but continues in e-mails among the students during the week. One of the great aspects of Coffee, Tea, and Prayer is that it has brought together graduate students from a variety of disciplines. Without this program, they probably would not have met; now they are a community. Also, because of their participation in Coffee, Tea, and Prayer, some of the students have connected with other Catholic groups on campus. A truly viable community of faith is never just focused on itself but looks beyond itself to spread the Word and build the Kingdom.

CHAPTER ELEVEN

Young Adults and Families

How can parishes support the faith lives of young families in the Church? This chapter reviews many opportunities the Church offers for permeating family life with faith. Through a process of invitation, catechesis, ritual, home activities, and mystagogy, the chapter suggests numerous ways in which leaders can support young adults as singles, married couples, and young parents. The chapter also addresses cultural considerations and suggests strategies for ministering to families of various cultures.

One important, and often overlooked, way to view ministry with young adults is through the lens of the family life cycle. Ministry with Young Adults: A National Catholic Initiative ("the Initiative") approached the challenge of ministering to all young adults—singles, married couples, young parents, those who are single again—without focusing on any specific group. The Initiative's research shows that young married couples without children have more in common developmentally with single adults than with those who do have children. Catholic young adult ministry has tried to focus on programs and strategies to reach young adults in every state of life, but in the last several years, the Church has recognized the abundance of opportunities to minister with young adults, especially through the family life cycle and the intergenerational faith community.

Ask a group of parish ministers about their ministry with young adults, and very few acknowledge that they have any such ministry. Yet ask them if their parish celebrates marriages of young adult couples, Baptisms of infants whose parents are young adults, and the First Eucharist and First Reconciliation of children whose parents are young adults, and they quickly discover that they do have a ministry with young adults. It may not be intentional and systematic; it may not attend to the particular faith development needs of young adults. However, numerous opportunities present themselves for intentional, purposeful, and systematic ministry with young adults when this ministry is viewed through the lens of the family life cycle.

YOUNG ADULTS AND THE FAMILY LIFE CYCLE

Family life cycle theory is one of the most useful methods for targeting the specific needs of entire families and of individual family members with life-cycle-appropriate programs, activities, and strategies. The unique characteristics of each stage and the passages between stages provide important clues for ministry with individuals and families. Distinct family life cycle stages involving young adults (defined here as adults between eighteen and thirty-nine years of age) include families with young adult children, single young adulthood, the new young adult couple, and young adult parents with young children.

Families with Single Young Adults: Becoming One's Own Person

The most significant aspect of this stage of life is that it is marked by the greatest number of exits and entries of family members. The stage begins when young adults move on to post-secondary education (college, technical school), the military, careers, and eventually homes of their own. For many young adults, it concludes with marriage. During this stage, there are challenges for both the single young adult and for the entire family system.

Single young adults confront some of the most important life tasks at this stage of the family life cycle. They reassess, evaluate, and take stock of what they have received from their families of origin (e.g., values, faith, styles of relating), and they identify what they plan to integrate into their own developing identity. Other tasks at this time of life include the following:

- Developing separation from one's family of origin, while maintaining emotional connection
- Accepting emotional and financial responsibility for self
- Formulating personal life goals
- Developing intimate peer relationships
- Establishing oneself in the world of work

The challenge for the family as a whole involves the following:

- Regrouping as a family, as each young adult moves out from the family
- Adjusting to changes in the marital relationship once parenting responsibilities are no longer constant

- Developing adult-to-adult relationships between grown children and their parents
- Realigning relationships to include in-laws and grandchildren
- Caring for the older generation (the grandparent generation) and dealing with disabilities and death

The New Young Adult Couple: Becoming a Couple

Marriage joins not only two individuals but also two families in a new relationship—a new family system. Marriage creates a change in status among all family members and generations, requiring that the couple negotiate new relationships between themselves and with their loved ones: parents, siblings, grandparents, extended family, and friends. The following challenges—some of the greatest they will negotiate through the family life cycle—face the new couple:

- Forming an intimate relationship
- Defining and learning the roles of each spouse, and establishing healthy gender roles
- Establishing new relationships as a couple with their families of origin and with each other's friends
- Committing to a new family, with its own rules, roles, responsibilities, values, and traditions

As they confront these challenges, the new couple often find themselves reflecting on the influence of their families of origin to draw insights about values and traditions that they want to include in their new family. This reflection helps them to sort out emotionally what they will bring from each family of origin, what they will leave behind, and what they will create for themselves.

Young Adult Parents with Children: Becoming a Parent

Becoming a parent is one of the most definitive stages of life. Once young adults have a child, their lives will never be the same again. With the arrival of the first child, the couple embarks on a new life task: to accept new members into the family and to adjust the rules, roles, responsibilities, and relationships of their family to include the needs of the youngest members. One of the key tasks for young adult parents is to continue to focus on their own development as they grow into their role as parents.

Families with young children face numerous challenges:

- Developing parenting roles and skills, and developing shared responsibilities for parenting
- Negotiating and joining in childrearing, work and financial responsibilities, and household tasks
- Making emotional and relational shifts to create a place for the new member of the family, and realigning relationships with extended family to include grandparenting roles
- Sharing the child's social development with the outside world
- Developing new patterns of family communication, traditions, and celebrations

OPPORTUNITIES FOR CAMPUS AND PARISH MINISTRY

The twin challenge of ministering with young adults within the context of the family system is (1) to address the family life cycle tasks for the family as a whole, and at the same time (2) to nurture the personal development and growth in faith of the young adult as an individual. This approach allows parishes to minister to and with the young adult in each of these stages, as well as within the broader family context.

This approach also recognizes that parishes and campuses are already ministering to young adults in the family context through religious education, sacramental preparation (e.g., RCIA, marriage, sacramental preparation for children), Sunday Mass, and service ministries. The challenge is to develop these ministries and programs so they are more responsive, both to the entire family and to young adults' developmental, social, and cultural needs. The response often means developing programs, activities, and resources within these ministries that are specifically designed for young adults. Young adult–responsive parishes need to keep several points in mind when ministering with young adults in the family context.

First, each of these distinct young adult stages of the life cycle provides opportunities for promoting the four goals of *Sons and Daughters of the Light*, the pastoral plan of the Catholic bishops of the United States for young adult faith formation:[1] (1) connecting young adults with Jesus Christ, (2) connect-

---

1   See United States Conference of Catholic Bishops (USCCB), *Sons and Daughters of the Light: A Pastoral Plan for Ministry with Young Adults* (Washington, DC: USCCB, 1996), 25-41.

ing young adults with the Church, (3) connecting young adults with the mission of the Church in the world, and (4) connecting young adults with a peer community. Parishes can structure efforts using these four goals as a framework. For example, when a parish celebrates the Baptism of an infant, it can use the opportunity to connect young adults with Jesus (through preparation and resources for their own growth in faith), with the Church and the mission of the Church (through involvement in the life of the parish), and with a peer community (through gathering the parents with other couples with infants). Preparation programs, resources for home use, the celebration of the sacrament itself, and follow-up ministry after the sacrament (mystagogy) can all serve as helpful tools in this process.

A second idea to keep in mind is that all efforts with new couples and with families of young children should be directed to helping families discover their sacred mission. In their pastoral message *Follow the Way of Love*, the Catholic bishops of the United States recognize the importance of the family and its mission:

> A family is our first community and most basic way in which the Lord gathers us, forms us, and acts in the world. The early Church expressed this truth by calling the Christian family a *domestic church* or *church of the home*. . . .
>
> The point of the teaching is simple, yet profound. As Christian families, you not only belong to the Church, but your daily life is a true expression of the Church.
>
> Your domestic church is not complete by itself, of course. It should be united with and supported by parishes and other communities within the larger Church. Christ has called you and joined you to himself in and through the sacraments. Therefore, you share in one and the same mission that he gives to the whole Church.[2]

The mission of the family, as presented in *Follow the Way of Love*, includes loving, fostering intimacy, professing faith in God, setting an example of Christian living, praying together, serving, sacrificing for one another, forgiving and seeking reconciliation, celebrating life's passages, celebrating the sacraments, acting justly, and affirming life.[3]

---

2   USCCB, *Follow the Way of Love: A Pastoral Message of the U.S. Catholic Bishops to Families* (Washington, DC: USCCB, 1994), 8.
3   See *Follow the Way of Love*, 9-10.

The third point to consider when ministering to young adults in a family context is a simple five-point framework that can guide efforts to nurture the faith of the family throughout the family life cycle. This framework provides a useful tool for creating parish programming and resources for the home. Imagine ways to use this framework—for example, creating a home kit for the new couple entering into the Sacrament of Marriage or for the family celebrating a Baptism.

1. *Learn.* Help families and individuals to explore the Scriptures and Catholic Tradition and to apply the Catholic faith to daily life as followers of Jesus Christ.

2. *Celebrate rituals.* Help families and individuals to develop patterns of ritual celebrations (daily, weekly, seasonal, annual) and to celebrate a variety of ritual experiences at home, such as church-year feasts and seasons (e.g., Advent, Lent), sacraments (e.g., Baptism, Eucharist), calendar-year events, and milestones (e.g., birthdays, anniversaries, graduations, retirements).

3. *Pray.* Help families and individuals to develop their prayer life and to experience a variety of prayer styles and settings, such as Morning and Evening Prayer, daily prayers for the season, table prayers, and traditional Catholic prayers.

4. *Enrich relationships.* Help families to develop skills for communal living, to deepen the marriage relationship, and to participate in common activities that build the family's strengths and celebrate its life. These elements help to strengthen the family's life together.

5. *Serve and work for justice.* Help families and individuals to discover and deepen their call to act justly and serve those in need, to relate the Scriptures and Catholic social teaching to local and global issues, to serve others and act for social justice, and to develop lifestyles based on gospel values.

Example 1: Graduation from College or Discharge from Military Service (Life Stage: Families with Young Adults)

Young adults undergo a number of important transitions at this stage of life: leaving home, starting a career or job or entering the military, graduating from college or being discharged from the military, and starting a new home. Ministry to young adults and their families in these transitions should include (1) invitation, (2) catechetical preparation, (3) ritual celebration, (4) home resources and activities, and (5) continuing ministry activities (mystagogy).

Here is a possible structure for a program in which a parish recognizes graduation from college or discharge from military service. Consider celebrating this process twice a year: December/January and May/June.

1. *Invitation.* Invite the young adult directly or through his or her family.

2. *Catechetical Preparation.* The catechetical preparation program serves as a "re-entry" educational process to help young adults and their families prepare for this new stage of life and to reconnect the young adults with the parish community. It could take one of many forms, such as a workshop or retreat experience, and might provide learning experiences for parents and young adults both together and separately. The content for the preparation program might center on the developmental tasks of young adults and their parents as well as themes of faith that are significant for parents and young adults (e.g., Christian vocation and lifestyle decisions, faith and work, involvement in the life and mission of the church community, and adult spirituality).

3. *Ritual Celebration.* At one or more Sunday liturgies, the parish might celebrate a special ritual for parents and young adults. The ritual marks the passage from college or the military into a new stage of life—for the young adult (career and work, vocation and ministry, adult responsibilities in the church community) and also for his or her parents (relationship with adult children, midlife vocation and ministry, renewal of marriage relationship). The ritual formally welcomes the young adult back into the life of the parish community.

4. *Home Activities.* Each young adult and each parent might be given a home kit of activities and resources for continuing their growth, together and separately. Include a parish calendar of events and a guide to parish ministries and involvement opportunities. Consider incorporating the following types of activities and resources that relate to each point in the five-point framework:

    • Learning—Short essays (such as *Catholic Updates*, which are four-page articles from St. Anthony Messenger Press, *www.americancatholic.org*, each with an imprimatur) on important themes related to faith; a reflection guide to the Sunday Mass readings; daily gospel readings
    • Ritual—Rite of leave-taking; blessing of a new home
    • Prayer—Guide to prayer practices; prayer journal for feasts of the Church throughout the year; Web sites for prayer and spiritual reflection
    • Enrichment—Information to help young adults and their parents better understand this stage of life[4]
    • Service—A guide to service projects and immersion trips for parents and young adults (together or separate; national and international), such as participating in a Habit for Humanity week-long building project

5. *Continuing Ministry (Mystagogy).* The ritual is not the end of a process; rather, it marks the beginning of continuing growth in faith. To continue the ministry that has begun, consider ways the parish community can become more responsive to young adults (and their parents) within its existing ministries, as well as new initiatives the parish can create to promote growth in faith. Some examples follow.

    • Become more responsive within existing parish ministries.
        — Provide gathering time after Sunday Mass for young adults to socialize and share insights on the Sunday Mass readings.

---

4   For example, see "Survival Guide for Parents of Young Adults" and "Survival Guide for Young Adults," in *Young Adult Works*, ed. Ronald Bagley, CJM, John Roberto, Susan Stark, and Joan Weber (Naugatuck, CT: Center for Ministry Development, 1997), Binder 5, Section 10.

— Make a conscious effort to invite young adults into church ministries, and provide them with training.
— Incorporate topics that are relevant to families with young adults into adult education programs (e.g., faith and midlife issues, spirituality of work, lifestyle decisions, marketplace morality, social issues, sexuality).
— If the parish sponsors intergenerational catechetical programs, provide specific learning activities for both young and middle-aged adults.
— If the parish sponsors small faith-sharing groups, provide small groups targeted to young adults. (See Chapter 10, "Forming Faith Communities of Young Adults," for ideas.)
— If the parish hosts an annual mission, incorporate features or activities targeted to young adults.

• Create new initiatives.
— Provide an annual retreat experience for parents and young adults.
— Organize service/immersion trips for parents and young adults—national or international.
— Develop and deliver targeted content (learning, rituals, prayers, service projects, enrichment, continuing faith-formation resources, and activities) to young adults and their parents through the parish Web site.

Example 2: Marriage
(Life Stage: New Couple)

Marriage marks the formal beginning of the "new couple" stage of the life cycle. Here is an example for ministering to the new couple and their families using the five program elements. This process can work for an individual couple or for groups of couples.

1. *Invitation.* When the couple comes to the church to schedule their marriage celebration, they can be invited to participate in the following process.

2. *Catechetical Preparation.* The catechetical preparation program should focus on the developmental tasks of the new couple, the faith-formation and learning needs of the young adult, and catechetical preparation for the Sacrament of Marriage. To bring a family perspective to the process, involve the parents and extended family members in specific aspects of the catechetical preparation, such as the following:

    - A "re-entry" catechesis (for those who have been inactive) that welcomes the couple back to the Church and refreshes their understanding and practice of the Catholic faith (primarily focused on the new couple, but with modifications for other inactive family members)
    - Suggestions for sharing faith, including specific ideas for interfaith couples
    - Knowledge and skills for addressing the developmental tasks of the "new couple" stage of life (for the new couple and family members)
    - Catechesis on the Sacrament of Marriage for the new couple as well as their parents, utilizing the rite itself as the catechetical content (e.g., the theology of marriage found in the introduction, order of service, Scripture readings, symbols, traditions, prayer texts, and the human experience being celebrated in the Sacrament)

    For groups of couples, preparation can include a series of workshops or extended time programs (day-long or weekend). For an individual couple, preparation might take the form of a mentored experience, with a married couple from the parish serving as guides through the learning experiences.

3. *Ritual Celebrations.* The wedding ceremony can best reflect a family perspective by including prominent roles for family members in the liturgy and a conscious effort to connect with the family through the homily. Incorporate special blessings for new couples at Sunday liturgies throughout the preparation process, as well as intentions for the new couple in the Prayer of the Faithful at Sunday Mass before and after the wedding ceremony.

When newlyweds return from their honeymoon (if taken directly after the wedding), introduce them *as a couple* to the parish at the first Sunday liturgy they attend. In addition, the parish can provide a ritual that helps the whole family to celebrate this rite of passage in which young adults formally leave their family of origin to begin a new family. This ritual could be celebrated at the rehearsal dinner. (See, for example, *Catholic Household Blessings and Prayers* for a "Blessing of an Engaged Couple" and "Blessing of a Son or Daughter Before Marriage."[5])

4. *Home Activities.* Parish leaders can give each new couple a home kit of activities and resources for continuing their growth in faith and their growth as a couple. Include a parish calendar of events and a guide to parish ministries and involvement opportunities. Include the following types of activities and resources, according to the five-point framework:

    - Learning—Short essays (e.g., *Catholic Updates*) on the Sacrament of Marriage and important themes of faith for the new couple, plus a reflection guide to the Sunday Mass readings and daily gospel readings
    - Ritual—A guide to creating and celebrating a regular calendar of family rituals as a new couple, as well as important rituals throughout the year (e.g., major feasts and seasons, anniversaries, birthdays)
    - Prayer—A guide and resources for developing family prayer and praying together as a couple, including table prayers for church-year feasts and Web sites for prayer and spiritual reflection
    - Enrichment—Information on skills for living as a married couple: emotional, financial, relational, practical
    - Service—Guides to charitable giving, community service projects, immersion trips (national and international), and service-oriented vacations

---

5   See USCCB, *Catholic Household Blessings and Prayers*, rev. ed. (Washington, DC: USCCB, 2007), 247-251, 253-254. This resource for families includes blessings and prayers suitable for adaptation to many suggestions in this chapter.

Sustain the momentum created by the home kit by developing a biannual newsletter in which new couples can suggest new resources and activities for each other. On the couple's first five wedding anniversaries, send them ideas for renewing their marriage commitment and living their faith in the coming year.

5. *Continuing Ministry (Mystagogy).* The ritual is not the end of the process; it marks the beginning of married life. To continue the ministry that has begun, consider ways in which the parish community can become more responsive to the new couple within its existing ministries and new initiatives the parish can create for promoting growth in faith:

- Become more responsive within existing parish ministries.
  — Celebrate six-month and annual anniversaries at Sunday Mass for married couples through the first five years of marriage.
  — Provide gathering time after Sunday Mass for new couples to socialize and share insights on the Sunday Mass readings.
  — Make a conscious effort to invite new couples into parish ministries, and provide them with training.
  — Incorporate topics of relevance to new couples into adult education programs. For ideas, visit the Web site of the bishops' pastoral initiative on marriage, *www.foryourmarriage.org.*
  — If the parish sponsors intergenerational catechetical programs, be sure to invite new couples to participate.
  — If the parish sponsors small faith-sharing groups, provide small groups targeted to new couples or to young adults in general.

- Create new initiatives.
  — Provide a one-year subscription to *Foundations: The Newsletter for Newly Married Couples.*[6]

---

6   *Foundations: The Newsletter for Newly Married Couples* is a publication of S & K Publishers in partnership with the National Association of Catholic Family Life Ministers. For more information, see *www. foundationsnewsletter.net.*

— Connect with newly married couples through evening, day-long, or weekend marriage-enrichment programming focused on the first years of married life. Provide a one-year anniversary retreat experience as a "refresher" on the sacramentality of marriage.

— Develop a program in which couples who have been married for several years mentor newly married couples.

— Organize a new-couples group that provides continued learning, sharing, socializing, prayer, and support.

— Develop and deliver targeted content (e.g., learning, rituals, prayers, service projects, enrichment, "marriage tips," ongoing faith-formation resources, and activities) to young couples through the parish Web site.

— Involve young couples in ministry and service together as a couple. Develop ministry opportunities designed for couples to work together (such as teaching or working with small groups). Organize a "couples volunteer weekend" with a variety of service projects. Build in time for couples to reflect on how service is important to their faith and their marriage.

Example 3: Birth and Baptism
(Life Stage: Young Adult Parents with Children)

Birth (or adoption) and Baptism mark the formal beginning of the "family with young children" stage of the life cycle. As new parents focus their energy on parenting, they still need to attend to their own continuing spiritual growth as young adults and as a couple. A possible structure follows for ministering to new young adult parents and the entire family, using the five program elements:

1. *Invitation.* Make expectant or adopting couples aware that they are invited into the baptismal preparation process. You might describe this as a faith-filled preparation for parents in anticipation of birth or adoption, particularly for those preparing for their first child. (The parish might also conduct "refreshers" for those expecting subsequent children.) A second opportunity for

invitation arises when the family schedules the Baptism of their new child.

2. *Catechetical Preparation.* The catechetical preparation program should focus on the developmental tasks of the family, the learning needs of the parents, the faith-formation learning needs of the young adults, and catechetical preparation for the Sacrament of Baptism. To bring a family perspective to the process, involve the parents, extended family members, and godparents in specific aspects of the catechetical preparation, such as the following:

    - A "re-entry" catechesis (for those who have been inactive) that welcomes the parents back to the Church and refreshes their understanding and practice of the Catholic faith (targeted to the parents, with modifications for other inactive family members)
    - Catechesis that nurtures young adults' growth in faith within their new role as parents, focusing on topics such as developing spiritual practices and a life of prayer, learning and sharing the great stories of the biblical tradition, understanding and communicating the moral values of the Catholic Tradition, understanding the ritual and theology of the sacraments, and understanding and celebrating the feasts and seasons of the church year
    - Knowledge and skills for addressing the developmental tasks of the "family with young children" stage of life and for parenting and nurturing the faith of young children (offered to parents, and possibly godparents and grandparents)
    - Catechesis on the Sacrament of Baptism for parents, godparents, and grandparents, using the rite itself as the catechetical content (e.g., the theology of Baptism and Initiation found in the introduction, order of service, Scripture readings, symbols, traditions, prayer texts, and the human experience being celebrated in the Sacrament)

For groups of parents, preparation can include a series of workshops or extended-time programs (day-long or weekend). For an individual couple, preparation might take the form of a mentored experience, with "veteran" parents from the parish serving as mentors through the learning experiences.

3. *Ritual Celebrations.* So that Baptism can reflect a family perspective, give prominent roles to family members in the celebration of Baptism, and make a conscious effort to connect with the family through the homily. Include special blessings for the parents and new child at Sunday liturgies through the preparation process, prayers for the expectant family at a Sunday Mass before the birth or adoption, and prayers for the new family after the child arrives. Celebrate a "rite of welcoming" several weeks prior to the Baptism, so that the parish community becomes aware of the forthcoming celebration. Consider creating a "parish book of blessings" from the parish community with words of welcome, support, and hopes and dreams for the child. The book could be a gift of joy, support, and inspiration to the child when he or she is older. Or consider providing copies of *Catholic Household Blessings and Prayers*, which contains many rituals appropriate for home celebration before, during, and after the arrival of a new child.[7]

4. *Home Activities.* Each family can be given a home kit of activities and resources for continuing growth through the early childhood years. Include a parish calendar of events and a guide to parish ministries and involvement opportunities. A variety of activities and resources can be included in a post-baptismal home kit. Include some of the following:

- Learning—Articles for young adult faith enrichment (e.g., *Catholic Updates*); children's storybooks and Bible stories; video and music recommendations; suggestions and activities for teaching values; recommended Web sites for families; short essays for parents on sharing the Catholic faith

---

7 See the section "Blessings and Prayers Before and After Birth or Adoption," in *Catholic Household Blessings and Prayers*, 224-238. The blessings and prayers include the following: "Prayer for Those Hoping to Conceive or Adopt a Child," "Blessing of Parents Before Childbirth," "Blessing Before Childbirth: For the Mother," "Blessings and Prayers Near the Time of Birth," "Thanksgiving for a Newborn or Newly Adopted Young Child," "Parents' Thanksgiving," and "Prayer on Bringing a Child into the Home."

and values; reflections and activities related to the Sunday Mass readings

- Ritual—Symbols and religious art (e.g., crucifix, holy water, family candle); ideas for a family altar or prayer space; bed-time rituals; ideas for important rituals throughout the year (e.g., major feasts and seasons, anniversaries, birthdays)
- Prayer—Ideas for prayer practices; resources for the young adult; a guide to praying with young children, including morning and evening prayer; simple first Catholic prayers and blessings; table blessings (before and after meals); prayers for special occasions; Web sites and resources for personal and family prayer and spiritual reflection
- Enrichment—Resources for parenting young children (e.g., skills, tools, information); activity suggestions for families with young children
- Service—Ideas and activities for family service, such as developing a lifestyle of stewardship, preparing and serving a meal at a soup kitchen, donating food and clothes for children in need, visiting the elderly, recycling, planting trees or a garden, reading Bible stories on service, and praying for those in need

Sustain the momentum created by the home kit by developing a biannual newsletter for families with young children, offering new resources and activities appropriate to the ages of their children.

5. *Continuing Ministry (Mystagogy)*. The ritual of Baptism is not the end of the process; it marks the beginning of family life with children. To continue the ministry that has begun, consider ways the parish community can become more responsive to the family with young children within its existing ministries as well as new initiatives the parish can create to promote growth in faith.

- Become more responsive within existing parish ministries.
    — Celebrate the baptismal anniversaries of young children at Sunday Mass.
    — Provide a special ritual or blessing for Mother's Day and Father's Day.

— Emphasize Holy Family Sunday as a time to recognize family life and the mission of the family with special rituals, blessings, and home resources.

— If the parish sponsors intergenerational catechetical programs, incorporate learning activities and a focused group for families with young children.

— If the parish sponsors a summer vacation Bible school, consider developing a family-centered version in which parents and children participate together.

— Provide family-centered service programs using existing service opportunities, such as Operation Rice Bowl (a project of Catholic Relief Services: *orb.crs.org*).

— Let young families know that they are welcome at liturgy as a family. The liturgy is tailor-made for families with young children because of the richness of its symbols, movements, word, and music.

• Create new initiatives.

— Develop a parents' support group (for mothers or fathers separately, or for both) for social and spiritual growth, mutual support, and learning.

— Host a reunion breakfast for families who have celebrated Baptism in the previous six or twelve months.

— Develop a family resource center of print, audio, and video resources that parents can use in sharing faith and values with young children.

— Develop a program for "veteran" parents to mentor new parents.

— Develop and deliver targeted content (e.g., learning, rituals, prayers, service projects, enrichment, ongoing faith-formation resources, and activities) for young adult parents and young children through the parish Web site.

— Organize regular parent education programs (with babysitting) that develop the understanding and practice of parenting young children and that build up the confidence and competence of parents.

— Provide seasonal catechetical programs that involve families with young children, such as an Advent or Lenten intergenerational learning program.

CULTURAL PERSPECTIVES ON THE FAMILY LIFE CYCLE

Unique cultural perspectives on family life need to be considered when doing ministry with young adults through the lens of the family life cycle. This section examines the perspectives of the Asian and Pacific Islander community and the Hispanic/Latino community as two examples. While the specific perspectives may be unique to those communities, the overall principle is the same: parishes that are responsive to young adults from a variety of cultures find out how young adults of a given culture understand family life and draw on this information to develop effective ministry to them.

The Asian and Pacific Islander Experience of Family

Family is a highly prized gift among Americans from countries in Asia and the Pacific islands. Young adults are socialized into traditional values: strong family ties and extended family structures, marriage stability, love for children, filial reverence, and respect for the elderly. Many young adults struggle with the conflict between continuing to practice these traditional family values and adapting to their new reality in the United States—including how to incorporate new values like individuality, independence, and competitiveness. As the Catholic bishops of the United States have observed, "Single Asian and Pacific young adults are often left alone to find their place either in society or in the Church. They need guidance during the difficult period of cultural adjustment, career change, vocation discernment, and other important decisions young people have to make."[8]

Entry points in the family life cycle often provide special opportunities to grab the attention of young adults from Asian and Pacific Islander backgrounds. For example, many Korean, Chinese, and Vietnamese Americans grow up in parishes where only their native language is used for faith formation and sacraments. Because some of them no longer speak their native language by the time they reach young adulthood, they may drop out of parish membership and go without much catechesis. But when these young adults

---

8   USCCB, *Asian and Pacific Presence: Harmony in Faith* (Washington, DC: USCCB, 2001), 23.

have families of their own, they tend to come back to the Church—just like the young adult population in general does. When this happens, young adults of Asian or Pacific Islander heritage may be hungry for catechesis—not just for their children, but for themselves as well. While they may search for a local parish to meet the needs of their children, they may be happily surprised to find one that also tends to their own needs.

Working with young adults from specific cultural backgrounds is also a great opportunity for parishes to adopt new celebrations that incorporate traditions from those cultures. A good example from the Asian and Pacific Islander community centers on the Sacrament of Marriage. Marriages are occasions for parishes to remind young adult Asian and Pacific Catholics of their "responsibility for the future of society and the Church."[9] Parishes can also reach Catholic families from Asia and the Pacific islands during marriage preparation, including pre-Cana programs. In the Asian and Pacific context, a wedding is a marriage of two families, not only of two people. Weddings include elaborate rituals to emphasize this relationship building. Handbooks for Catholic wedding rituals in the Vietnamese, Filipino, Chinese, and other cultural traditions are available and can be rich resources for local churches. According to Fr. Peter Phan,

> the essential meaning of the wedding remains: it is a celebration of the two extended families and not simply of the couple by themselves. The ancestors are invoked, the new husband and wife are introduced to them, each of them acquiring a new set of relationships . . . [with] those who have died. In fact, each of them marries a whole new family, composed of the living and the dead. It is this (in addition to the sacrament or the ritual at the pagoda) that makes a wedding a sacred, and not simply civil and social, ceremony for the Vietnamese. These new relationships will sustain the new couple in their marriage, in good health and in sickness, in want and in plenty.[10]

Parishes can also incorporate traditional practices that celebrate the birth of a child. For example, Koreans often hold a hundred-day celebration for infants. Much like a birthday party, it is a celebration of life, health, and future

---

9   Pope John Paul II, *The Church in Asia* (*Ecclesia in Asia*), no. 47, *www.vatican.va/holy_father/john_paul_ii/ apost_exhortations/documents/hf_jp-ii_exh_06111999_ecclesia-in-asia_en.html.*

10   Peter Phan, *Vietnamese-American Catholics*, Pastoral Spirituality Series (Mahwah, NJ: Paulist Press, 2005), 60-61.

prosperity. Parishes could offer this festive event for groups of infants, perhaps starting with a special blessing at a Sunday liturgy, and then providing a social occasion afterward for young adult families to join together, get to know each other, and begin new friendships based on their faith, their stage in the life cycle (as new parents), and a beautiful tradition.

The Hispanic/Latino Experience of Family

Hispanics/Latinos constituted more than 35 percent of all Catholics in the United States in the year 2000,[11] and there is no more important ministry with Hispanic/Latino young adults than the ministry of promoting and supporting healthy marriages and families. Looking out at any congregation with a significant Hispanic/Latino population, one is overwhelmed by the great percentage of young adult families. Family is the crucible where God's love is experienced or not, where discipleship is modeled or not, where mission is awakened or suffocated. The vocation to marriage and family is truly a sacred mission.

The tensions that many Christian homes experience with the values of a secular, consumer culture are accentuated in Hispanic/Latino families of all socioeconomic groups. Clashes over food, modesty standards in clothing, family rules of respect, discipline, roles, and obligations are common. Effective communication is vital, yet it is sometimes compromised. Immigrant parents who are still learning English may experience an upsetting sense of powerlessness when they try to exercise authority and discipline with children who are their translators in visits with doctors and school officials. Stresses sometimes lead to depression or domestic violence. In the face of these challenges, parishes can play an important role in advocating for adequate and affordable bilingual services and in providing timely referrals. Catechesis and liturgies can help families celebrate the richness of having two cultures to draw from and can thereby help ease the stresses of life.

As effective parish leaders consider how to make current ministries more responsive to all young adults, and as they initiate new ways to support and enrich all families in life transitions, they also think creatively of ways to involve Hispanic/Latino family members from all stages of the family life cycle.

Within the family life cycle, Baptism and marriage preparation work particularly well as key entry points for young adult ministry among Hispanics/ Latinos. Learning about the theology of marriage and of Baptism—reflecting

---

11   See *www.usccb.org/hispanicaffairs* and the U.S. Census Bureau.

on the symbolism, traditions, Scriptures, prayer texts, and human experiences of the sacraments—can help enrich young Hispanics/Latinos' bonds with the Church. Extended family members or friends can be chosen as *padrinos*, who serve as godparents or sponsors for Baptism and also develop a strong relationship with the child's parents, mentoring the child throughout life and "walking with" the parents as extended family. *Padrinos* should be invited to participate in the catechetical preparation for sacraments, which can be a vital route of re-entry for inactive Catholics. In addition, older parish couples can be assigned as mentors to offer young adult couples the opportunity to talk about cultural traditions, values, and clashes—an opportunity that helps the young adults sort out what traditional practices to keep, what new ones to adopt, and how to resolve conflicts peacefully. Finally, parishes can create a take-home kit of activities and Spanish resources that Hispanic/Latino families can use to continue their growth in faith through the early years of marriage or after Baptism—a wonderful way to continue the parish ministry.

The number of common-law and civil marriages among Hispanics/Latinos is a reality that heightens the importance of warm invitation and welcome when a young adult Hispanic/Latino couple is expecting a child. Parishes with Hispanic/Latino families might start by incorporating a blessing for pregnant mothers into their liturgies. A flyer or brochure could be developed and offered to women who come forward for the blessing. This printed piece could identify social service resources that are available (e.g., prenatal care, women's support, La Leche League, fair housing), names of physicians in the parish, and Catholic Charities services. The brochure should also include bilingual prayers highlighting the sacred mission of the family, as well as an invitation to participate in the parish's baptismal preparation process (including a description of the process and a schedule of baptismal preparation meetings). Baptismal preparation provides an opportunity to explicitly invite couples who are in a civil marriage to consider making their marriage sacramental by preparing for and celebrating the Sacrament of Marriage. This invitation can include the powerful witness of peers who have chosen to celebrate the Sacrament of Marriage in a simple ceremony, enlivened with Hispanic/Latino traditions but without the need to spend a great deal of money.

Outside of sacramental preparation itself, one successful program for strengthening Hispanic/Latino family life and encouraging sacramental marriage is the Movimiento Impacto de Cristiandad, a program spearheaded by Hispanic/Latino families, for Hispanic/Latino families, in the Archdiocese of

Miami.[12] Migrant farmworker families of Our Lady of Guadalupe Parish in Immokalee, Florida, have especially welcomed Impacto teams year after year for the annual family retreat. Designed for couples with children between the ages of three and eleven, Impacto is a weekend retreat where volunteer teams of couples lead sessions throughout the day, and then families return home in the evenings. Impacto focuses on strengthening the Catholic family, with much attention given to developing mutuality in relationships. Couples are not required to be married in the Church in order to attend. During the weekend, retreat leaders warmly and directly invite couples to consider entering into the Sacrament of Marriage as a way to strengthen family life in Christ. Children meet in different age groups for fun and reflective activities. Times are woven in for families to gather for meals, prayer, and celebration. In addition to Impactos, several other dynamic family or marriage-oriented weekend experiences have invigorated Hispanic/Latino Catholic families and parishes, including Encuentros Familiares (Ignatian), Cursillos de Cristiandad, and Camino del Matrimonio.

Many young adult Hispanics/Latinos have known much suffering and loss in their lives, but they also know a depth of faith and trust in God and the Blessed Virgin, and they know the rewards of determination, sacrifice, and unrelenting hope. Bringing with them a connection to a rich faith tradition, young Hispanic/Latino families who are invited and welcomed into parishes find that the Church helps them negotiate life's challenges and celebrate its surprises. They develop their gifts for the service of their family, Church, nation, and world.

CONCLUSION

Viewing ministry with young adults through the lens of the family life cycle stages offers parishes and campuses a wide variety of opportunities for ministry. The examples in this chapter only hint at the possibilities for becoming more intentional, purposeful, and systematic in ministry with young adults. The approach described in this chapter recognizes that parishes and campuses are already ministering to young adults in the context of their families through existing ministries. The challenge is to develop these ministries and programs so they are more intentional in their purpose and more responsive

---

12   For information about Impacto, see *www.impacto.org*.

to the entire family system and to young adults' developmental, social, and cultural needs.

The five-point framework proposed in this chapter can be used in a wide variety of ways to nurture the faith of the young adult and of the family. Parishes and campuses can use the framework to target the major transitions and milestones in the lives of young adults and their families. And they can use it to guide young adults through the feasts and seasons of the church year and the calendar year. This framework provides a useful tool for creating parish programming and resources for the home.

Consider how these ideas can spark your own creativity and help your campus or parish become more responsive to the needs and hungers of young adults and their families.

CHAPTER TWELVE

Young Adult Ministry: Hispanic/Latino Perspectives

How can parishes address the specific pastoral needs of Hispanic/Latino young adults, one of the fastest-growing groups in the Catholic Church in the United States today? In the not-too-distant future, Hispanics/Latinos are expected to account for half of the Catholic population in this country. This chapter addresses the unique challenges and graces that parish leaders encounter in ministering to Hispanic/Latino young adults. The chapter also offers both parish and diocesan strategies for supporting these young adults.

Ministry with Hispanic/Latino young adults presents a complex, challenging, and marvelously rewarding experience to parish leaders.[1] In the Catholic Church in the United States today, this work represents a vital cooperation with the work of the Spirit in building up the Reign of God. The following recommendations are offered to help strengthen parish leaders' confidence and resolve in this work as they strive to achieve the communion and solidarity to which all Catholics are called.

Hispanic/Latino young adults cross every spectrum of American society: from the third-generation resident of the United States, working as a chemical engineer in Miami and holding a master's degree, to the immigrant Spanish-speaking migrant worker; from the diocesan director of youth ministry in San Diego to the undocumented packing house employee in the Midwest. The research of Instituto Fe y Vida has highlighted four distinct groups of Hispanic/Latino young adults:

---

1   The United States Conference of Catholic Bishops (USCCB) offers this explanation of the terms "Hispanic" and "Latino": "The term 'Hispanic' was used during the 1970 Census and was adopted by the church leadership of the time to help define a people with a common identity, vision, and mission. It has been integral to the *memoria histórica* [historical record] of Hispanic ministry since 1970 and continues to be integral to the pastoral efforts of the entire Church today. In recent years, the term 'Latino' has become widely used by church and community leaders, particularly in urban areas. It is a self-identifying term that has emerged from the community and is embraced by the Church. . . . it is essential for understanding and for effective working relationships to recognize that the people come from different countries and come with special identities. The binding forces are the faith tradition, language, and values" (USCCB, *Encuentro and Mission: A Renewed Pastoral Framework for Hispanic Ministry* [Washington, DC: USCCB, 2002], note 5). For other discussion of the terms "Hispanic" and "Latino," see *Hispanic Young People and the Church's Pastoral Response*, Prophets of Hope 1 (Winona, MN: St. Mary's Press, 1994), nos. 38-43.

1. *Immigrant workers* speak primarily Spanish, are mostly of Mexican origin, are often undocumented, have little formal education, usually come from large families, are motivated and hopeful and willing to work hard, seek moral and spiritual support from the Church, and are mostly at the lower end of the economic spectrum. They need faith to confront the great challenges they face in life.

2. *Mainstream movers* mostly speak English, were mostly born in the United States, might have left the Catholic Church, are college-educated, are also motivated and hopeful and willing to work hard, and are mostly in the middle to upper end of the economic spectrum. They need faith to develop a sense of hope.

3. *Identity seekers* were mostly born in the United States, are children of immigrants, struggle to finish school, are mostly bilingual, often have low self-esteem, may be unmotivated or apathetic, may find hope in work or family relationships, might seek refuge in substance abuse or promiscuity, and are at the lower to middle end of the economic spectrum. They need faith to overcome consumerism and individualism.

4. *Gang members and high-risk youth* typically have limited bilingual abilities and little formal education, were mostly born in the United States, live in inner cities, are often unemployed, have anger towards society, experience despair, are often incarcerated, may become habitual drug users/sellers, and are mostly at the lower end of the economic spectrum. They need faith to move from anger and hatred to forgiveness.[2]

The challenge for parish leaders is to keep all four groups in mind when reaching out and ministering to this fast-growing segment of the Catholic population in the United States.

---

2   The four groups and their characteristics are summarized from Instituto Fe y Vida, "Fast Facts About U.S. Hispanic Catholics," *www.feyvida.org/research/fastfacts.html*.

PRACTICAL STRATEGIES FOR PARISH LEADERS

1. Be Conscious of Culture

Along with becoming fluent in Spanish, young adult ministers in the United States need to develop cultural competency with Hispanics/Latinos. Hispanics/Latinos vary in culture, but all identify with the common Spanish language, and many identify with certain cultural and Christian symbols and values. Many also identify with the richness of *mestizaje*—the mixing of indigenous, Spanish, and African cultural heritages, forming a new cultural identity—because most Hispanics/Latinos are interracial. Effective leaders recognize the multi-dimensionality of the Hispanic/Latino presence, and they learn the social, economic, and political features and histories of the various sub-groups. No longer are different sub-groups of Hispanics/Latinos concentrated only in certain regions of the country: e.g., Mexicans in the Southwest, Cubans in the Southeast, and Puerto Ricans in the Northeast. Today these sub-groups, as well as many more from Central and South America, "are all mixed together everywhere."[3]

Understanding history and culture will help tremendously in understanding relationships between sub-groups and changing expectations of the Church. This understanding will also serve efforts to ensure that parishes respect religious sensitivities and meet the spiritual needs of such a variety of peoples. "Prayer is different. Reasons for coming together for worship are different. What is looked for in preaching is different. What is expected of Church is different," states Bishop Ricardo Ramirez, Bishop of Las Cruces, in New Mexico, in an address to Hispanic/Latino liturgical leaders.[4] Ministry leaders need to learn and know the cultural values that impact and shape *pastoral juvenil hispana* (that is, ministry with Hispanic/Latino young adults): values such as a deeply Catholic cultural orientation, a strong affinity for relationships and family, and a deep devotion to our Blessed Mother.

2. Honor and Appreciate Cultural Expressions of Faith

Just as Chapter 11 of this book, "Young Adults and Families," urges parish leaders to develop a family consciousness, the work of the Church in the

---

3   Bishop Ricardo Ramirez, "Envisioning Hispanic Liturgy: Challenges for the Instituto at the Beginning of the Millennium" (presentation to Instituto de Liturgia Hispana Board Meeting, February 23, 2001), 5, *www.dioceseoflascruces.org/root/bishop/PDF/speeches/bp_sp_08.pdf*.

4   "Envisioning Hispanic Liturgy," 3.

modern world requires a "culture consciousness": a sensitivity toward and appreciation of not only Scripture, church teaching, and Tradition, but also human cultures and popular religious expressions.[5] This consciousness allows leaders to affirm faith and foster cultural identity and human community within each cultural group, and also to work to build community across all Hispanic/Latino subcultures. Theologians such as Virgilio Elizondo, Roberto Goizueta, and Jaime Vidal have suggested that the virtues of Hispanic/Latino popular religiosity offer avenues for the renewal and revitalization of the entire worshiping community in the United States.[6]

3. Commit Personnel and Resources

At the current crossroads in the Church, with the Hispanic/Latino population growing so rapidly, effective parish leaders direct church personnel and resources toward ministry and ministry formation with Hispanics/Latinos in order to enable them to be agents of the Church in its mission of liberation. Hispanic/Latino young adults today are in key positions in the Church to be agents of the New Evangelization, to bring forth the best of both cultures to promote the Gospel, and to denounce the values and practices that degrade life and promote social fragmentation.

There is much work to do. Some Hispanics/Latinos are more "churched" than others. "The majority," states Bishop Ramirez, "have yet to be fully initiated into the Church."[7] "All our traditions are being and will continue to be challenged in the future."[8]

The predominance of the Protestant work ethic in the United States, the persistent reality of poverty, ongoing discrimination, and the pressures and attractions of Western consumer culture greatly affect many Hispanic/Latino young adults today. This community is in a crisis: a time of great need but also of great opportunity. It will take cooperation among all Catholics to help young Hispanic/Latino generations receive the great traditions of faith and culture and find their place in the Church, for the sake of their own flourishing and that of the world.

---

5   See Second Vatican Council, *Pastoral Constitution on the Church in the Modern World* (*Gaudium et Spes*), in *Vatican Council II: Volume 1: The Conciliar and Post Conciliar Documents*, ed. Austin Flannery (Northport, NY: Costello Publishing, 1996), no. 53.

6   For more information about these theologians, see Eduardo C. Fernandez, SJ, *La Cosecha: Harvesting Contemporary United States Hispanic Theology, 1972-1998* (Collegeville, MN: Liturgical Press, 2000), 60.

7   "Envisioning Hispanic Liturgy," 6.

8   "Envisioning Hispanic Liturgy," 3.

4. Be Educated and Aware

A parish that is responsive to its Hispanic/Latino young adults makes sure its leaders are familiar with the contributions of Hispanic/Latino ministry in the United States, especially the *encuentros pastorales*, regional institutes, and national groups that provide leadership and resources.[9] Effective parish leaders take steps to learn the history and language of Hispanics/Latinos in the parish, and they follow the priorities that the Catholic bishops of the United States set forth in their *National Pastoral Plan for Hispanic Ministry* and the more recent *Encuentro and Mission: A Renewed Pastoral Framework for Hispanic Ministry*.[10]

5. Study the Conclusions of the First National Hispanic Youth and Young Adult Ministry Encounter

The first Encuentro Nacional de Pastoral Juvenil Hispana (or National Hispanic Youth and Young Adult Ministry Encounter), on the theme of "Encuentro: Weaving Together the Future," was held at the University of Notre Dame in June 2006. The regional gatherings leading up to the Encuentro Nacional came to several significant conclusions regarding the needs of young adults in relation to the Church. These needs include the following:

- Support and accompaniment of priests and those in ministry with young adults
- Material resources, including funding, for young adult ministry
- Personnel trained in *pastoral juvenil hispana* in diocesan offices and parishes
- Training and formation programs that empower young adults to assume leadership
- Evangelization efforts that recognize the lived realities of young adults and that present the Good News as an answer to consumerism and individualism

---

9   The National Catholic Council for Hispanic Ministry (see *www.ncchm.org*) has sixty-nine member associations representing a wide variety of groups, including religious orders, educational institutions, publishing companies, and national Catholic Hispanic/Latino ministry organizations. One of its explicit goals is to promote "fuller participation of Hispanics/Latinos, especially youth and young adults, in church and society, by assisting through higher and advanced education in pastoral and theological studies" (*www.ncchm.com/membership-objectives.php*).

10   See USCCB, *National Pastoral Plan for Hispanic Ministry* (Washington, DC: USCCB, 1987); see also *Encuentro and Mission*.

- Catechetical programs, targeted to Hispanic/Latino young adults, about the sacraments, especially the Eucharist, and about Catholic values and principles
- Materials targeted to Hispanic/Latino young adults on biblical topics, sexual orientation, current events, and so forth
- Guidance from church leaders[11]

The regional gatherings at the Encuentro Nacional also offered young adults' insights into strategies for parishes and dioceses, including the following:

- Encourage pastors to support *pastoral juvenil hispana* financially and spiritually.
- Give priority to a comprehensive young adult formation.
- Reach out to Hispanic/Latino young adults who have left the Church.
- Collaborate with other parish ministries to encourage Hispanic/Latino participation.
- Offer social gatherings, retreats, and activities to enliven young adult ministry.
- Seek continuity in all *pastoral juvenil hispana* programs.[12]

At the Encuentro Nacional, young adult participants compiled a list of what they need from the Church:

- Equality and rights in activities
- More participation by young adults in the mission of the Church
- Guidance in vocational and professional discernment
- Priests and leaders who are familiar with their language and culture, and more bilingual priests and parish staff
- A Web site that connects Hispanic/Latino young adults nationally
- Facilities in the parish where young adults can gather
- Parishes that are more actively involved with young adults

---

11   See National Catholic Network/De Pastoral Juvenil Hispana, *Cuaderno de Trabajo Workbook/Encuentro Nacional* (St. Louis, MO: Primer Encuentro Nacional de Pastoral Juvenil Hispana, 2006), 8.
12   See *Cuaderno de Trabajo Workbook/Encuentro Nacional*, 38.

- Greater acceptance between adults and young people
- Greater acceptance of different cultures
- More volunteer opportunities
- More space for young adults[13]

The final conclusions from the Encuentro Nacional will be studied and applied for years to come. The following pastoral principles were offered by the young adult participants as guidelines for future efforts in ministry with Hispanic/Latino young adults:

- Hispanic/Latino young adult ministry needs to be from young adults, with young adults, and for young adults.
- Christ must be the source, center, and summit of this ministry; young adult ministry should lead to an encounter with Christ, conversion, and discipleship.
- Evangelizing young adults through a living and active and prophetic ministry is critical.
- Characteristics of effective Hispanic/Latino young adult ministry include promoting the sacredness of life and a critical social conscience in young adults; being joyful, festive, and welcoming; standing in solidarity with young adults who are poor or marginalized; preserving the language, beliefs, and traditions of the culture; collaborating; conducting ongoing evaluation; including a full-time Hispanic/Latino young adult ministry coordinator on the parish level; holistically forming young adults through sacramental experiences; promoting a life of prayer; having a missionary spirit; having the support of the pastor; including both short- and long-term vision for ongoing faith formation; offering workshops for young adult faith formation; promoting education; and providing resources for higher levels of training.[14]

To become more responsive to Hispanic/Latino young adults, parish leaders can learn more about the results of the Encuentro Nacional de Pastoral Juvenil Hispana and apply the findings to parish ministry where appropriate. Parishes can also find out if their diocese has a pastoral plan for Hispanic minis-

---

13   See "Contributions from the National Encuentro—Session: Focus on Hispanic Young Adult Ministry," in *Cuaderno de Trabajo Workbook/Encuentro Nacional.*

14   See "Session 3: Pastoral Principles (Young Adults)," in *Cuaderno de Trabajo Workbook/Encuentro Nacional.*

try and, if so, what priorities are its mission focus as well as what opportunities exist for ministry formation and celebrations.

6. Think Small at First

Parishes that seek to minister effectively to Hispanic/Latino young adults set small goals and build on small successes. They develop relationships and then invite leadership and participation from Hispanic/Latino young adults. Eric Law writes that "invitation becomes a spiritual discipline for multicultural leaders."[15] When interest grows, set an achievable goal for making one parish event or ministry more responsive to Hispanic/Latino young adults (e.g., a parish mission). Then evaluate, learn from experience, and try again, building on the new relationships and positive energy generated. Go easy. Keep people excited and wanting more.

7. Link Action with Reflection, and Liturgy with Justice

All ministry planning needs to consider Hispanic/Latino young adults, and especially the need to break down the division between the spiritual and the social in their lives. Young-adult–responsive parishes help young adults view the complexity of this lived reality through the lens of Catholic social teaching about justice.

8. Preach Through Action

Formation happens through work and life. Incorporate prayer, evangelization, and catechesis into all efforts. Parishes that are responsive to Hispanic/Latino young adults are conscious of modeling ministry in all they do. They continually assess whether current methods and processes are conveying the message of the Good News of God's love, his embrace of all, and his baptismal call for all to be missionaries in the Church and the world.

9. Celebrate and Engage Different Gifts

Responsive parishes strive to involve Hispanic/Latino young adults with different personalities, interests, talents, and educational and cultural backgrounds. It is important to focus not just on those who are extroverts and naturally good speakers, but also on the quiet types.

---

15   Eric H. F. Law, *The Wolf Shall Dwell with the Lamb* (St. Louis: Chalice Press, 1993), 81.

10. Seek Funding for Special Efforts

Groups such as the Lilly Foundation, the Raskob Foundation, and the University of Notre Dame have given commendable support to research and program development in innovative ministry for young adults and Hispanic/Latino groups. Those working with Hispanic/Latino young adults can apply for grants to obtain creative sources of funding for Hispanic/Latino young adults interested in ministry and theology, as well as for ongoing development of effective, culturally sensitive, celebrative, and prophetic resources.[16]

11. Provide Leadership Training for Hispanic/Latino Young Adults

Parishes that seek to be more responsive to Hispanic/Latino young adults work with Hispanic/Latino young adult leaders in the parish to generate interest in bilingual ministry institutes, conferences, and certification and degree programs. Then the parishes help to arrange the registration, transportation, and lodging to enable these leaders to attend. Such programs exist to inspire and train them, to help them network with peers, and to connect them with mentors in their dioceses, around the country, and even throughout the continent. Universities, seminaries, religious orders, retreat centers, national conferences of ministers, and faith-based organizing groups can all reach out to and offer scholarships for Hispanic/Latino young adults. Connecting these young adults with the finest of the Catholic spiritual, intellectual, and organizational tradition will help them build their capacity to work together in "*pastoral de conjunto*," communion in mission,[17] to lead within the Church and contemporary society.

None of these efforts will bear fruit, however, without nurturing Hispanic/Latino young adults in their faith and connection with the Church and their culture in families, small church communities, and local parishes. All groups of Hispanic/Latino youth and young adults urgently need ministries on the local level that evangelize them, empower them, and accompany them on their journeys.

---

16   Contact Foundations and Donors Interested in Catholic Activities (FADICA); see *www.fadica.org*.
17   *Pastoral de conjunto* is an important concept for conducting successful Hispanic ministry. See *Encuentro and Mission*, no. 33.

12. Encourage and Affirm the Development of Resources in Spanish

Catholic publishers are making available a larger selection of resources in Spanish, and some, like St. Mary's Press, are trying to make original contributions in this area through projects like the Prophets of Hope series, in partnership with Instituto Fe y Vida. Yet all agree that many more resources are needed.

In addition to translating most statements of the bishops into Spanish, the United States Conference of Catholic Bishops (USCCB) has also developed original materials in Spanish, such as *Discípulos Jóvenes: Corresponsables de los Dones de Dios en Misión* (a statement on stewardship for teenagers) as well as retreats, reflections, and prayer services for the celebration of Catechetical Sunday.[18] Many USCCB resources for adult faith formation, catechesis, and small faith-sharing groups, including the *United States Catholic Catechism for Adults* (*Catecismo Católico de los Estados Unidos para los Adultos*) are available in Spanish as well as English.

The Southwest Liturgical Conference and Oregon Catholic Press hold music competitions to recognize new talent and encourage the composition of bilingual music for various seasons and liturgical celebrations, including music for the Rite of Christian Initiation of Adults. The Diocese of Richmond, in Virginia, lists a variety of Hispanic ministry resources and helpful descriptions at *www.richmonddiocese.org/oha/pubs.htm*. Our Sunday Visitor Curriculum Division (formerly Harcourt Religion Publishers) offers a Spanish-language magazine for families to use at home, *La Fe en Familia*, to accompany its *Un Llamado a la Fe* faith formation curriculum for elementary-school children. *La Fe en Familia* magazine offers families the opportunity to deepen their understanding of Catholic teaching and Tradition through practical suggestions and articles about real families today.

Spiritual, family, and other apostolic movements, such as those that flourish in the Archdiocese of Miami, offer many "schools of ministry" in Spanish. These schools prepare movement members to lead their peers on topics like conversion to faith in Jesus, greater discipleship through the spiritual exercises,

---

18   Visit *www.usccbpublishing.org* for USCCB resources. For Catechetical Sunday resources, see *www.usccb.org/catecheticalsunday*.

addiction-free life, mission trips to Latin America, and spiritual, countercultural parenting.[19]

Leaders from North America, like Carmen Cervantes from Instituto Fe y Vida, have been gathering with peers in Latin America involved in a network of youth centers and institutes: Red Latinoamericana de Centros e Institutos de Juventud.[20] Much fruitfulness may come from this collaboration, as fellow leaders from different countries share not only publications, resources, and program models, but also the energy and vision for the work.

13. Learn Spanish

More and more Americans are speaking Spanish—including more and more Catholic young adults and families.[21] For some parish leaders, it is hard to imagine that nearly half of the child, youth, and young adult Catholic population of the United States is Hispanic/Latino.[22] Many in this population prefer to speak Spanish. Therefore, effective parish leaders in the United States learn

---

19   For more information on current activities in the Archdiocese of Miami, see the "Calendario" page on the Web site of *La Voz Catolica*, *www.vozcatolica.org*.

20   See *www.ipadej.org*.

21   A growing percentage of Hispanics/Latinos in the United States are immigrants and children of immigrants. Currently, 39 percent of Hispanics/Latinos are foreign-born, 33 percent are U.S.-born children of foreign-born parents, and 28 percent are children of U.S.-born parents. With regard to language, 54 percent speak exclusively or primarily Spanish at home, 22 percent speak equal amounts of Spanish and English, and 22 percent speak exclusively or primarily English at home. See Ken Johnson-Mondragón, *The Status of Hispanic Youth and Young Adult Ministry in the United States: A Preliminary Study* (Stockton, CA: Instituto Fe y Vida, 2002).

According to the *Official Catholic Directory*, the number of Catholics in the United States in 2002 was 65.2 million. In 2000 the United States Census reported 35.3 million Hispanics/Latinos in the United States; overall, 70 percent of Hispanics/Latinos are Catholic. Putting the numbers together, in 2000 there were 24.7 million Hispanic/Latino Catholics in the United States, for roughly 39 percent of the Catholic Church in the United States.

Sixty-four percent of all Hispanics/Latinos attend church regularly, based on an August 2002 survey conducted for the Latino Coalition (by McLaughlin and Associates' affiliate Opiniones Latinas). Forty-five percent attend religious services weekly; among them, 43 percent primarily attend services in Spanish, 30 percent attend bilingual services, and 27 percent attend services in English (Thomas Rivera Policy Institute, May 2001). By 2010, it is commonly estimated that half of all Catholics in the United States will be Hispanic/Latino. Since 1960, 71 percent of the growth in the Catholic population in the United States has been due to Hispanics/Latinos (Stewart Lawrence, study for the USCCB Committee on Hispanic Affairs [1999], 5). By 2050, the Hispanic/Latino population in the United States is expected to reach 96.5 million, or 24.5 percent of the total U.S. population (Census Bureau, Middle Series Population Projections).

All of the above data are summarized in the USCCB newsletter *En Marcha*, Fall/Winter 2002, 16-23.

22   Presently Hispanics/Latinos account for more than 45 percent of all Catholics under the age of thirty in the United States, and more than half of all Hispanics/Latinos are under twenty-six years of age. Both of these factors contribute to the projected rapid growth of the Hispanic/Latino population in the coming decades. From 2000 to 2003, the young Hispanic/Latino population has grown about 9 percent, while the young white population has decreased about 1 percent. See Instituto Fe y Vida Research and Resource Center, *Changing the Face of Ministry with Catholic Hispanic Youth and Young Adults* (Stockton, CA: Instituto Fe y Vida), cited in the USCCB newsletter *En Marcha*, Winter/Spring 2004, 15.

Spanish and implement helpful bilingual programs. "Special efforts to acquire the languages of the new immigrants by all church ministers constitute an essential, concrete step towards a full and effective welcome."[23]

The use of Spanish in the home and in society, in business and in politics, is only becoming more prevalent and valuable. Therefore, effective parish leaders value this skill and acquire it as part of their formation, knowing that it supports the current and future vitality of the Church in the United States. They also take into consideration that learning a new language requires time and resources that are already in high demand. To build connections, they identify and empower Hispanic/Latino young adults who can serve as bridges of communication because they are both bilingual *and* bicultural. These young adults can bring unity and provide insight to serve the ministry of *pastoral juvenil hispana* at large.

PRACTICAL STRATEGIES FOR DIOCESAN DIRECTORS

Church leaders have used different strategies to delegate Hispanic/Latino young adult ministry in different dioceses across the United States. One common strategy is to give diocesan directors of youth and young adult ministry the responsibility for ministry to, and formation of, Hispanic/Latino young adults. Some recommendations for these diocesan leaders follow:

- Where there is no paid leader of *pastoral juvenil hispana*, budget a stipend for a consultant who will serve as a liaison between the diocese and the lay ecclesial ministers carrying out *pastoral juvenil hispana*. The consultant can represent the diocese at special events and help coordinate leadership development opportunities.
- To best serve the *pastoral juvenil hispana* leadership in the parishes, effective diocesan leaders maintain direct personal contact (e.g., pastoral visits, personal phone call, personal invitations). E-mail, mailers, and flyers are not always the most effective methods of outreach, being more impersonal. Personal contact is also vital for reaching out to young adults and young adult ministry teams.
- Apostolic movements such as Jornadas de Vida Cristiana, Encuentros de Promoción Juvenil, and Renovación Carismática are very

---

23   USCCB, *Welcoming the Stranger Among Us: Unity in Diversity* (Washington, DC: USCCB, 2000), 36.

effective when it comes to bringing Hispanic/Latino young adults back to the fold. Diocesan leadership would do well to collaborate with them, keeping in mind that they are a great resource for creating opportunities for the initial encounter with Christ. However, movements may sometimes present a challenge if they pull active *pastoral juvenil hispana* leaders away from involvement in their parish groups. Remind leaders that the ultimate goal of apostolic movements and small church communities is to bring the young adult into the life of the parish.

CONCLUSION

Half of all Catholics in the United States under the age of ten are Hispanic. In 2005, there were 29,600,000 Hispanic Catholics in the United States—37 percent of the total Catholic population of the country.[24] The Catholic Church has a significant opportunity in this new millennium: to embrace the gifts, deep faith, joy, and religious practices of Hispanic/Latino young adult Catholics, while advocating for and providing concrete aid for the undocumented, the marginalized, the illiterate—the ones left behind. One of the most important things parish leaders can do today is to listen to the voices of young Hispanics/Latinos, whose hunger for a vibrant relationship with Christ and the Church teaches leaders how to minister to them.

---

24   See "Fast Facts About U.S. Hispanic Catholics."

CHAPTER THIRTEEN

Taking the Next Steps

How can parishes move forward in welcoming young adults into the Catholic Church in the twenty-first century? This chapter addresses the challenges facing the Church in its attempt to live out the vision for ministry with young adults laid out in the bishops' pastoral plan for young adult faith formation, Sons and Daughters of the Light. *The chapter invites parish leaders to be bridge builders for young adults and to remember that we are all part of the Church—and we need each generation in order to make a complete community of faith.*

Catholic parishes have a unique opportunity today to live out the vision of the bishops' pastoral plan for young adult faith formation, *Sons and Daughters of the Light*,[1] by welcoming the gifts and responding to the needs of their young adults. This book, which lays out ways to take advantage of that opportunity, closes with these reflections on the implications of the pastoral plan and of Ministry with Young Adults: A National Catholic Initiative ("the Initiative") for parish life in the twenty-first century.

In the early 1990s, the situation for young adults (those between the ages of eighteen to thirty-nine) in most parishes in the United States could be accurately described as hit-or-miss. While some dioceses and a handful of parishes were doing effective, intentional ministry with young adults, most parish leaders were less intentional about making young adults an integral part of the faith community. Existing ministries in the average parish were tailored to the needs of Catholic education in grade school and high school, and to some extent through college. Then, with a few exceptions, effective outreach to young adults ceased until they were married, had children, and re-entered the cycle through their children's sacramental preparation and education. After their children grew up, adults could avail themselves of excellent programs and ministries for seasoned members of the parish.

The largest problem in this arrangement was the gap between ministry to teenagers and ministry to young adults preparing for marriage. In the 1950s, 1960s, and 1970s, this was not a major issue: because most people married

---

1   See United States Conference of Catholic Bishops (USCCB), *Sons and Daughters of the Light: A Pastoral Plan for Ministry with Young Adults* (Washington, DC: USCCB, 1996).

soon after high school or college, the gap was minimal or non-existent. But as more and more young adults began to delay marriage and family life until their thirties, the gap between outreach efforts began to span ten years or more. Many Catholics were set adrift until they married and started a family— and many did not come back to the faith after living so long without it.

In the 1980s, young adult initiatives developed in more dioceses, parishes, and faith communities. More ministry was being targeted to young adults; unfortunately, this young adult ministry was often separate from the ministry to the intergenerational parish community. When the Initiative and *Sons and Daughters of the Light* converged in the 1990s, a new paradigm emerged for ministry with young adults. Church leaders recognized a two-fold need: (1) to integrate young adults into the overall faith community and, within that context, (2) to provide specific programming to meet young adults' specific needs. This development has made a tremendous impact on the lives of thousands of young adults. As the previous chapters in this book have described, many wonderful and exciting models now effectively connect young adults with Jesus Christ, with the Church, with a peer community, and with the mission of the Church in the world.

Yet the challenge to be responsive to the needs of young adults remains today. Several years into the twenty-first century, the gifts and talents of a vital segment of the intergenerational faith community are still not being used to their fullest. A 2002 study by the Catholic Pluralism Project attests to this fact, finding that only 26 percent of Catholics born after 1961 are active in their parish, compared to 64 percent of Catholics born before the Second Vatican Council.[2]

A VISION FOR THE FUTURE

In the years ahead, the Catholic Church in the United States has an opportunity to complete the circle. Catholic leaders can work together to create a world where ministry with and by young adults exists in all Catholic faith communities—where parishes are complete and united in the love and service of God's will, and where they value the diversity of gifts from all age groups.

Effective Catholic leaders can work to create a new covenant between two key populations in the Church. In this covenant, the gifts of seasoned

---

2   See Center for Applied Research in the Apostolate (CARA), *Special Report: Young Adult Catholics* (Washington, DC: CARA, 2002), 4.

adults—time, wisdom, wealth, and a desire to leave a legacy—and the gifts of young adults—time, energy, enthusiasm, and a desire to make their mark—combine to welcome the Holy Spirit into Catholic communities and to spread the Good News of Jesus Christ.

An intergenerational Church will bring about what Pope John Paul II referred to as a *"new springtime of Christian life."*[3] Imagine a community where young Catholic nurses and doctors are mentored by seasoned Catholic medical professionals regarding how to bring the healing love of Christ to all of their patients. Imagine a community where young Catholic parents are matched with an "empty nest" couple in their parish as a resource for advice and guidance on passing on the faith and raising their children. Imagine a community where young adults become mentors for youths in the parish. Imagine a community where all parish ministries are led by teams that combine the optimism and idealism of young adults with the wisdom and understanding of mature adults.

Eighty-six-year-old Regina Westhoff is the last of her generation in a family that produced twenty-two children, seventy-six grandchildren, and more than forty-two great-grandchildren. She captured the situation in a letter to her family:

> When we were all growing up on 51st Street, the one constant was our Catholic faith, and even though Mama and Papa didn't have a lot of material things to share with us, they did leave us *a lasting legacy in our faith*. As we all got older and various adversities beset us, it was our faith in God's Providence that sustained us, and consequently, we all had our children baptized and tried to the best of our limited abilities to hand down that faith to each of you. But it seems to me that some of you have either lost your faith, or allowed it to grow cold, and so, I wonder, *what are you passing on to your children that will sustain them?*[4]

It is a question for the ages—for older adults who may or may not have passed on the faith to young adults, and to young adults who are now parents and looking for ways to share their faith with their own children. It is also a question for all Catholic communities of faith. In *Sons and Daughters of the*

---

3   Pope John Paul II, *On the Coming of the Third Millennium* (*Tertio Millennio Adveniente*) (Washington, DC: USCCB, 1994), no. 18.

4   Regina Westhoff, letter to author, 2002.

Light, the bishops recall the best order in which to engage young adults in their faith:

1. To connect young adults with Jesus Christ
2. To connect young adults with the Church
3. To connect young adults with the mission of the Church in the world
4. To connect young adults with a peer community[5]

The opportunity and challenge for the future is to give primary focus to connecting young adults with Jesus Christ. If young adults are evangelized, they will naturally desire to be catechized, which will make their experience of the sacraments the rich, grace-filled experiences they should be for all Catholics.

Evangelization involves our own relationship with Jesus and sharing the Good News of Jesus with others. That concept has such strong appeal for young adults who hunger for spirituality and thirst for fellowship. The challenge is to be sure that our actions declare to others that the good we do is done out of Christian conviction. We cannot evangelize others if we are not on fire with the love of the Lord ourselves. Or as we read in 1 Peter 3:15-16, "Sanctify Christ as Lord in your hearts. Always be ready to give an explanation to anyone who asks you for a reason for your hope, but do it with gentleness and reverence." If faith communities can bring young adults to know Jesus Christ, everything else will follow.

BUILDING BRIDGES, NOT WALLS

In July 2000, Ministry with Young Adults: A National Catholic Initiative included a national symposium on ministry with young adults, held in Omaha, Nebraska. The resulting *Symposium Report* identified six challenges to be solved in order for ministry to young adults to move to the next level: to transform parishes into robust intergenerational communities.[6]

1. *Challenges to Church Leadership.* "Many church leaders still do not know *how* to generate a welcoming presence to young adults; nor do they realize the importance of fully integrating them into the

---

5   See *Sons and Daughters of the Light*, 28-41.
6   See John Roberto and Joan Weber, eds., *Meeting the Challenges of Ministry with Young Adults in a New Millennium: Symposium Report* (Naugatuck, CT: Center for Ministry Development, 2000).

faith community. We also need to *facilitate* young adults at the ground level in parish ministry by helping them discern their gifts and recognize their talents. We need to equip young adults with the *language* of theological reflection and discernment."[7]

2. *Catechesis.* "We must translate our sacramental system authentically to touch the lives of today's young adults by applying faith to life. We need to know how, when and where to transmit the rich tradition of the Catholic Church to young adults. We need honest, non-judgmental responses and 'safe space' in the face of young adults' questioning and scrutiny of the Church's teachings and traditions. The Church must provide an *experience* of faith so as to draw young adults to greater love and service to God and God's people."[8]

3. *Connecting Faith and Life.* "The Church must make connections between culture and gospel and discover how the Jesus story is being lived by young adults. Then we must learn to honor their experience. Church leaders should plunge in relationally with young adults and learn their culture, finding the Christ there. The Church must affirm lay spirituality and empower young adults to live out this spirituality in family, work, society and in the church itself."[9]

4. *Evangelizing Young Adults.* "The Church must walk with young adults on their faith journeys, listening to them and using their everyday experiences as 'openings' for evangelization and faith/life integration. Parishes and campuses need to accept young adults' experience of being Catholic and use their talents to enhance our parish communities and strengthen their Catholic identity. We need to do better at reaching non-practicing young adults, listening to their critiques of the Church and finding ways to respond as Church in order to grow with young adults."[10]

5. *Ministry to a Diverse Generation.* "The Church needs to work outside of the box of single culture and modernism to allow a new model to emerge from young adults' lived experiences. We need to discover the diversity of young adults in gender, culture,

---

7   *Symposium Report*, 15.
8   *Symposium Report*, 15.
9   *Symposium Report*, 15.
10   *Symposium Report*, 15.

education, money, customs, etc. through a *catholic* (i.e., universal) perspective, open to all expressions and experiences. And we need to bridge the 'generational gaps' in the Church, learning how to be a truly inclusive communion of believers where all are valued, honored and ministered to so that they can live out their baptism and minister to others."[11]

6. *Using Media and Technology.* "We must *use* the market research/ analysis to develop ministry with young adults and to spread the gospel through the use of technology. We need to balance community and interaction with technology as we welcome young adults into the Church and use modern concepts to reach them and work with them."[12]

Parishes could see any one of these six challenges as a reason not to engage in young adult ministry. Similarly, young adults could see any of these challenges as a reason not to get involved in their parishes. But effective parishes and motivated young adults will see the challenges as an opportunity to determine how to overcome these obstacles. The real challenge, as modeled by Jesus Christ, is to look at these stumbling blocks and—instead of piling them up to create a wall that will keep people in or out—lay them next to each other and create a bridge for both sides to cross. This will take a significant investment of time and energy, but the investment is worth the reward.

Take technology as an example. Rather than lamenting the work involved in using media effectively to communicate the faith, Catholic leaders can engage young people in solving this problem for the Church. Web sites like *www.bustedhalo.com* and *www.catholicexchange.com*, as well as local Web sites constructed by numerous dioceses and campus ministries, have engaged young adults' help, with tremendous results. Leaders of these efforts saw technology as a bridge to the future, not a wall holding them back.

Theology on Tap, discussed several times in this book, is another bridge joining church theologians and catechists with young adults in a safe space for exploration and learning. Still another bridge can be found in the Little Books series from the Diocese of Saginaw, in Michigan;[13] these books, which are revised regularly to follow the liturgical season and lectionary cycle, offer

---

11   *Symposium Report*, 15-16.
12   *Symposium Report*, 16.
13   For more information on the Little Books of the Diocese of Saginaw series, see *www.littlebooks.org* and *saginaw.org*.

daily six-minute devotionals that combine the Scripture of the day with a commentary. By word of mouth, awareness of these books has expanded from Michigan to parishes throughout the United States, where the books have been particularly effective in bridging faith with everyday life.

And, of course, this book, *Connecting Young Adults to Catholic Parishes: Best Practices in Catholic Young Adult Ministry*, is filled with examples of obstacles that creative and visionary leaders have, with God's help, turned into bridges to the new springtime of evangelization.

THE CHURCH IS ALL OF US

Sons and Daughters of the Light challenges young adults to take the initiative and be leaders. This book challenges all parish leaders to think of the Church in the first person—as "we," not as "it" or "they." We are all members of the Catholic Church and the Body of Christ. Not only does the Church have room for all of us, it needs all of us as well.

When all can embrace the Church, the Body of Christ, in the first person, God's amazing grace will transform this world. Being more responsive to young adults throughout the Church will benefit more than just young adults. The more faith communities open up to the gifts and fresh ideas of young adults, the more the entire intergenerational parish will be renewed and blessed. Ultimately, what young adults want from the Church—a sense of community and belonging, a chance to grow more deeply into a relationship to Jesus, and an opportunity to serve and lead—is what all Catholics want. Are you ready to do your part?

The History of Ministry with Young Adults: A National Catholic Initiative

1993: THE INITIAL GRANT

In January 1993, the Raskob Foundation for Catholic Activities sent a request for proposals (RFP) to eighteen Catholic organizations and individuals, inviting them to submit a plan for developing and sustaining ministry with young adults in the Catholic Church. This RFP was influenced by particular members of the Raskob Foundation's board of trustees: young adults themselves, who were motivated by their own lived experience of feeling excluded from the Church's ministry. They shared their hopes that the Church would consciously and deliberately reach out to young adults.

In response to the RFP, the National Catholic Young Adult Ministry Association (NCYAMA) submitted a request for a small grant that would bring together people in the field to assess the needs of Catholic young adults. The Raskob Foundation funded the NCYAMA proposal, and NCYAMA hosted the gathering in Philadelphia in October 1993. Based on the results, NCYAMA wrote and submitted its grant proposal. Meanwhile, the Catholic Campus Ministry Association (CCMA) and the Center for Ministry Development (CMD) also submitted applications.

The Raskob Foundation reviewed the proposals and asked the three organizations to work together to develop a single, combined proposal. After the organizations met to explore the possibilities, CCMA and NCYAMA submitted a joint proposal for a five-year, multi-phase plan, which the Raskob Foundation accepted in 1994. The Center for Ministry Development and the St. John Eudes Center were hired to administer and staff the plan for Ministry with Young Adults: A National Catholic Initiative ("the Initiative").

1993: WORLD YOUTH DAY

Even as the Raskob Foundation was encouraging the enhancement of ministry with young adults, the United States was hosting its first World Youth Day in Denver, Colorado. The Holy Father started the tradition of World Youth Day in 1984 when he invited young Catholics to Rome to celebrate and enhance their faith. This international gathering has since been held every few years in a different country.

The Denver experience proved to be a watershed event in the history of young adult ministry for the Catholic Church in the United States. The then-National Conference of Catholic Bishops (now the United States Conference of Catholic Bishops [USCCB]) had already begun to recognize the need for ministry with young adults when the bishops saw that, unlike the World Youth Day participants from other countries, the majority of the American participants in World Youth Day in Denver were teenagers, not young adults. This observation contributed to a growing awareness that the Church had no "delivery system" to reach young adults, except through campus ministry. In November 1993, three months after the Denver experience, the bishops authorized the drafting of a pastoral plan for ministry with young adults in the United States—to be published in 1996 as *Sons and Daughters of the Light* (see below). While the bishops had already been looking at the need to connect with young adults, World Youth Day in Denver gave added impetus to their decision to do something about it.

1994: THE INITIATIVE

Ministry with Young Adults: A National Catholic Initiative was launched with hearings across the country to listen to young adults and to those who minister with them. Both groups were asked to comment on two primary questions:

1. What do young adults look to the Church to provide in their faith journeys?
2. What strengths and gifts could young adults bring to church life?

Based on the information gathered, the Initiative staff created a list of what young adults seek from the Church. They then invited fifty-five people from various ministries around the country to a design meeting in Buffalo to develop the resources needed to address those issues that young adults identified as crucial.

After two years of research and development, the Initiative published several resources and sponsored three national conferences to share the insights and sources gathered and created by the participants. The Initiative's printed resources (published through the Center for Ministry Development) included the following:

- *Young Adult Works*. A five-binder series full of programs and resources for doing comprehensive ministry with young adults in parishes and on campuses. (Fr. Ronald Bagley, CJM, John Roberto, Susan Stark, and Joan Weber, eds., *Young Adult Works* [Naugatuck, CT: CMD, 1997].)

- *Leadership for Life*. A book for young adults on the vision and practice of Christian leadership. (Michael Poulin, Lori Spanbauer, Joan Weber, and Jennifer Willems, *Leadership for Life: Discovering Your Gifts for Christian Leadership* [Naugatuck, CT: CMD, 1997].)

- *Leader's Guide to "Leadership for Life."* A guide to using *Leadership for Life* in a group setting through seven two-hour workshops. (John Roberto, *Leader's Guide to Leadership for Life: Discovering Your Gifts for Christian Leadership* [Naugatuck, CT: CMD, 1997].)

- *Connecting Young Adults with the Word*. A guide for homilists and liturgy planners, in three volumes: one for each cycle of the lectionary. (Fr. Ron Bagley, CJM, *Connecting Young Adults with the Word: A Guide for Homilists and Liturgy Planners* [Naugatuck, CT: CMD, 1997-1999].)

- *Sharing God's Word Through the Year*. A Sunday Scripture guide in three volumes (one for each cycle of the lectionary) for use in young adult small faith-sharing groups. (Fr. Ron Bagley, CJM, ed., *Sharing God's Word Through the Year: A Guide for Small Groups of Young Adults* [Naugatuck, CT: CMD, 1997-1999].)

- *Becoming a Young Adult Responsive Church*. A booklet used to implement the bishops' statement *Sons and Daughters of the Light*. (Fr. Ron Bagley, CJM, John Roberto, and Joan Weber, *Becoming a Young Adult Responsive Church* [Naugatuck, CT: CMD, 1997].)

- *Ideas and Strategies for Connecting with Young Adults*. A poster filled with more than one hundred ideas for ministry with young adults. (John Roberto, ed., *Ideas and Strategies for Connecting with Young Adults* [Naugatuck, CT: CMD, 1997].)

1996-1997: *SONS AND DAUGHTERS OF THE LIGHT*

After the awakening brought about by the 1993 World Youth Day in Denver, the Catholic bishops of the United States unanimously approved the final draft of *Sons and Daughters of the Light: A Pastoral Plan for Ministry with Young Adults*.[1] This statement aimed to provide a foundation for ministry with young adults. *Sons and Daughters of the Light* was published in early 1997, and a plan for its implementation began. (*Sons and Daughters of the Light* has since been made available in Spanish, Vietnamese, and Korean.)

1998-1999: THE INITIATIVE CONTINUES

The Initiative team crisscrossed the country, providing in-services on young adult ministry in more than sixty dioceses and regions. The target audience included young adults who were leaders in their faith communities, as well as pastors, parish staff, campus ministers, and diocesan staff.

2000: NATIONAL SYMPOSIUM

The Initiative sponsored a national symposium in Omaha, Nebraska, to process and synthesize its findings and fruits from the previous six years—including the document *Meeting the Challenges of Ministry with Young Adults in a New Millennium: An Evaluation Project for Ministry with Young Adults—A National Catholic Initiative*, the project evaluation conducted by the Center for Applied Research in the Apostolate (CARA).[2] The symposium also worked to identify where the Church would need to move in the first decade of the twenty-first century in order to continue to connect with young adults. A synthesis of the findings of the symposium was published under the title *Meeting the Challenges of Ministry with Young Adults in a New Millennium: Symposium Report*.[3]

---

1   See USCCB, *Sons and Daughters of the Light: A Pastoral Plan for Ministry with Young Adults* (Washington, DC: USCCB, 1997).

2   See Mary E. Bendyna, RSM, Mary Gautier, and Paul Perl, *Meeting the Challenges of Ministry with Young Adults in a New Millennium: An Evaluation Project for Ministry with Young Adults—A National Catholic Initiative* (Washington, DC: CARA, 2000).

3   John Roberto and Joan Weber, eds., *Meeting the Challenges of Ministry with Young Adults in a New Millennium: Symposium Report* (Naugatuck, CT: CMD, 2000).

2000-2008

In the first decade of the new millennium, church leaders have been implementing *Sons and Daughters of the Light* and struggling to meet the needs of the generations of young adults born after the Second Vatican Council. Leaders are also learning how to more effectively incorporate technology (e.g., podcasts, blogs) into their ministry. The 2006 Encuentro Nacional de Pastoral Juvenil Hispana (or National Hispanic Youth and Young Adult Ministry Encounter) also provided insights into ministry with the growing number of Hispanic/Latino young adults in parishes and dioceses in the United States.

BEYOND 2008

The present book, *Connecting Young Adults to Catholic Parishes: Best Practices in Catholic Young Adult Ministry*, was developed from the symposium conclusions, the post-Initiative lived experiences of those ministering with young adults, and new insights into outreach with young adults gained through successes and struggles with implementing *Sons and Daughters of the Light* in the years since the pastoral document was published.

Acknowledgments

This book was made possible in part by generous grants from the Raskob Foundation for Catholic Activities, Inc., and the Louisville Institute. The Raskob Foundation was the major funder for Ministry with Young Adults: A National Catholic Initiative. Both foundations supported the young adult ministry symposium held in Omaha, Nebraska, in 2000.

About the Authors

Fr. Ronald Bagley, CJM (*Chapter 7*), is the former pastor of St. Bonaventure Parish in West Seneca, New York. He serves as director of the Pastoral Ministry Program at Divine Word Seminary in Tagaytay, Cavite, in the Philippines. He is also a formator at several seminaries in the Diocese of Imus.

Alicia Bondanella (*Chapter 9*) is the executive director of the Corporate Work Study Program of Don Bosco Cristo Rey High School in the Archdiocese of Washington. Alicia is the former youth and young adult coordinator for the Catholic Campaign for Human Development at the United States Conference of Catholic Bishops.

Cindee Case (*Chapter 2*) is the director of the Office of Youth and Young Adult Ministry for the Diocese of Youngstown in Ohio. She previously served in the Archdiocese of Atlanta and in the Dioceses of St. Augustine and Cleveland. She was on the board of directors for the National Catholic Young Adult Ministry Association and spent three years as its president.

Michele Castle (*Chapter 3*) was director of young adult ministry for the Diocese of Raleigh for seven years. She now resides in North Carolina, where she is a wellness and success coach in her own business. She serves on the advisory board of Busted Halo (*www.bustedhalo.com*).

Tom East (*general editor*) is the director for the Center for Ministry Development. Previously, he was the associate director of religious education for the Archdiocese of Los Angeles and a campus minister for Citrus College in Azusa, California.

Marissa Esparza-Garcia (*Chapter 12*) is the associate director for *pastoral juvenil* and was the director of the Office for Youth Ministry in the Diocese of San Diego, California. She provides training, in English and Spanish, for adult, youth, and young adult leaders on Catholic youth ministry and *pastoral juvenil hispana*. Her training sessions especially address the challenges of ministering to the various cultures in the Church.

Maria Teresa Gaston (*Chapter 12; contributor, Hispanic/Latino culture*) is the director of the Creighton Center for Service and Justice at Creighton

University. Born in Havana, Cuba, she has degrees in theology and Hispanic ministry and is working on a graduate degree in organizational psychology. She is the mother of three young adult sons.

Mary Jansen (*Chapter 10*) is the director for the Office of Young Adult Ministry, Campus Ministry, and Evangelization in the Archdiocese of San Francisco. Mary lives in San Francisco and received her master's degree in theology from the University of San Francisco in 2004.

Paul Lavallee (*Chapter 5*) lives in suburban Philadelphia and works as an engineer. He was a founding member and the first chairperson of YASKI (Young Adults of St. Katharine's and St. Isaac's in Wayne, Pennsylvania), and he remained an active member afterward. He also volunteers for pro-life causes.

Raquel Lopez (*Chapter 12*) is completing her studies in business management and working full-time at Mater Dei Catholic High School in San Diego, California, as the Juan Diego Adult Center coordinator. She is the former assistant director for *pastoral juvenil hispana* for the Diocese of San Diego.

Matthew Manion (*Chapters 8, 13*) is the president and CEO of the Catholic Leadership Institute. He is the former director of young adult ministry for the Archdiocese of Philadelphia and lives in Devon, Pennsylvania, with his wife, Kerri, and their three children, Grace, James, and Kathleen.

Mariette Martineau (*Chapter 6*) was a project coordinator with the family and intergenerational ministry team of the Center for Ministry Development. Previously she was the coordinator of youth ministry and of the young adult retreat team for the Diocese of Saskatoon, Saskatchewan.

Michelle Miller (*general editor*) is recently married and presently lives in Canada. She previously worked at the United States Conference of Catholic Bishops and is also the former executive director of the National Catholic Young Adult Ministry Association.

Eunice Park (*contributor, Asian/Pacific Islander culture*) is the former coordinator of young adult ministry in the Diocese of Oakland in California. She is a student at the Franciscan School of Theology in Berkeley, California, where she is a candidate for both MTS and MAMC degrees, with an expected date of graduation in 2009.

Fr. Charles Pfeffer *("The Campus Connection" sections)* was the director of campus ministry for the University of Pennsylvania. He was formerly the director of the Office of Youth and Young Adult Ministry for the Archdiocese of Philadelphia.

John Roberto *(Chapter 11)* is the founder and president of Lifelong Faith Associates, an organization dedicated to nurturing growth in faith for all ages and generations in the parish and at home. He is the founder and former director of the Center for Ministry Development.

Sonji Robinson *(contributor, African American culture)* serves as the assistant director of the Clinical Trials Financial Management Division at Children's Hospital of Philadelphia. She served in the Archdiocese of Philadelphia as founding program coordinator at the St. Peter Claver Center for Evangelization and as coordinator for young adult ministry.

Kristi Schulenberg *(Chapter 9)* is the former director of parish social ministry for Catholic Charities USA. She is active in Amnesty International USA and in the movement to end the death penalty. She is currently the vice president of operations for Kamakura Corporation in Honolulu, Hawaii.

Joan Weber *(Chapter 1; general editor)* is the coordinator for young adult ministry services at the Center for Ministry Development. She was the president of the National Catholic Young Adult Ministry Association from 1990 to 1992 and is a former coordinator of young adult ministry for the Archdiocese of Omaha.

Sr. Christine Wilcox, OP *(Chapter 4)*, is assistant director of campus ministry at the Dominican University of California in San Rafael. She holds master's degree in theology and another in linguistics. She is the former director of young adult and campus ministry for the Archdiocese of San Francisco.

Index